FUNDAMENTALISM REBORN?

Fundamentalism Reborn?

Afghanistan and the Taliban

Edited by
WILLIAM MALEY

HURST & COMPANY, LONDON

First published in the United Kingdom by
C. Hurst & Co. (Publishers) Ltd.,
38 King Street, London WC2E 8JZ
© William Maley and the Contributors, 1998
New preface © William Maley, 2001
Third impression, 2001
All rights reserved
Printed in England

ISBNs
1-85065-346-1 (cased)
1-85065-360-7 (paperback)

PREFACE

AFGHANISTAN AND THE TALIBAN, 1998-2001

William Maley

On Sunday 9 September 2001, two Moroccan journalists carrying Belgian passports arrived to conduct an interview with the military leader of the forces of the Islamic State of Afghanistan, Ahmad Shah Massoud, in the northern Afghan town of Khwaja Bahauddin. But it was not an ordinary interview. When one of the 'journalists' began to film the renowned commander, a bomb hidden in his video camera exploded, inflicting injuries on Massoud from which he reportedly died six days later. In normal circumstances this would have been a shattering blow to the 'Islamic State', and grounds for wild celebration within the puritanical Taliban movement which controlled Afghanistan's main cities, and which Massoud had for years opposed. Yet the circumstances by then were anything but normal. For just two days after the suicide attack on Massoud, suicidal terrorists had struck again, not this time in the remote reaches of Afghanistan, but in the commercial and military heartland of the United States of America, hijacking planes from Logan and Dulles airports and crashing them into the Pentagon and the twin towers of the World Trade Center, which collapsed in ruin with astronomical casualties and dispelled forever the sense of security which most ordinary Americans felt in the continental United States.

The prime suspect in both the attacks was the same man: Osama Bin Laden, a wealthy Saudi extremist who had helped finance the Taliban seizure of Afghanistan's capital Kabul in September 1996, and had ever since enjoyed the Taliban's hospitality.[1] Within a few days of the attack on 11 September, the US Administration of George W. Bush had assembled a powerful circumstantial case pointing to his involvement. But it went further than this: rather than simply focussing on Bin Laden and his terrorist networks, it also focussed

---

[1]   For Bin Laden's background, see Gilles Kepel, *Jihad. Expansion et déclin de l'islamisme* (Paris: Gallimard, 2000), pp. 309-316; Michael Griffin, *Reaping the Whirlwind: The Taliban Movement in Afghanistan* (London: Pluto Press, 2001), pp. 133-140.

directly on the circles which had nurtured him. The Taliban had reached their moment of truth. In many ways it was unsurprising that they had arrived at such a point. As the contributions to this book detail, the Taliban movement was a terrifying oddity in the politics of the modern world, dependent upon support from its allies in Pakistan's military intelligence, eccentric in its ideological disposition, ruthless in dealing with those it categorised as opponents, and utterly unequal to the tasks of either comprehending the global environment within which it operated, or crafting solutions to the enormous problems by which Afghans were confronted after two decades of mayhem and disruption in their homeland. While the Taliban attempted to legitimate their power by reference to their provision of 'security', with the passage of time it became clear that, as Tacitus wrote in the *Agricola*, they had made a wilderness and called it peace. And although the US State Department had responded to the Taliban takeover of Kabul in a way which was frightening in its sheer naiveté, the passage of time had punctured most of the illusions on which American policy towards the Taliban was based. But it still took the horror of a bright and sunny September morning in Washington and New York to turn the last of these illusions into dust.

When the Taliban first appeared, some observers at least were prepared to give them the benefit of the doubt, and although their gender policies earned them extremely adverse publicity, the belief that they could be a force for stability persisted in some quarters. However, from 1998 it became clear that this could never be the case. In August of that year, Taliban forces renewed their assault on the northern city of Mazar-e Sharif, and finally overran it. The consequences were revolting. Urged on by incendiary broadcasts from the Taliban 'Governor', Mullah Mohammad Niazi, Taliban forces embarked on the slaughter of ethnic Hazaras, whom they blamed for the losses they had suffered during their short-lived occupation in May 1997. In the three days from 8-11 August, an estimated 2,000 Hazaras were slain.[2] Eight staff of the Iranian Consulate were also killed, reportedly at the hands of Pakistani extremists in the Taliban force, and a war between Iran and the Taliban nearly resulted. These events did not, however, receive quite the attention they deserved, for on 7 August 1998, bombs had wrecked the US Embassies in Kenya and Tanzania, causing extensive loss of life, and the Clinton Administration concluded that Bin Laden was to blame. Two weeks later, the US fired Tomahawk cruise missiles at training camps run by Bin Laden in Afghanistan, but if he was the target, they missed, and an Italian adviser to the UN

---

2   *Afghanistan: The Massacre in Mazar-i Sharif* (New York: Human Rights Watch, 1998).

Special Mission to Afghanistan, Lieutenant-Colonel Carmine Calo, was murdered as the UN moved to evacuate some of its staff from Kabul.[3] This breakdown in relations destroyed the Taliban's hopes, up to then pursued with some vigour, of reaching agreements with energy companies for the construction of pipelines from Central to South Asia through Taliban territory.[4] From this point, the radicalisation of the Taliban became ever more palpable. In July 1999, a leading moderate Pushtun whose family had had some association with the Taliban in their early days, Abdul Ahad Karzai, was murdered in Quetta: this came less than a week after the US had imposed unilateral sanctions on the Taliban over their hospitality to Bin Laden, and clearly indicated that the Pushtun moderates, always regarded with suspicion by the Taliban's military backers in Pakistan, were expendable. Further sanctions against the Taliban, imposed in 1999 by UN Security Council resolution 1267 and in 2000 by Security Council resolution 1333, built on the earlier foundation established by Washington in response to the attacks on its enemies: their direct effects on ordinary Afghans were limited,[5] but as rhetoric from Pakistani circles made clear, they were certainly felt by the Taliban leaders and their backers. Much more dramatic evidence of anti-modernism in Taliban ranks came in February 2001, when in an act of almost unbelievable cultural vandalism, Taliban under Commander Dadullah dynamited two of Afghanistan's greatest treasures, the ancient Buddhas of Bamiyan.[6] This reflected the disappearance of almost any semblance of real consultation in Taliban decision-making, and the increasing influence of narrow-minded bigots with little understanding of the messages which their actions would send. Yet here too, as in the arrests of Christian aid workers later in the year, there may have been an underlying political strategy, namely to force the international community into dialogue with the Taliban, something Pakistan had long been urging, despite the barriers to interaction which the Security Council had sought to impose.

---

3   See William Maley, *The Foreign Policy of the Taliban* (New York: Council on Foreign Relations, 2000), p. 24.

4   See William Maley, 'The Perils of Pipelines', *The World Today*, vol. 54, nos. 8-9, August-September 1998, pp. 231-232; Ahmed Rashid, *Taliban: Militant Islam, Oil and Fundamentalism in Central Asia* (New Haven: Yale University Press, 2000), pp. 157-182.

5   See *Report of the Secretary-General on the humanitarian implications of the measures imposed by Security Council resolutions 1267 (1999) and 1333 (2000) on Afghanistan* (New York: United Nations, S/2001/695, 13 July 2001), para. 67.

6   See Pierre Centlivres, 'Adieu aux Bouddhas de Bamiyan', *Afghanistan Info*, no. 48, March 2001, pp. 6-7; Véra Marigo, 'Bamyan: Naissance et destruction de deux géants', *Les Nouvelles d'Afghanistan*, no. 93, April-June 2001, pp. 16-21.

Pakistan's own relationship with the Taliban had remained firm. In October 1999, the civilian government of Nawaz Sharif was overthrown in a military coup mounted by General Pervez Musharraf, but Islamabad's backing for the Taliban did not weaken at all. In July 2001, Human Rights Watch reported on Pakistan's support in the following terms: 'Of all the foreign powers involved in efforts to sustain and manipulate the ongoing fighting, Pakistan is distinguished both by the sweep of its objectives and the scale of its efforts, which include soliciting funding for the Taliban, bankrolling Taliban operations, providing diplomatic support as the Taliban's virtual emissaries abroad, arranging training for Taliban fighters, recruiting skilled and unskilled manpower to serve in Taliban armies, planning and directing offensives, providing and facilitating shipments of ammunition and fuel, and on several occasions apparently directly providing combat support.'[7] The system of Deobandi madrassas provided a ready supply of manpower: according to Ahmed Rashid, 'an estimated 80,000 to 100,000 Pakistanis trained and fought in Afghanistan' between 1994 and 1999.[8] This reflected an alarming rise in Sunni militancy within Pakistan itself.[9] Yet the Taliban still were not able to eliminate their opponents, who retained control over Afghanistan's seat in the United Nations General Assembly and received an unexpected boost when the former leader of Herat, Ismail Khan, sensationally escaped from a Taliban prison on 26 March 2000 and resumed his anti-Taliban activities.

The lives of ordinary Afghans were beset with misery. From 1999, a drought struck the country, the most serious for thirty years, and the economy was devastated. Distorted by the effects of war and by the perverse incentive structures arising from Afghanistan's open borders and Pakistan's high tariffs, the economy was skewed towards illicit activities such as smuggling and opium growing,[10] although from

---

[7] *Afghanistan—Crisis of Impunity: The Role of Pakistan, Russia and Iran in Fueling the Civil War* (New York: Human Rights Watch, July 2001), p. 23.

[8] Ahmed Rashid, 'The Taliban: Exporting Extremism', *Foreign Affairs*, vol. 78, no. 6, November-December 1999, pp. 22-35 at p. 27. See also Amin Saikal, 'The Lineup Looks Like: Bin Laden, Taleban, Pakistan', *International Herald Tribune*, 14 September 2001.

[9] See Muhammad Qasim Zaman, 'Sectarianism in Pakistan: The Radicalization of Shi'i and Sunni Identities', *Modern Asian Studies*, vol. 32, part 3, July 1998, pp. 689-716; S.V. R. Nasr, 'The Rise of Sunni Militancy in Pakistan: The Changing Role of Islamism and the Ulama in Society and Politics', *Modern Asian Studies*, vol. 34, part I, January 2000, pp. 139-180; Vali R. Nasr, 'International Politics, Domestic Imperatives, and Identity Mobilization: Sectarianism in Pakistan, 1979-1998', *Comparative Politics*, vol. 32, no. 2, January 2000, pp. 171-190.

[10] See William Maley, 'Reconstructing Afghanistan: opportunities and challenges', in Geoff Harris (ed.), *Recovery from Armed Conflict in Developing Countries: An*

2000 the Taliban, perhaps in the hope of securing international acceptability, rigorously enforced a ban on poppy cultivation (but without offering any alternative economic activity for the farmers whom they targeted). The immiseration of the Afghan people has so dominated their lives that political action has scarcely been an option for them: survival from day to day is more important.

How can Afghanistan escape from its rut? The abandonment under US pressure of Pakistan's support for the Taliban has the capacity to create an unmanageable crisis within the Taliban movement, but Afghanistan's problems run deeper than the character of any single internal actor, for the Afghanistan conflict has become a transnational struggle which requires a synoptic and integrated solution.[11] It is necessary to find means of reconstructing the Afghan state along sustainable lines, and this will require from the international community a long-term commitment, in which moderate Afghans are partners, a new Marshall Plan is devised for the region, and the Afghan people are identified not as sinners to be punished, but as victims to be rescued.[12]

Afghanistan stands on the brink of a humanitarian disaster of unimaginable dimensions. But it is not a situation altogether without hope. The Taliban emerged in large measure because, after the collapse of the Soviet Union at the end of 1991, the United States lost interest in the politics of southwest Asia, and left Afghanistan exposed to the predations of its self-interested neighbours. The costs of such an approach, both for the Afghans and the wider world, are now all too obvious, and it is unlikely that Washington would wish to repeat its earlier mistake. Intervention can be a blunt tool for addressing complex problems, and it is best that it be attempted, if at all, with a full awareness of its limitations. But neglect of Afghanistan is no longer an option. That, at least, became clear from the dreadful events of September 2001.

---

economic and political analysis (New York: Routledge, 1999), pp. 225-257; Barnett R. Rubin, 'The Political Economy of Peace and War in Afghanistan', *World Development*, vol. 28, no. 10, October 2000, pp. 1789-1803; Peter Marsden and Emma Samman, 'Afghanistan: The Economic and Social Impact of Conflict', in Frances Stewart, Valpy Fitzgerald and Associates, *War and Underdevelopment* (Oxford University Press, 2001), vol.II, pp. 21-55.

[11] For more detailed discussion, see Barnett R. Rubin, Ashraf Ghani, William Maley, Ahmed Rashid and Olivier Roy, *Afghanistan: Reconstruction and Peacebuilding in a Regional Framework* (Bern: KOFF Peacebuilding Reports no. 1/2001, Swiss Peace Foundation, 2001).

[12] See Ahmed Rashid, 'Wretched Afghanistan', *The Washington Post*, 21 September 2001; Barnett R. Rubin, 'Afghans Can Be Our Allies', *New York Times*, 22 September 2001.

ACKNOWLEDGEMENTS

This book had its origins in a suggestion by Michael Dwyer that the Taliban phenomenon demanded more careful and detailed attention than it had received in the tumultuous days and weeks following the Taliban seizure of Kabul in September 1996. For this, and for his enthusiasm and support during the preparation of the volume, I owe him a great debt. Beyond his pivotal role, the book owes what merits it possesses largely to the energy and scholarship of the contributors, for whose efforts and patience I am deeply grateful. Beyond asking them to address particular topics, I have made no effort to impose any particular line of argument or methodology upon their contributions.

A number of people have helped shape my own thinking about Afghanistan, and in turn this book. Apart from the contributors, I have greatly profited from discussions at different times with Nasiba Akram, Anthony Arnold, Grahame Carroll, Pierre Centlivres and Micheline Centlivres-Demont, Gilles Dorronsoro, Patricia Garcia, Ravan Farhadi, Ashraf Ghani, Frédéric Grare, Habib R. Hala, Connie Lenneberg, Susie Low, Sayed Askar Mousavi, Kabir Osman, Abdul Rahim, Barnett R. Rubin, Fazel Haq Saikal, Fiona Terry, Bill Van Ree, and Marvin G. Weinbaum, as well as other Afghan and non-Afghan friends, currently working in Afghanistan or Pakistan, whom I should not name, but who will know of my gratitude.

It was my good fortune to be able to begin work on the book during a period of leave granted to me by the University of New South Wales. The first part of this leave I spent as a Visiting Research Fellow in the Refugee Studies Programme at Oxford University, and I would like to thank the RSP Director Dr David Turton, and the staff of the RSP Documentation Centre, for their hospitality. I was also able during my leave to do work at the ACBAR Resource and Information Center (ARIC) in Peshawar, and thank the superb staff of ARIC, and especially Fahim Rahimyar, for their kind assistance during my stay. I owe a particular debt of gratitude to officials of the United Nations Office for Coordination of Humanitarian Assistance to Afghanistan, and the International Committee of the Red Cross, for their generous assistance in a number of ways.

Finally, I wish to thank Beverley Lincoln of the University of New South Wales, who prepared the map with great patience.

Canberra, January 1998   WILLIAM MALEY

CONTENTS

Part IV: Paths to the Future

THE AUTHORS

ANWAR-UL-HAQ AHADY is Professor of Political Science at Providence College. He obtained his PhD from Northwestern University, and has published widely on Middle Eastern and West Asian security issues.

ANTHONY DAVIS is a frequent visitor to Afghanistan, and reports on Afghan affairs for *Asiaweek* and the Jane's Information Group. He graduated in Chinese from the Australian National University, and has been a Macarthur Fellow. He is currently completing a book on the Afghan war.

NANCY HATCH DUPREE is Senior Consultant to the Agency Coordinating Body for Afghan Relief (ACBAR) in Peshawar. She holds degrees from Barnard College and Columbia University, is a member of the Gender Advisory Group, and her publications include *An Historical Guide to Afghanistan*, *The Road to Balkh*, and a co-edited volume on *The Cultural Basis of Afghan Nationalism*.

BERNT GLATZER is a researcher at the Zentrum Moderner Orient in Berlin. He has served at different times as the Representative in Pakistan of the Südasien Institut, Heidelberg University, and as a consultant to the Danish Committee for Aid to Afghan Refugees (DACAAR). He is author of *Nomaden von Gharjistan: Aspekte der wirtschaflichen, sozialen und politischen Organisation nomadischer Durrani-Paschtunen in Nordwestafghanistan*.

ANTHONY HYMAN was Associate Editor of *Central Asian Survey*, and author of *Afghanistan under Soviet Domination,1964-91*. He was Visiting Fellow at Queen Elizabeth House, Oxford University and a Senior Fellow of the SSRC-Macarthur Foundation (New York) on Peace and Security; and he published widely on post-Soviet Central Asia. He died in 1999 after a long illness.

MICHAEL KEATING was Director of Media Natura in London for five years until September 1997, when he took up a UN assignment as Senior Adviser, Strategic Framework for Afghanistan. His chapter was commissioned before he took up this appointment, and was refined subsequently.

RICHARD MACKENZIE is a journalist and regular visitor to Afghanistan, on which he has written for *National Geographic*. He has also worked as a Producer for CNN, and serves as Editor-in-Chief of Global News Services.

WILLIAM MALEY is Senior Lecturer in Politics, University College, University of New South Wales, Australian Defence Force Academy. He has co-edited *The Soviet Withdrawal from Afghanistan*, and co-authored *Regime Change in Afghanistan: Foreign Intervention and the Politics of Legitimacy* and *Political Order in Post-Communist Afghanistan*.

AHMED RASHID, a graduate of Cambridge University, is Pakistan and Afghanistan correspondent of the *Far Eastern Economic Review*, and author of *The Resurgence of Central Asia: Islam or Nationalism?*

OLIVIER ROY is Director of Research at the Centre National de la Recherche Scientifique in Paris. His wrote his doctoral dissertation on state and society in Afghanistan, and his books include *Islam and Resistance in Afghanistan*, *Afghanistan: From Holy War to Civil War*, *The Failure of Political Islam*, *Généalogie de l'islamisme*, and *La Nouvelle Asie Centrale*.

AMIN SAIKAL is Professor of Political Science and Director of the Centre for Middle Eastern and Central Asian Studies at the Australian National University. He has held visiting appointments at King's College, Cambridge; the Institute of Development Studies at the University of Sussex; and the Center of International Studies at Princeton. He is author of *The Rise and Fall of the Shah*, and many articles and chapters.

M. NAZIF SHAHRANI is Professor of Anthropology and Central Asian Studies at Indiana University, and a Scholar-in-Residence at the Woodrow Wilson International Center for Scholars in Washington DC. He obtained his PhD at the University of Washington. He is author of *The Kirghiz and Wakhi of Afghanistan: Adaptation to Closed Frontiers*, and co-edited *Revolutions and Rebellions in Afghanistan: Anthropological Perspectives*.

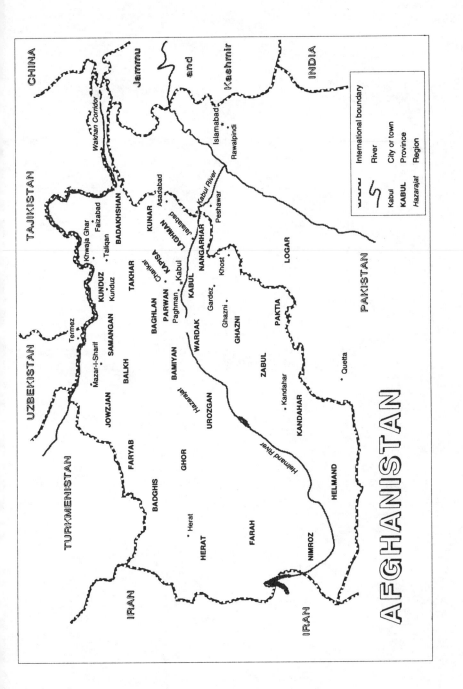

AFGHANISTAN

INTRODUCTION

INTERPRETING THE TALIBAN

William Maley

'He who seeks the salvation of the soul, of his own and of others, should not seek it along the avenue of politics, for the quite different tasks of politics can only be solved by violence'–*Max Weber*

On 26-27 September 1996, the Afghan capital Kabul was overrun by an armed force known as the 'Taliban', a name taken from the Persianised plural form of the Arabic word 'Talib', which means religious student. Seemingly indifferent to the gaze of the wider world, they set out to impose a new order on the city. Kabul residents awoke to find the battered body of the former communist president Najibullah hanging from a pylon in Ariana Square, alongside the corpse of his hapless younger brother who happened to have been visiting Najibullah in the UN compound in central Kabul when the city fell. This, however, was only the beginning of a much more extensive set of changes. Within a matter of days, the new leadership had issued decrees on a range of social matters which produced widespread if nonetheless muted consternation. Women, who in Kabul had been permitted to move freely around the city for nearly four decades, and made up the majority of the student body at Kabul University, were henceforth to venture out of their homes only if swathed in the stifling *burqa*. Their male relatives were curtly informed that they were obliged, in accordance with the dictates of the Islamic faith, to grow beards; and that if they did not, punishment under Islamic Sharia law would follow. Within days, foreign journalists were filing stories on the beating of women in public places by zealots armed with car-radio antennae, and on the prohibition of music, cassette tapes, kite flying, homing pigeons, and chess.[1] Furthermore, significant numbers of

---

[1] For the texts of Taliban decrees, see *Final report on the situation of human rights in Afghanistan submitted by Mr. Choong-Hyun Paik, Special Rapporteur, in accordance with Commission on Human Rights resolution 1996/75* (United Nations: E/CN.4/1997/59, 20 February 1997), pp. 32-36. For samples of the press reporting, see Sarah Horner, 'Kabul falls under the Islamic lash', *The Sunday Times*, 29 September 1996; Christopher Thomas, 'Militants bring a veil down on battered Kabul', *The Times*, 30 September 1996; John F. Burns, 'For Women in Kabul, Peace at the Price of Repression', *The New York Times*, 4 October 1996; Jon Swain, 'Kabul hushed by Taliban dark age', *The Sunday Times*, 6 October 1996. My own initial observations on the Taliban takeover of Kabul can be found

1

people were arrested in house-to-house searches, prompting the human rights organisation Amnesty International to warn that a 'reign of terror' had struck the city.[2] Religious fundamentalism of a particularly virulent kind seemed to be on the march.

Yet as so often is the case in Afghanistan, the tale of the Taliban's activities was more complex than some of the immediate reporting suggested. The Taliban had attempted hardly more in Kabul than they had already carried out in the southern city of Kandahar (from late 1994), and in the western city of Herat (from September 1995), which had drawn little in the way of adverse comment from the international community. The identity of Najibullah's killers remained somewhat mysterious, with suspicion falling increasingly on ethnic Pushtun members of the Khalq communist faction, notoriously hostile to Najibullah, who had penetrated Taliban ranks. As time went by, it became clear that while the Taliban continued to seek international recognition on the basis of their occupation of Kabul, the heart of their operations remained in Kandahar from which their elusive leader, a one-eyed cleric named Mohammad Omar who had never been openly photographed, continued to operate. Perhaps because the heartland of Taliban power was so remote, the implementation of Taliban decrees in Kabul proved sporadic.[3] Furthermore, there was considerable evidence to suggest that the Taliban were being strongly supported by the Pakistani government led by Benazir Bhutto, ironically a woman educated at Oxford and Harvard. There was also for outside observers the remarkable spectacle of a muted reaction to the Taliban takeover on the part of the US State Department, normally allergic to the slightest sign of resurgent 'Islamic extremism' or of involvement by groups in opium poppy cultivation, from which the Taliban were profiting in areas they claimed to control.[4] In Afghanistan at least, 'narco-

---

in William Maley, 'Taliban Triumphant?', *The World Today*, vol. 52, no. 11, November 1996, pp. 275-276.

2 *Afghanistan: Taleban Take Hundreds of Civilians Prisoner* (London: Amnesty International, ASA/11/07/96, 2 October 1996).

3 This led to some indulgent reporting of Taliban activities from journalists not noted for longstanding involvement with the Afghanistan issue: see, for example, James Fergusson, 'Afghanistan: The Peace Brought by the Taliban', *The Independent*, 19 February 1997. Sentimental reporting of the Taliban was pioneered by Nancy DeWolf Smith, 'These Rebels Aren't So Scary', *The Wall Street Journal*, 22 February 1995. For a more recent (and slightly less effusive) sample of this writer's work, see Nancy DeWolf Smith, 'The Warriors Time Forgot', *The Wall Street Journal*, 27 March 1997.

4 That the Taliban obtained revenue from a tax on opium sales was admitted by Mohammad Omar in an interview with the journalist Bizhan Torabi: see 'Entretien avec Mollah Mohammad Omar', *Politique internationale*, no. 74, Winter 1996-97, pp. 135-143 at pp. 141-142.

fundamentalism' seemed somehow to have become acceptable to Washington, possibly because of lobbying by firms hoping to transport energy resources from Turkmenistan to Pakistan via Afghanistan, and by opponents of Iran, a country which had no sympathy whatsoever for the Taliban.

Within a relatively short space of time, Western aid agencies based in Kabul found themselves entangled in a troubling debate over whether it was better to work with the Taliban, in order to ensure that local people received some material assistance, or to isolate them entirely, in order to signal that their policies were unacceptable to a world in which international instruments had increasingly demanded respect for the rights of both men and women. This debate raised obvious questions about the likely effects of different policy positions, given the characteristics of the Taliban. So did the significant military setbacks suffered by the Taliban in May-June 1997. Their attempt to take over northern Afghanistan by orchestrating an internal coup by General Abdul Malik Pahlavan against northern warlord Abdul Rashid Dostum failed disastrously. Malik's forces turned ferociously on their Taliban 'allies' only four days after Dostum's flight to Turkey on 24 May–an exit which had prompted an outburst of premature triumphalism amongst the Taliban, and lured Pakistan, Saudi Arabia and the United Arab Emirates to accord the Taliban diplomatic recognition, a hasty step which wiser heads in these states doubtless later regretted.

Yet the characteristics of the Taliban have received far less attention than one might have expected, and that is a problem which this book aims to rectify. Are the Taliban a transient phenomenon, or a permanent fixture with which the international community will have to deal for years to come? Do they reflect intransigent 'fundamentalism', are they a recrudescence of tradition, amenable to reform by persuasion and example, or are they simply a manifestation of the totalitarian drive to subordinate the whole of private life to public control? The contributors all shed light on different aspects of the ways in which the Taliban emerged, and in which they have affected Afghanistan's region, the prospects for postwar reconstruction in Afghanistan, and the likely course of Afghanistan's social and political futures. The question of whether the Taliban represent the rebirth of fundamentalism is an enormously difficult and complex issue, and ultimately one we leave for readers of this book to confront. However, to assist in the formulation of this question, I wish in this introduction to do five things. The first is to set recent developments in Afghanistan in historical context. The second is to explore the dimensions of the crisis which the Taliban unexpectedly confronted in mid-1997, and to reflect on how these might shed light on the characteristics, the strengths, and the weaknesses of the movement.

The third is briefly to examine the social and doctrinal roots of the Taliban. The fourth is to explore some of the dimensions of 'fundamentalism', both conceptually and historically, as well as of various alternative concepts by which one might wish to characterise the Taliban. The fifth is to highlight some of the conclusions offered by the contributors to this volume.

Afghanistan's path to crisis

Afghanistan is a landlocked country in Central Asia, bordered by Pakistan, Iran, Turkmenistan, Uzbekistan, Tajikistan, and China. Its population has never been fully counted by census, but at present probably stands somewhere between 15 and 20 million people.[5] The overwhelming majority of its people are Muslims, although a significant minority—between 10 and 20 per cent—adhere to the heterodox Shiite rather than the orthodox Sunni confession. The population is also diverse in both ethnic and linguistic terms.[6] While two Indo-Iranian languages—Persian and Pushto—are the ones most widely heard in the country, one also encounters speakers of Turkic, Dravidian, Nuristani, and other languages. This linguistic diversity tends to reinforce some manifestations of ethnic identification, as also

[5] Thomas H. Eighmy, *Afghanistan's Population Inside and Out* (Islamabad: Office of the A.I.D. Representative for Afghanistan Affairs, 1990), p. 11, estimates an internal population of 12,363,255; this has since been swelled by the voluntary repatriation of perhaps two-thirds of the 5-6 million Afghan refugees in Pakistan and Iran, as well as by natural growth. Unpublished 1997 estimates by the UN put the internal population at 20.1 million, with about half in the centre and north, and half in the east, west, and south.

[6] On Afghanistan's ethnic and linguistic diversity, see H.F. Schurmann, *The Mongols of Afghanistan: An Ethnography of the Môghols and Related Peoples of Afghanistan* (The Hague: Mouton, 1962); Louis Dupree, 'Ethnography', in Ehsan Yarshater (ed.), *Encyclopædia Iranica* (London: Routledge & Kegan Paul, 1985), Vol. I, pp. 495-501; Erwin Orywal (ed.), *Die ethnischen Gruppen Afghanistans: Fallstudien zu Gruppenidentität und Intergruppenbeziehungen* (Wiesbaden: Dr. Ludwig Reichert Verlag, 1986); Pierre Centlivres and Micheline Centlivres-Demont, *Et si on parlait de l'Afghanistan?* (Paris: Éditions de la Maison des science de l'homme, 1988); Jean-Pierre Digard (ed.), *Le fait ethnique en Iran et en Afghanistan* (Paris: Éditions du Centre National de la Recherche Scientifique, 1988); Robert L. Canfield, 'Afghanistan: The Trajectory of Internal Alignments', *The Middle East Journal*, vol. 43, no. 4, Autumn 1989, pp. 635-648; Pierre Centlivres, 'La nouvelle carte ethnique de l'Afghanistan', *Les Nouvelles d'Afghanistan*, no. 47, 1990, pp. 4-11; Nassim Jawad, *Afghanistan: A Nation of Minorities* (London: Minority Rights Group, 1992); Pierre Centlivres, 'Les groupes ethniques et les "nationalités" dans la crise afghane', in Riccardo Bocco and Mohammad-Reza Djalili (eds.), *Moyen-Orient: Migrations, Démocratisation, Méditations* (Paris: Presses Universitaires de France, 1994), pp. 161-170.

do group norms and practices which socialisation within the household or family tends to replicate across generations. Afghanistan is further divided economically and spatially, with the bulk of the population based in villages and engaging in sedentary agricultural and pastoral activities. Social organisation, diverse and complex, has not reflected any simple stratification along lines of class–a concept with limited value in the analysis of Afghanistan's micro-societies–but tends rather to reflect the importance of bonds of kinship and reciprocity. To the extent that groups have suffered systematic disadvantage it tends to reflect Weberian-style social closure, to which the Hazaras, by virtue of their distinctively oriental appearance, have particularly been victim.[7] The web-like character of Afghan society explains its remarkable resilience, a resilience which has been repeatedly confirmed by its capacity to resist and survive threats to its existence.

The images of Afghanistan which occupy the minds of lay readers are frequently tinged with the romanticism of an earlier era. Tales of the rout of the British during the First Anglo-Afghan War of 1838-42, and Sir Frederick Roberts's memoir of his march to Kandahar during the Second Anglo-Afghan War of 1878-9, have merged with the poetry of Rudyard Kipling, and the *Flashman* novels of George Macdonald Fraser, to create an image of wild, heavily-armed and hirsute tribesmen seeking to hold back the forces of modernity–an image which the behaviour of the Taliban has reinforced in diverse ways. But for many years, Afghanistan has reflected much more complex realities than these.

While the emergence of Afghanistan as a territorial unit is often dated from the rule of Ahmad Shah Durrani (1747-72), the political disarray which followed his death left the Afghan 'polity' debilitated for much of the nineteenth century.[8] Abdul Rahman Khan, who ruled from 1880 to 1901 with British backing, and was even appointed a Knight Grand Commander of the Order of the Star of India, created a

---

[7]   See Hassan Poladi, *The Hazaras* (Stockton: Moghul Press, 1989); Kristian Berg Harpviken, *Political Mobilization among the Hazaras of Afghanistan: 1978-1992* (Oslo: Report no. 9, Department of Sociology, University of Oslo, 1996); Sayed Askar Mousavi, *The Hazaras of Afghanistan: An Historical, Cultural, Economic, and Political Study* (Richmond: Curzon Press, 1997). On the contemporary political activities of Hazaras, see Hafizullah Emadi, 'Exporting Iran's Revolution: The Radicalization of the Shiite Movement in Afghanistan', *Middle Eastern Studies*, vol. 31, no. 1, January 1995, pp. 1-12; Hafizullah Emadi, 'The Hazaras and their role in the process of political transformation in Afghanistan', *Central Asian Survey*, vol. 16, no. 3, September 1997, pp. 363-387.

[8]   For a detailed discussion, see Christine Noelle, 'The Interaction between State and Tribe in Nineteenth-Century Afghanistan: The Reign of Amir Dost Muhammad Khan (1826-1863)', Unpublished PhD thesis, University of California at Berkeley, 1995.

consolidated central state, but at terrible human cost.[9] His son Habibullah, who ruled from 1901 until his assassination in 1919, was far more moderate than his father, and this eroded the accumulated capital of fear upon which his father's rule had thrived. Consequently, when the ambitious modernisation plans of his son Amanullah (and the tax collection processes needed to finance them) provoked opposition, neither Amanullah nor his court possessed the authority to override the forces ranged against them.[10] Yet those forces, led by Habibullah Ghazi, were themselves rapidly overthrown; Habibullah Ghazi was an ethnic Tajik, whereas for centuries Afghanistan's rulers had been drawn from the ranks of the numerically dominant Pushtuns. Indeed, for those who believe in the capacity of history to repeat itself, there are striking parallels between the overthrow in 1929 of the Tajik Habibullah Ghazi, and that of the Tajik President Burhanuddin Rabbani and his military supremo, the Tajik Ahmad Shah Massoud, in 1996. Yet there are significant differences as well. General Nadir Khan, who overthrew Habibullah, immediately re-established a monarchical system, which he headed until his assassination in November 1933. The Taliban, by contrast, moved to establish a theocracy, and showed no interest in facilitating the return to Afghanistan of Nadir's son Zahir, who had ruled Afghanistan as King from 1933 until overthrown in a palace coup mounted by his cousin Mohammad Daoud in 1973, and some of whose supporters had naively favoured the Taliban as a means of restoring the remnants of the *ancien régime*.

The legitimacy of the Afghan state was at all times shaky.[11] As David Edwards has recently argued, a range of potentially conflicting value systems are to be found in Pushtun society–values of honour,

9   For various perspectives on this period, see Vartan Gregorian, *The Emergence of Modern Afghanistan: Politics of Reform and Modernization 1880-1946* (Stanford: Stanford University Press, 1969); M. Hasan Kakar, *Afghanistan: A Study of Internal Political Developments 1880-1896* (Kabul and Lahore: Punjab Educational Press, 1971); M. Hasan Kakar, *Government and Society in Afghanistan: The Reign of Amir Abd-al Rahman Khan* (Austin: University of Texas Press, 1979); J.L. Lee, *The 'Ancient Supremacy': Bukhara, Afghanistan and the Battle for Balkh, 1731-1901* (Leiden: E.J. Brill, 1996).

10 Leon B. Poullada, Jr., *Reform and Rebellion in Afghanistan, 1919-1929: King Amanullah's Failure to Modernize a Tribal Society* (Ithaca: Cornell University Press, 1973); M. Nazif Shahrani, 'State Building and Social Fragmentation in Afghanistan: A Historical Perspective', in Ali Banuazizi and Myron Weiner (eds.), *The State, Religion, and Ethnic Politics: Afghanistan, Iran, and Pakistan* (Syracuse: Syracuse University Press, 1986), pp. 23-74.

11 For more detailed discussion, see Amin Saikal and William Maley, *Regime Change in Afghanistan: Foreign Intervention and the Politics of Legitimacy* (Boulder: Westview Press, 1991), pp. 9-32.

kingship, and religion.[12] But of course, ethnic Pushtuns made up only one element of the population of Afghanistan, and the more extreme forms of Pushtun chauvinism left a bitter taste in the mouths of many non-Pushtuns, setting the scene for diverse political mobilisation once the authority of the state was compromised. This came about in the late 1970s. The Afghan government, which faced a decline in foreign aid, proved unable to satisfy the aspirations of those Afghans who having been given a Western-style education confidently expected to secure bureaucratic employment.[13] This, together with the penetration of the armed forces by Soviet-trained personnel, created the conditions for a radical shift in Afghanistan's politics, which came about with the coup of April 1978, in which President Mohammad Daoud was killed. This event ruptured once and for all the delicate equilibrium by which the state had survived, one in which strategic distribution of resources and respect for the prerogatives of local élites had secured the prudential support of those whom the central authorities were unable to intimidate. As the extremists of the communist People's Democratic Party of Afghanistan, and particularly its hardline Khalq faction, sought from a very narrow support base to impose policies of land redistribution, re-education, and secularisation based on a profound misunderstanding of the complexity of Afghanistan's mechanisms for preserving social order and solidarity, they confronted increasingly ferocious popular resistance, as well as heightened tension between the Khalq and its more 'moderate' partner, the Parcham faction. The combination of popular resistance and intra-élite antagonism set the scene for the invasion of Afghanistan in December 1979 by the regime's Soviet backer.[14]

The communist regime installed by the Soviet invasion survived until April 1992, first under Babrak Karmal (1979-86) and then under Dr Najibullah (1986-92).[15] By judicious use of the massive material support which the USSR continued to supply the regime following

[12] David B. Edwards, *Heroes of the Age: Moral Fault Lines on the Afghan Frontier* (Berkeley & Los Angeles: University of California Press, 1996).

[13] Barnett R. Rubin, *The Fragmentation of Afghanistan: State Formation and Collapse in the International System* (New Haven: Yale University Press, 1995), p. 77.

[14] For detailed discussion of events leading to the Soviet invasion, see Odd Arne Westad, 'Prelude to Invasion: The Soviet Union and the Afghan Communists, 1978-1979', *International History Review*, vol. 16, no. 1, 1994, pp. 49-69; Raymond Garthoff, *Détente and Confrontation: American-Soviet Relations from Nixon to Reagan* (Washington DC: The Brookings Institution, 1994), pp. 977-1075.

[15] On the communist regime, see Rubin, *The Fragmentation of Afghanistan*; Anthony Arnold, *Afghanistan's Two-Party Communism: Parcham and Khalq* (Stanford: Hoover Institution Press, 1983); Anthony Arnold, *The Fateful Pebble: Afghanistan's Role in the Fall of the Soviet Empire* (San Francisco: Presidio Press, 1993).

the completion of the withdrawal of Soviet troops from Afghanistan in February 1989, Najibullah managed to buy enough support at the local level to cling to power for a further three years. But with the cut-off of all aid following the failure of the August 1991 coup attempt in Moscow (which destroyed the political position of those committed to assisting him), his regime was doomed, and it collapsed in April 1992. The story of what happened thereafter is taken up in this book.[16] But to set the scene for this discussion, it is important to say a little more about the Islamic resistance which emerged after the April 1978 coup, and the influences to which it was exposed during its long years of struggle.

Historically, the role of organised religious groups in Afghanistan's politics had not been in any sense a dominant one, although insensitivity to key interests of the religious establishment could cause problems for a ruler, as Amanullah discovered to his cost in 1928-29. However, in the years preceding the communist coup, religious mobilisation had proved ineffective. Those who sought to oppose the unveiling of women from 1959 were swiftly repressed, and while a significant Muslim youth movement (*Sazman-e Javanan-e Musulman-e Afghanistan*) took shape, those of its members who attempted an uprising against the Daoud regime, in the Panjsher Valley in 1975, were crushed with ease by the Afghan army.[17] The communist coup changed the situation decisively. Symbolic steps taken by the new regime highlighted its atheism and attachment to the (atheistic) Soviet Union. It is therefore hardly surprising that opposition to the regime was rhetorically articulated in religious terms. Islam provided legitimacy for challenges to the kind of regime for which the cadres of the People's Democratic Party purported to stand. Yet the vocabulary of Islamic resistance embraced a remarkably diverse range of politico-religious forces, varying from the intensely ideological to the avowedly rustic. The Afghan resistance,[18]

---

[16]   I have sought to tell parts of the story in William Maley and Fazel Haq Saikal, *Political Order in Post-Communist Afghanistan* (Boulder: Lynne Rienner, 1992); William Maley, 'The Future of Islamic Afghanistan', *Security Dialogue*, vol. 24, no. 4, December 1993, pp.383-396; and William Maley, 'The dynamics of regime transition in Afghanistan', *Central Asian Survey*, vol. 16, no. 2, June 1997, pp. 167-184.

[17]   On Islam in the Afghan political process, see Olivier Roy, *Islam and resistance in Afghanistan* (Cambridge: Cambridge University Press, 1990); Asta Olesen, *Islam and Politics in Afghanistan* (Richmond: Curzon Press, 1995).

[18]   For more detailed discussion of the Afghan resistance, see Roy, *Islam and resistance in Afghanistan*; Olesen, *Islam and Politics in Afghanistan*; Eden Naby, 'The Afghan Resistance Movement', in Ralph H. Magnus (ed.), *Afghan Alternatives: Issues, Options, and Policies* (New Brunswick: Transaction Books, 1985), pp. 59-81; Eden Naby, 'The Changing Role of Islam as a Unifying Force in

collectively known by the title Mujahideen (meaning 'Warriors in the Way of God'), ranged from 'parties' (*tanzimat*) with headquarters outside Afghanistan, to forces organised on a regional basis, to scattered groups of fighters with local interests and agendas whose attachment to the wider resistance was dictated by a need for access to weaponry, but whose tactics resembled those of seasonal tribal warfare and whose ideological affinity with the parties they nominally represented was potentially quite tenuous.

Some parties sought to bolster their status by pointing to the achievements of commanders linked with them: the largely-Tajik Jamiat-e Islami, headed by Professor Burhanuddin Rabbani (who was to become President of Afghanistan in June 1992), drew credit from association with Tajik commanders such as Ahmad Shah Massoud (in the Panjsher Valley north of Kabul) and Ismail Khan (in the Herat area). By contrast, the Pushtun Hezb-e Islami of Gulbuddin Hekmatyar had limited popular support but flourished on the strength of long-term patronage from Pakistan's Inter Services Intelligence Directorate (ISI), while the Ittehad-e Islami of Abdul-Rab al-Rasul Sayyaf received generous financial support through charitable trusts established in Saudi Arabia. These parties also differed markedly in ideology: while those of Pir Sayed Ahmad Gailani, Sebghatullah Mojadiddi, and Mohammad Nabi Mohammadi were well disposed to the idea that Zahir Shah should play a role in solving Afghanistan's crisis, and the Jamiat-e Islami adopted a moderate Islamist position, Hekmatyar's Hezb took an extremely uncompromising stance–labelled 'fundamentalist' by some– which complemented its Leninist approach to political organisation. These differences were accentuated by personal antagonisms: in April 1992, Hekmatyar's spokesman candidly observed that 'Hekmatyar can't agree to anything that includes Ahmed Shah Masoud'.[19] It is hardly surprising that the politics of post-communist Afghanistan proved troubled.

Afghanistan', in Ali Banuazizi and Myron Weiner (eds.), *The State, Religion, and Ethnic Politics: Afghanistan, Iran, and Pakistan* (Syracuse: Syracuse University Press, 1986), pp. 124-154; Eden Naby, 'Islam within the Afghan Resistance', *Third World Quarterly*, vol. 10, no. 2, 1988, pp. 787-805; Graham Fuller, *Islamic Fundamentalism in Afghanistan: Its Character and Prospects* (Santa Monica: RAND R-3970-USDP, 1991); Olivier Roy, *Afghanistan: From Holy War to Civil War* (Princeton: The Darwin Press, 1995); Assem Akram, *Histoire de la guerre d'Afghanistan* (Paris: Balland, 1996).
19 *International Herald Tribune*, 22 April 1992.

The northern crisis

After the Taliban seized Kabul, their opponents appeared in considerable disarray. The Taliban controlled four of the country's five main cities, namely Kabul, Kandahar, Herat, and Jalalabad, and only a fifth, Mazar-e Sharif, lay outside their grasp. Bringing Mazar under their control was therefore an important objective for the Taliban: if they succeeded in taking over the north, their claim to be rulers of the whole country would be difficult to contest. For a brief moment in May 1997, such domination appeared to be within their grasp, but ultimately it eluded them.[20] Rarely have events in Afghanistan moved so fast, or fortunes changed so rapidly. The crisis broke out on 14 May 1997, when an armed commander named Abdul Rahman Haqqani was shot dead in Mazar-e Sharif. The following fortnight witnessed an escalating drama which culminated in the arrival of Taliban in the north, followed by gruesome massacres of Taliban in the streets of Mazar. The northern crisis had significant regional and international ramifications, exposing the depth of Pakistan's entanglement with the Taliban. It left Pakistan painfully isolated as virtually all major powers declined to follow the lead of its maladroit Foreign Minister, Gohar Ayub, in according diplomatic recognition to the Taliban 'government'. It furthermore placed a question mark over the durability of the Taliban phenomenon as a whole. For if nothing succeeds like success, nothing fails like failure.

The killing of former President Najibullah in September 1996 set off reverberations well beyond the Kabul conurbation. In the months before the Taliban took Kabul, the government of Pakistan, undoubtedly their most important backer, had been cultivating the former communist militia leader Abdul Rashid Dostum, who was based in Mazar. Dostum's defection to the resistance in early 1992 had helped precipitate the collapse of the communist regime, but thereafter he had pursued a complex strategy of power balancing, seeking above all to preserve a northern fiefdom under his dominion, which had led him not only to join Hekmatyar in his blistering assault on Kabul at the beginning of 1994, but after the flight of Hekmatyar in 1995, to provide technical support to the Taliban as they moved into the west of Afghanistan. Pakistan's strategy seems to have been to leave Dostum in position in the north, under nominal Taliban authority, in order to allay the fears of 'fundamentalism on the march' which Russia and the republics of Central Asia would certainly have entertained had real Taliban approached their borders. The death of Najibullah derailed

---

[20] For a more detailed discussion of the events of May 1997, see Anthony Davis, 'Taliban found lacking when nation-building beckoned', *Jane's Intelligence Review*, vol. 9, no. 8, August 1997, pp. 359-364.

any such strategy, and instead drove Dostum into the arms of his erstwhile enemy Ahmad Shah Massoud. This alliance, in tandem with the negative publicity which accompanied the Taliban occupation of Kabul, thwarted the Taliban's objective of securing Afghanistan's seat at the UN, which remained in the hands of the Rabbani government. But Pakistan's hopes of establishing a nominally-Taliban buffer in the north did not wane altogether, and the assassination of Haqqani triggered a new attempt to bring this about.

On 19 May, reports emerged that Dostum's foreign affairs spokesman, General Abdul Malik Pahlavan, whose power base lay to the west of Mazar near the frontline with Taliban forces in Badghis, had defected to the Taliban.[21] Rumour had held Dostum responsible for the murder of Malik's ambitious brother Rasul Pahlavan in 1996; and Haqqani was also allied to Malik. Malik's handing over to the Taliban of the Herat resistance leader Ismail Khan suggested that his intention, at least at this point, was indeed to change his allegiance. But most analysts on the spot saw a Pakistani hand at work, since Malik would scarcely have moved against Dostum in the name of the Taliban unless he had very firm guarantees that he would remain in charge if Dostum were overthrown. On 23 May, the staff of the Pakistani consulate in Mazar were suddenly evacuated on a UN flight to Islamabad; and the following day, as fighting broke out in the city, Dostum fled to Turkey, paving the way for the return of the Pakistani consular staff one day later. The afternoon of 25 May saw Pakistan recognise the Taliban at a hastily-summoned press conference. At the same time, Afghan and Pakistani Taliban were heading in large numbers from Peshawar towards the Afghan border;[22] a number of senior Taliban leaders flew to Mazar to claim 'their' victory; and an expeditionary force of Taliban led by other senior figures headed north from Kabul, and surprisingly found themselves able to cross the Hindu Kush mountain range thanks to the wholly unexpected 'defection' of a senior Massoud commander, Bashir Salangi.

Three days later, on 28 May, everything fell apart. By this time, bands of young Taliban students had begun to arrive in Mazar from the west. Their attempts to disarm some of Malik's forces led to an exchange of fire; more Taliban were killed by an anti-tank missile as their truck sped towards the centre of the city; and soon an orgy of slaughter began as Taliban were hunted down in side streets by locals. As night fell, more than a hundred Taliban bodies littered the road outside the Sub-Delegation of the International Committee of the Red

21 Significant military movements to the east of Mazar on the previous evening, witnessed by the author, suggest that Dostum may have become aware of Malik's defection at least a day before it became publicly known.
22 Witnessed by the author in Peshawar, 25 May 1997.

Cross,[23] and the alliance between Malik and the Taliban was dead as well–notwithstanding an almost pathetic effort by Pakistan to revive it on 5 June, one which succeeded only in making public what were most likely the terms of the original agreement.[24] The whole débâcle showed Pakistan to be not a master puppeteer, but rather a clumsy apprentice sorcerer, reminiscent of the central character in Goethe's poem *Der Zauberlehrling* who fell victim to forces he had blithely liberated but then could not control. The consequences of this carnage were widely felt. Militarily, the Taliban suddenly were in a far more parlous position than they had expected. Key leaders were caught in Mazar, while others found themselves trapped north of the Salang tunnel, as Bashir Salangi sprang what was almost certainly a trap behind the expeditionary force. Kabul was suddenly under threat again, as Massoud's forces surged out from the Panjsher Valley to seize the Parvan provincial capital of Charikar, and thereafter headed south along the roads of the Shomali Valley, which the Taliban had earlier largely depopulated by force. The Taliban found themselves so thinly stretched that Pakistani Taliban had to be sent to the front line at Charikar, where their lack of proper military training left them brutally exposed to Massoud's firepower.[25]

[23] Overall Taliban casualties in the north were of course far higher than this: in November 1997, a number of mass graves were opened in the Shiberghan area, and from inspection of the bodies by Western journalists, it was clear that many of the victims were *hors de combat* when they were killed. See Barbara Crossette, 'Up to 2,000 Taliban Fighters Reported Slain', *The New York Times*, 18 November 1997. According to a subsequent report, 'U.N. investigators said mass killings were committed by both sides in the fighting, adding that they also had found evidence of mass slaughter of ethnic Uzbeks by Taliban troops. U.N. officials said the killings appeared to be ethnically motivated. "It appears that everybody was butchering everybody up there," one U.N. official said': *Associated Press*, 13 December 1997.

[24] See BBC *Summary of World Broadcasts*, FE/2938/A/1, 6 June 1997.

[25] Pakistani deaths in Afghanistan began to be reported in the Pakistani press in mid-June: see Shamim Shahid, 'Is there jihad in Afghanistan?', *The Nation*, 15 June 1997. The danger to which Pakistanis were being exposed with the apparent passive acceptance–if not active support–of their government was revealed by the case of Maroof Ahmed, a 13-year old student from an impoverished family at the Jamia Islamia madrassa in Karachi's Clifton district, who was sent into Afghanistan in May by clerics, and whose experience came to light only when his distraught father commenced legal action in the High Court of Sindh. See Zahid Hussain, 'Pakistan pupils sent to aid Taleban', *The Times*, 4 August 1997. On 6 August 1997, Pakistani authorities charged the madrassa with kidnapping, and on 8 August Maroof finally returned home, saying 'I cried all the way but they would not listen': *Associated Press*, 8 August 1997. In September 1997, the UN Secretary-General reported that a number of prisoners interviewed in Afghanistan by UN staff 'freely admitted that they came from various areas in

More damaging to the Taliban was the psychological impact of the deflation of their aura of invincibility, which was potentially threatening because continuing success, and the desire to be part of it, can be one of the main sources of cohesion for social movements. But perhaps most damaging of all to the Taliban was the way in which the Mazar experience put an end to the hope that like some Hobbesian sovereign, they could rapidly bring 'order' to Afghanistan by subordinating other power centres to their control.[26] After Mazar, it was clear that this would most likely be a process with huge costs attached to it, something confirmed when a renewed three-week Taliban assault on the town from 9 September 1997 brought a great deal of bloodshed to civilians (including a grisly massacre of Hazaras in the nearby village of Qizilabad on 14 September)[27], the return of Dostum from exile in Turkey, but ultimately no improvement in the Taliban's military position in the north. With the erosion of the hope of a 'Hobbesian solution', a significant basis of the Taliban's claim to legitimacy, namely their proclaimed ability to put an end to 'anarchy', was also threatened. It is now more than likely that even should the Taliban at some stage succeed in taking Mazar, this would not bring about 'peace', but rather trigger mass ethnic conflict of a scale and ferocity that Afghanistan has thus far largely been spared.

At heart, the northern crisis sprang from the difficulty which the Taliban movement faced in compromising with its opponents. I use the word 'movement' advisedly: there is no doubt that elements of the Taliban *leadership* had been prepared to compromise with General Malik, and on terms which hardly resonated with the longstanding Taliban claim that all forces of 'corruption' should be disarmed. But it was clear that the students who perished in Mazar had not been appraised of the details of the compromise, and perhaps their loyalty to the movement would have been sorely tested had they known what their leaders planned. To explore this matter further, it is necessary to

---

Pakistan': *The Situation in Afghanistan and its Implications for International Peace and Security: Report of the Secretary-General* (United Nations: S/1997/719, 17 September 1997), para. 17. Earlier reports on Pakistani prisoners were provided by Edward Barnes, 'Friends of the *Taliban*', *Time*, 4 November 1996, and Anthony Davis, 'The not so hidden hand: how Pakistanis help the Taliban crusade', *Asiaweek*, 29 November 1996.

26 For somewhat innocent statements of the Hobbesian argument, see Ben R. Goldsmith, 'A Victory to Fear or a Source of Hope?', *The World Today*, vol. 53, no. 7, July 1997, pp. 182-184, and Ralph H. Magnus and Eden Naby, *Afghanistan: Mullah, Marx, and Mujahid* (Boulder: Westview Press, 1998) p. 195.

27 Personal communication from an official of a Western aid agency in Mazar-e Sharif, 30 September 1997; *Afghanistan: Continuing Atrocities Against Civilians* (London: Amnesty International, ASA/11/09/97, September 1997); *Reuters*, 20 October 1997.

discuss in more detail the origins of the Taliban and how they might be categorised, since different movements facilitate different patterns of relations between leaders and followers.

The social and doctrinal roots of the Taliban

The Taliban did not emerge from nowhere, although the precise milieu which nurtured them has not been widely studied.[28] The figure of the Talib is a relatively familiar one in the Northwest Frontier: as long ago as 1898, Winston Churchill penned some cutting remarks about 'a host of wandering *Talib-ul-ilms*, who correspond with the theological students in Turkey [and] live free at the expense of the people'.[29] In Afghanistan, the establishment in the twentieth century of state-supported venues for religious education such as the Faculty of Islamic Law at Kabul University, and state madrassas (Islamic colleges), did not mean the end of private madrassas 'in which the talib proceeded at his own individual speed with one subject at a time'.[30] The advent of war in Afghanistan in the 1980s saw talibs taking to the battlefield; they were witnessed in 1984 by Olivier Roy in Uruzgan, Zabul and Kandahar.[31] Other students emerged not from madrassas in Afghanistan, but from those run by the Jamiat-e Ulema-i Islam, a Pakistani political party headed by Maulana Fazlur Rahman, which offered a conservative religious education to boys from Afghan refugee camps, especially orphans or sons of very poor families. The religious training of these students was heavily influenced by the Deobandi school, which originated in the Dar ul-Ulum Deoband, an institution established in the Indian town of Deoband in 1867.[32] The Deobandi school preached a form of conservative orthodoxy, and madrassas under

---

[28] Notably perceptive works so far which have sought to account for the origins and character of the Taliban include Barnett R. Rubin, 'Women and pipelines: Afghanistan's proxy wars', *International Affairs*, vol. 73, no. 2, April 1997, pp. 283-296; Rameen Moshref, *The Taliban* (New York: Occasional Paper no. 35, The Afghanistan Forum, May 1997); Kristian Berg Harpviken, 'Transcending Traditionalism', *Journal of Peace Research*, vol. 34, no. 3, August 1997, pp. 271-287; Bernt Glatzer, 'Die Talibanbewegung: Einige religiöse, lokale und politische Faktoren', *Afghanistan Info*, no. 41, October 1997, pp. 10-14.

[29] Winston Churchill, *The Story of the Malakand Field Force* (New York: W.W. Norton & Company, 1990), p. 7.

[30] Olesen, *Islam and Politics in Afghanistan*, p. 188.

[31] Olivier Roy, 'Le mouvement des tâlebân en Afghanistan', *Afghanistan Info*, no. 36, February 1995, pp. 5-7 at p. 5.

[32] For a detailed discussion of the Deobandi tradition, see Barbara D. Metcalf, *Islamic Revival in British India: Deoband, 1860-1900* (Princeton: Princeton University Press, 1982).

its influence provided the bulk of the Afghan ulema.[33] In this orthodoxy, evil and apostasy could be defined at least in part in terms of departure from *ritual*–that is, 'action wrapped in a web of symbolism'[34]–and it is for this reason that the Taliban emphasise the enforcement of modes of behaviour which to the outside observer seem peripheral to solving Afghanistan's major problems. It is scarcely surprising that the most cohesive organisation in the Taliban's otherwise-inchoate structure is the much-feared religious police force (*Amr bil-Maroof wa Nahi An il-Munkir*, the department responsible for the 'Promotion of Virtue and Suppression of Vice'[35]).

It is important, however, to distinguish between on the one hand those *talibs* whose activities observers such as Roy witnessed, and on the other the *Taliban movement*, which comprises more than just students from madrassas. First, its leadership is drawn from former Mujahideen–many of them affiliated with Mohammad Nabi Mohammadi's Harakat-e Enqelab-e Islami, an overwhelmingly Pushtun party which many traditional clerics joined during the war against the USSR. Its senior leaders–such as Mohammad Omar, Mohammad Rabbani, Mohammad Ghaus, Mohammad Abbas, Mohammad Hassan, and Wakil Ahmad–all claim titles such as 'Mawlawi' or 'Mullah', which signify that they have moved beyond the simple status of talib. Second, the Taliban movement has accommodated Pushtuns with notably secular backgrounds, including, in the words of prominent spokesman Mohammad Masum Afghani, 'communists ... who have abandoned their old ideas', as well as 'supporters from the era of Zahir Shah'.[36] The former expression is almost certainly code for members of the Khalq faction of the People's Democratic Party of Afghanistan, to which Pushtun communists gravitated. Third, the Taliban movement seems also to have accommodated at least some of the Kandahari *Pai luch* brotherhood, a secret society with a distinctive uniform whose members could be seen in company of the Taliban in Kabul in mid-1997, and which had been involved in anti-modernist disturbances at the instigation of conservative clerics in Kandahar in 1959.[37] Fourth, through much of the country, but especially in its ventures in the north, the movement has willingly opened its doors to armed Pushtuns who 'reflagged'

33 Roy, *Islam and resistance in Afghanistan*, p. 58.
34 David I. Kertzer, *Ritual, Politics and Power* (New Haven: Yale University Press, 1988), p. 9.
35 This expression is derived from the Holy Koran: see *Sura al-Imran*, 3: 104 and *Sura al-Hajj*, 22: 41. There is a similarly-named religious police in Saudi Arabia.
36 BBC *Summary of World Broadcasts*, FE/2234/A/1, 22 February 1995.
37 See Louis Dupree, *Afghanistan* (Princeton: Princeton University Press, 1980), p. 537.

themselves as Taliban for reasons of expediency: it appears to have been Taliban of this type who committed the Qizilabad atrocity. But fifth, and most importantly, the Taliban movement draws on human and financial resources from Pakistan and Saudi Arabia, which have transformed it from a disorganised collection of fronts with local agendas into an organised political force with countrywide objectives. This external factor distinguishes the Taliban from earlier movements amongst Pushtuns which might seem to offer illuminating historical analogues. The Roshani movement of the late sixteenth and early seventeenth centuries founded by Bayazid Ansari (1525-85?), and the anti-Sikh Mujahideen movement promoted in the early nineteenth century amongst Pushtuns by Sayed Ahmad Barelvi (1786-1831), were able to mobilise many followers, but suffered from a lack of organisational resilience in times of adversity which external support could have supplied.[38] That the Taliban movement has survived for as long as it has tells us something about its nature, since social movements are notoriously fissile for reasons clearly set out by Sidney Tarrow: 'Internally, a good part of the power of movements comes from the fact that they activate people over whom they have no control. This power is a virtue because it allows movements to mount collective actions without possessing the resources that would be necessary to internalize a support base. But the autonomy of their supporters also disperses the movement's power, encourages factionalism and leaves it open to defection, competition and repression'.[39] Resources supplied by external backers permit movements to construct prudential support based on clientelism and patronage, which can make them appear deceptively robust. The loss of such support can devastate a movement politically. Thus, while Islamabad finds it extraordinarily difficult to manipulate the Taliban on a day-to-day basis, not least because of the movement's loose structure, the Taliban may be more vulnerable than they realise to dangers arising from a breakdown in their relationship with Pakistan.

On fundamentalism, traditionalism, and totalitarianism

The behaviour of the Taliban may lend credence to those who characterise them as *fundamentalist*. But if a Hekmatyar could be described as fundamentalist as well, the question arises as to what characteristics, if any, unite them; and whether these are characteristic

---

38 On the Roshani movement, see Olaf Caroe, *The Pathans 550 B.C.-A.D. 1957* (Karachi: Oxford University Press, 1980), pp. 200-204. On the Mujahideen movement, see Roy, *Islam and resistance in Afghanistan*, pp. 56-57.

39 Sidney Tarrow, *Power in Movement: Social Movements, Collective Action, and Politics* (Cambridge: Cambridge University Press, 1994), p. 23.

of fundamentalism, or fundamentalism *alone*, or some other definable political dispositions. It is to disentangle some of these issues that the following remarks are directed.

At its simplest, fundamentalism implies the 'activist affirmation of a particular faith that defines that faith in an absolutist and literalist manner'.[40] Originally used to describe strands within Protestant Christianity, since the Iranian revolution of 1979 it has been popularly and rhetorically used to identify what scholars have dubbed 'resurgent Islam', 'radical Islam', or 'Islamist' movements in Muslim countries.[41] Of course, 'fundamentalism' is only one of a number of strands of politics and thought to be found in Muslim countries,[42] and 'Islamic fundamentalism' has been subject to searching criticism in terms both of its coherence, and its political potency.[43] Fortunately, recent scholarship has offered a more nuanced interpretation of fundamentalism than accompanied the earlier, polemical usages. According to Parekh,[44] fundamentalism presupposes a separation between religion and society; the existence of a single sacred text or a set of texts in hierarchical relation with each other; direct access for the believer to the text or texts; and authority within the religion for using the state to enforce religious identity. The fundamentalist accepts no

[40] John O. Voll, 'Fundamentalism', in John L. Esposito (ed.), *The Oxford Encyclopedia of the Modern Islamic World* (New York: Oxford University Press, 1995) vol. II, pp. 32-34.

[41] For a sampling of relevant literature, see Mohammed Ayoob (ed.), *The Politics of Islamic Reassertion* (London: Croom Helm, 1981); John L. Esposito (ed.), *Voices of Resurgent Islam* (New York: Oxford University Press, 1983); Emmanuel Sivan, *Radical Islam: Medieval Theology and Modern Politics* (New Haven: Yale University Press, 1985); Shireen T. Hunter (ed.), *The Politics of Islamic Revivalism: Diversity and Unity* (Bloomington: Indiana University Press, 1988); Martin E. Marty and R. Scott Appleby (eds.), *Fundamentalisms and the State: Remaking Polities, Economies, and Militance* (Chicago: The University of Chicago Press, 1993); John L. Esposito, *The Islamic Threat: Myth or Reality?* (New York: Oxford University Press, 1993); Olivier Roy, *Généalogie de l'islamisme* (Paris: Hachette, 1995); John L. Esposito (ed.), *Political Islam: Revolution, Radicalism, or Reform?* (Boulder: Lynne Rienner, 1997).

[42] See Dale F. Eickelman and James Piscatori, *Muslim Politics* (Princeton: Princeton University Press, 1996).

[43] For samples of such criticism, see Hamid Enayat, *Modern Islamic Political Thought* (London: Macmillan, 1982) pp. 83-110; As'ad AbuKhalil, 'The Incoherence of Islamic Fundamentalism: Arab Islamic Thought at the End of the 20th Century', *The Middle East Journal*, vol. 48, no. 4, Autumn 1994, pp. 677-694; Olivier Roy, *The Failure of Political Islam* (Cambridge: Harvard University Press, 1994).

[44] Bhikhu Parekh, 'The Concept of Fundamentalism', in Alexsandras Shtromas (ed.), *The End of "Isms"?: Reflections on the Fate of Ideological Politics after Communism's Collapse* (Oxford: Blackwell, 1994), pp. 105-126.

separation of politics and religion; aims to capture and use the state; rejects the authority of interpretive tradition, but nonetheless reads the text in light of political objectives, seeking in the process 'to challenge and remake the world'.[45] The fundamentalist is a modernist, responsible not merely for obeying the dictates of the faith, but for ensuring that others do as well. For Parekh, fundamentalism differs radically from the non-modernist ultra-orthodox disposition in religion, since the latter retreats from the world, leaves God to rectify its evils, and denies all dynamic readings of Scripture.

A further point, often overlooked but of some importance, relates to the role of the leader in fundamentalist movements. Since sacred texts cannot interpret themselves authoritatively, fundamentalist movements typically depend upon an authority figure to play this superordinate role.[46] In practice, fundamentalism entails loyalty not so much to a particular doctrine as to a particular leader. From Mohammad Ibn Abdul Wahhab,[47] whose beliefs were so strongly contested in nineteenth-century Afghanistan, to Gulbuddin Hekmatyar,[48] whose views were to prove controversial in the twentieth, movements have been built around men as well as texts. But there is an additional reason, beyond the silence of texts, why leadership is so important to fundamentalist *movements*, and that is their low level of political institutionalisation. In communist systems, 'cults of personality' characteristically emerged where the party was weakly institutionalised.[49] Similar cults can be found in the Muslim world, with the most obvious example being that surrounding Ayatollah Khomeini in Iran.

Whether the Taliban are 'fundamentalist' in this nuanced sense is a question on which opinions may differ. While they hardly strike one as modernist, their appetite for theocracy, desire to remake the world, and creative approach to scriptural interpretation all have fundamentalist overtones. But perhaps the characteristic most starkly redolent of fundamentalism is the special role accorded to the Taliban leader Mohammad Omar, who is identified by his followers by the

---

45 Ibid., p. 116.

46 On the 'silence of the text', see E.D. Watt, *Authority* (London: Croom Helm, 1982), p. 68.

47 See Christine Noelle, 'The Anti-Wahhabi Reaction in Nineteenth-Century Afghanistan', *The Muslim World*, vol. 85, nos. 1-2, January-April 1995, pp. 23-48.

48 See David B. Edwards, 'Summoning Muslims: Print, Politics, and Religious Ideology in Afghanistan', *Journal of Asian Studies*, vol. 52, no. 3, 1993, pp. 609-628.

49 Graeme Gill, 'Personality Cult, Political Culture and Party Structure', *Studies in Comparative Communism*, vol. 17, no. 2, Summer 1984, pp. 111-121.

title of *Amir al-Momineen* ('Commander of the Faithful'),[50] and who has reportedly exploited one of the holiest relics of Afghanistan, namely the Cloak of the Prophet Mohammad (*Khirqa-e mubarak*), as a source of symbolic legitimation for his authority.[51] Omar's proclaimed path to politics–allegedly through a call to action in a visionary dream, of a kind similar to those by which Amir Abdul Rahman Khan claimed to have been inspired over a century earlier–had a mystical dimension to set him apart from 'ordinary' politicians, and bears the hallmarks of an attempt to synthesise a charismatic basis for personal authority. Here we find virtually a paradigm case of a fundamentalist leader in the making.

Other analysts have argued that the Taliban reinvigorate established modes of behaviour, and thus implicitly characterise them as *traditionalist*. At a seminar held in Washington DC on 6 November 1996, former US Ambassador to Pakistan Robert Oakley suggested that what the Taliban represented was the arrival of 'village' values and attitudes in the cities.[52] While this view was strongly contested, it does allow us to ask questions over the extent to which tradition is a factor which shapes the Taliban phenomenon. However, the substance of 'tradition' is not quite as clear as the casual reader might think.

A useful starting point in the discussion of tradition is the definition offered by Martin Krygier, who sees in tradition three key elements, namely:

pastness: the contents of every tradition have or are believed by its participants to have, originated some considerable time in the past. Second is authoritative presence: though derived from a real or believed-to-

---

50 On the origins of this title, see Matthew S. Gordon, 'Amir al-mu'minin', in John L. Esposito (ed.), *The Oxford Encyclopedia of the Modern Islamic World* (New York: Oxford University Press, 1995) vol. I, pp. 86-87. The title had previously been used in the nineteenth century to refer to Amir Dost Mohammad Khan: see Sayed Qassem Reshtia, *Afghanistan dar qarn-e nozdeh* (Kabul: Dawlati metbaeh, 1967), p. 63; R.D. McChesney, *Central Asia: Foundations of Change* (Princeton: The Darwin Press, 1997), pp. 142-143. It was also used by the followers of Sayid Ahmad Barelvi to describe their leader: see Barbara D. Metcalf, 'Sayyid Ahmad Barelwi', in Esposito (ed.), *The Oxford Encyclopedia of the Modern Islamic World*, vol. I, p. 200. More recently it has been used by King Hassan of Morocco: see Ibrahim A. Karawan, *The Islamist Impasse* (Oxford: Oxford University Press, Adelphi Paper no. 314, International Institute for Strategic Studies, 1997), p. 13. By May 1997, preachers in Kabul mosques had begun to accord Mohammad Omar an additional title: *Sultan-e zaman* ('Lord of Time').

51 See Andrew Meier, 'Stoners', *The New Republic*, 7 October 1996; Tim McGirk and Rahimullah Yusufzai, 'Mullah with a Mission', *Time*, 31 March 1997.

52 For a report on this seminar, see *The Future of Afghanistan: The Taliban, Regional Security and U.S. Foreign Policy* (Washington DC: United States Institute of Peace, March 1997).

be-real past, a traditional practice, doctrine or belief has not, as it were, stayed there. Its traditionality consists in its *present* authority and significance for the lives, thoughts or activities of participants in the tradition. Third, a tradition is not merely the past made present. It must have been, or be thought to have been, passed down over intervening generations, deliberately or otherwise; not merely unearthed from a past discontinuous with the present.[53]

Traditions can be manifested in patterns of social authority, in values, and in modes of comportment, as well as in schools of interpretation of sacred or secular doctrine. While some see tradition as a deadweight on the present, for others tradition 'has a moral and epistemological authority not merely because of its age but because it has been vitalized by many minds and different kinds of historical experiences'.[54] What is implicit in Krygier's definition, however, and explicit in a range of other writings, is that 'traditions' are not fixed but in a constant process of reformulation or even invention.[55]

It is more this kind of 'imagined' tradition of which the ordinary Taliban are bearers, rather than 'pure' traditions with genuine as opposed to mythologised historical referents. It is not the values of the village, but the values of the village *as interpreted by refugee camp dwellers or madrassa students most of whom have never known ordinary village life* that the Taliban seek to impose on places like Kabul. This accounts for their ability to do things which would be unthinkable in a typical Afghan village–for example beat up women from a stranger's family, a step which would typically activate powerful norms of revenge. There are obvious complexities in assessing in different spheres the extent to which the 'traditions' which the Taliban might be seen to reflect tend more towards the 'real' or more towards the 'imagined', and here is not the place to undertake such an inquiry. But the mere plasticity of tradition should not mask the radical departure which the Taliban represent from established patterns of social authority (in which the Talib is not a dominant figure), and in modes of comportment (which socially-transmitted codes of etiquette regulated strictly in Afghan society).

A third approach to characterising the Taliban sees them as an example of *totalitarianism* in the making. The concept of totalitarianism seems to have originated in Italy[56] but became widely

53 Martin Krygier, 'Law as Tradition', *Law and Philosophy*, vol. 5, no. 2, 1986, pp.237-262 at p. 240.
54 Parekh, 'The Concept of Fundamentalism', p. 121.
55 See Edward Shils, *Tradition* (Chicago: University of Chicago Press, 1981); on the functions of constructed *ritual*, see Eric Hobsbawm and Terence Ranger (eds.), *The Invention of Tradition* (Cambridge: Cambridge University Press, 1983).
56 See Leonard Schapiro, *Totalitarianism* (London: Macmillan, 1972), p. 13.

used only after the Second World War, largely as a result of the publication of Hannah Arendt's influential book *The Origins of Totalitarianism*. Arendt's study, the first two parts of which dealt with anti-Semitism and imperialism rather than totalitarianism, burrowed deep into the experience of Europe in order to explain the emergence of the forms of social organisation found in Nazi Germany and Stalinist Russia. She focussed in particular upon a small number of characteristics which in combination she found distinctively present in these states. The liberal notion that positive law bound rulers as well as ruled found no analogue in such states. Behind a facade of constitutional rule the power of the state could be exercised in untrammelled fashion. But two particular factors were even more important. The first was the rationalisation of the activities of the state in terms of a perfectibilist ideology. 'Over and above the senselessness of totalitarian society', she wrote, 'is enthroned the ridiculous supersense of its ideological superstition'.[57] Ideology rather than law became the guiding principle for individual behaviour within society. The second factor was the use made of terror: 'If lawfulness is the essence of non-tyrannical government and lawlessness is the essence of tyranny, then terror is the essence of totalitarian domination'.[58] Terror served the ends of the totalitarian leader by severing the social bonds on which the emergence of opposition to the leader would depend.

The subsequent history of the concept has been a chequered one,[59] and much of the literature on totalitarianism relates only to highly developed systems of domination and has no real bearing on the situation in Afghanistan. However, there is one usage of the term which is potentially of value, namely that which describes a force as totalitarian if it seeks to monopolise the political sphere, and to assimilate all of social life to it. It distinguishes pluralistic movements from those which recognise no private sphere beyond the reach of political authority. The late Isaiah Berlin reputedly described the Communist Party as a cross between a church and an army, and it is not difficult to see the Taliban as meriting this description as well. What distinguishes the Taliban as a totalitarian movement from the familiar totalitarianisms of the twentieth century is that they emerged in a country in which state institutions had collapsed, as a result of which the institutional resources for enforcing totalising objectives are not available on a national as opposed to local scale. This may be an

---

57 Hannah Arendt, *The Origins of Totalitarianism* (New York: Harcourt Brace Jovanovich, 1973), p. 457.
58 Ibid., p. 464.
59 See Abbott Gleason, *Totalitarianism: The Inner History of the Cold War* (New York: Oxford University Press, 1995).

important factor in explaining the sporadic and inconsistent application of Taliban decrees.

But one important qualification is also in order. The Taliban's base of power cannot be reduced simply to terror. Terror is important above all for the psychological effects which it produces:[60] during the French Revolution, as Norman Davies points out, it 'was designed to create such a climate of fear and uncertainty that the very thought of opposition would be paralysed'.[61] Hazaras in particular have been victims of repression under the Taliban, since they are tragically exposed both to the Taliban's militant anti-Shiism, and to persecution on the basis of deep-rooted racialist hatreds. Furthermore, the activities in Kabul of the Taliban's *Amr bil-Maroof wa Nahi An il-Munkir* under Mawlawi Qamaluddin (and particularly their repression of women, which symbolises not only the vulnerability of women, but the impotence of their male relatives) certainly have had an intimidating psychological effect on the population as a whole. Nowadays, the word 'terror' (*wahshat*) is commonly used by Kabulis, albeit in barely more than a whisper, to describe the state of mind to which Taliban rule has brought them.[62] The Taliban's 'Deputy Foreign Minister', Sher Mohammad Abbas Stanekzai even admitted in September 1997 that it 'is a fact our rules are obeyed by fear', something he justified by claiming that 'people are addicted to sin'.[63] The combination of a repressive ideological framework, an obsessively energetic and thuggish religious police, and a lot to hide, accounts for Taliban actions which otherwise would seem massively self-destructive, such as the detention and intimidation of European Union Commissioner for Humanitarian Affairs Emma Bonino, and distinguished journalists William Shawcross and Christiane Amanpour, in Kabul on 29 September 1997 on the grounds that members of their party had taken photographs.[64] Outside urban areas, however, the grip of the Taliban on the population is much lighter,[65]

---

60 See William Maley, 'Social Dynamics and the Disutility of Terror: Afghanistan, 1978-1989', in P. Timothy Bushnell, Vladimir Shlapentokh, Christopher K. Vanderpool, and Jeyaratnam Sundram (eds.), *State Organized Terror: The Case of Violent Internal Repression* (Boulder: Westview Press, 1991), pp. 113-131.

61 Norman Davies, *Europe: A History* (Oxford: Oxford University Press, 1996) p. 709.

62 John F. Burns, 'A Year of Harsh Islamic Rule Weighs Heavily for Afghans', *The New York Times*, 24 September 1997.

63 *Agence France Presse,* 23 September 1997.

64 See Christiane Amanpour, 'Tyranny of the Taliban', *Time*, 13 October 1997. This episode prompted a scathing attack on the Taliban by German Foreign Minister Klaus Kinkel, who stated that the justification for the detentions was 'unbelievable and shameful in every respect': *Reuters*, 29 September 1997.

in part because of a shortage of cadres. The Taliban can reasonably claim to have less Afghan blood on their hands than the Soviet Army, associates of the Khalqi dictator Hafizullah Amin, or the Hezb-e Islami of Hekmatyar, although Afghans whose homes were destroyed and families killed by Taliban rockets and shells in Kabul in 1995 and 1996 and Mazar in 1997 may reasonably ask just how much less.

Making sense of the Taliban

The chapters in this book, as I noted earlier, are not designed to address directly the question of whether the Taliban should be described as 'fundamentalist'–or 'traditional' or 'totalitarian'–but they do provide the reader with a firm basis from which to reflect upon this question. It is dangerous to treat the Taliban as if they are a monolithic force, and the individual contributors in their own ways highlight this point. However, they also draw attention to important distinctive features of the Taliban phenomenon.

Amin Saikal examines why the Rabbani Government was unable to consolidate its position during the period it occupied the Afghan capital. He highlights both internal and external factors which militated against stability, with the intransigence of Gulbuddin Hekmatyar and the support from Pakistan for Hekmatyar and then the Taliban standing out as especially important considerations. He also notes the major problems which Rabbani faced as a result of factional divisions within his political organisation, and is particularly critical of the reappointment of Hekmatyar as Prime Minister in June 1996, when to many Kabul residents he represented only the bloodshed which had engulfed them since shortly after the communist regime collapsed. He concludes by noting that since the Rabbani government continues to occupy Afghanistan's UN seat, it remains a potential actor in the country's political future.

Anthony Davis offers a detailed account of how the Taliban became a military force. He traces their campaigns from their earliest major operations in October 1994 to their seizure of Kabul in September 1996. He notes that the early Taliban operations involved substantial hostilities and human losses, and argues that with the important exception of Kandahar, it is a myth that the areas into which the Taliban pushed were racked by lawlessness and anarchy. He concludes that the Taliban were pre-eminently a military organisation rather than a political movement, and that covert Pakistani support for the Taliban has been broader in its scope and ultimately far more

---

[65] See Bernt Glatzer, 'Aid, Development and Human Rights in Afghanistan' (Peshawar: mimeo, November 1996).

ambitious in its goals than that of other regional powers for their
Afghan candidates. Ahmed Rashid takes up the complexities of Pakistan's relations
with the Taliban. He outlines the nature and character of their links
with different Pakistani groups–not simply the ISI, but also the
Jamiat-e Ulema-i Islam, the transport mafia, the Bhutto government,
and some of Pakistan's provincial governments as well–and shows
how the exploitation of these links by the Taliban, combined with the
lack of institutional means to ensure coherence in Pakistan
government policy towards Afghanistan, served to whittle away
Pakistan's authority and respect among many Afghans. His
conclusions are sombre: many Pakistanis find the Taliban an
inspiration; any mass Islamic movement in Pakistan is likely to
secure support from Pakistani madrassa students who have fought
alongside the Taliban in Afghanistan; and the threat of an Islamic
revolution in Pakistan has never been greater.

Richard Mackenzie examines the way in which the USA has come
to terms with the Taliban phenomenon. He finds no 'smoking gun' to
establish direct involvement by US state agencies in the Taliban's
rise, but in a real sense the picture he paints is even more damning:
until very recently, one of drift in policy, and indifference to the fate of
a people in whose country unattractive forces were blithely loaded with
American-funded arms, at the expense of hopes for political order once
they had served their purpose of undermining the geopolitical position
of the USSR. While Afghan critics of the Taliban see Washington as
the Taliban's Svengali, Mackenzie's analysis suggests other
metaphors: a Procurator of Judea washing his hands, or a Levite
giving a wounded man a wide berth.

Anthony Hyman traces the differing reactions of the Russian and
Central Asian governments to the rise of the Taliban. While the
general reaction to the Taliban seizure of Kabul was one of
consternation, with Uzbek President Karimov strongly reaffirming his
country's support for Dostum, the Government of Turkmenistan,
which had significant interests in seeing its oil and gas exported
through Afghanistan, opted to stand apart from its neighbours, and
reacted calmly to Afghan developments. Somewhat similar patterns
emerged following the May 1997 northern crisis, with Uzbekistan in
particular fearing the impact of Taliban success in terms of refugees,
drugs, and ideology, rather than any direct military threat from roving
Taliban bands. Hyman concludes that the real targets of statements and
communiques issued by the Russian and Central Asian governments
were not the Taliban as such, but rather their Pakistani and Saudi
backers, whom the Russians blamed (along with US oil interests) for
orchestrating Taliban successes.

Anwar-ul-haq Ahady traces the history of Saudi and Iranian interest in Afghanistan, which he sees as falling into three phases: 1980 to 1988, 1988 to 1992, and 1992 to the present. During the first, the Saudi involvement was much more striking than was the Iranian. In the second period, Saudi Arabia was keen to see a pro-Saudi, pro-Pakistani Islamic government in Kabul, and was not interested in self-determination for the people of Afghanistan. This was not well received in Tehran, which, freed from the burdens of the Iran-Iraq war, increased its involvement in Afghanistan. In the post-communist period, the situation became even more complex, with alliances shifting frequently until the emergence of the Taliban. At this point, Massoud and Rabbani moved closer to Iran, since the USA had not responded to their efforts to align with America; and the Saudis provided financial support to the Taliban. This rivalry between foreign powers, played out on Afghan soil, is one of the factors which helps to sustain the ongoing conflict.

Michael Keating examines the dilemmas of providing humanitarian assistance in Afghanistan. Is humanitarian assistance contributing to or facilitating the conflict? Should the international community's political activities be more closely tied to its social and humanitarian agenda? Should aid be conditional on adequate regime performance in the spheres of human rights? The answers to these questions are not simple, but the emergence of the Taliban has sharpened the debate considerably, since a non-confrontational approach to the Taliban may be poorly received by donors to whom their gender policies appear a brazen insult. Further questions affect the nuts and bolts of assistance. How should the world deal with a group which claims to be a government but lacks any significant administrative capacity? These are matters which are troubling for NGOs and the UN alike, and the UN has begun to address them, not only through its PEACE ('Poverty Eradication and Community Empowerment') Initiative, but also through a Strategic Framework process which has sought to bring structure and coherence to project planning.

Nancy Hatch Dupree takes up gender issues in her discussion of the position of Afghan women under the Taliban. In contrast to those who have favoured a revolutionary approach to gender issues,[66] she emphasises the extreme complexity of defining gender roles and of determining appropriate means for their realisation. She notes the dependence of the Taliban movement on young, very narrowly-educated troops, whose leaders fear how they might behave in a relatively cosmopolitan city if given the opportunity. The result in

---

[66] For a critique of such an approach, see William Maley, 'Women and Public Policy in Afghanistan: A Comment', *World Development*, vol. 24, no. 1, January 1996, pp. 203-206.

Kabul has been a retreat of nearly forty years to the period before the voluntary unveiling of women was permitted, and the effective exclusion of women from most spheres of education and employment, with consequent effects on economic security, and of course on the well-being of women themselves. While the Taliban ask for time, visible action, not rhetoric, is required. Dupree concludes by noting the loss to Afghanistan, either through resettlement or social marginalisation, of the talents of thousands of educated, professional women who wish neither to deny their society's values nor compromise Islam: it is these women who must be 'uncaged' if Afghanistan is to move forward.

Bernt Glatzer looks at the ways in which ethnic and tribal identifications affect social and political stability in Afghanistan. He finds only a grain of truth in the view of the current conflict as an *ethnic* war, and further argues the tribal system is an element of resilience and stability in times of turmoil, and that where it is functioning well, the Taliban have not dared to touch it. Ethnicity is concerned with social boundary-making; in itself it contributes neither to stability nor instability; and it has been an epiphenomenon in the Afghan war. The disintegration of Afghanistan is seen across ethnic groups as a terrifying prospect to be avoided. It is local, cultural, and religious autonomy for which groups struggle, not the breakup of the country.

William Maley examines the performance of the United Nations in seeking to promote a political solution to the Afghanistan problem. He argues that UN efforts have been thwarted not simply by intransigence on the part of the Afghan combatants, but also by neglect of relevant issues and parties–both internal and external–as well as by UN actions which have undermined parties' confidence in the mediation process, and by excessive publicity surrounding mediation activities. He is particularly critical of the UN's failure to speak candidly and specifically about the external interference to which Afghanistan has been subject, and sees a real danger that this 'studied blindness' will legitimate a model of 'creeping invasion' for other states to follow, with potentially disastrous consequences for world order.

Olivier Roy directs his attention to the future of Islamism in Afghanistan. He notes the long-term dependence of Afghan Islamism on other Islamic movements, and the consequent hostility to Shiism, Sufism and western culture which these links either injected into or accentuated in Afghanistan. The rise of the Taliban he sees as a clear case of 'neo-fundamentalism', focussed on Sharia law rather than the idea of an Islamic state. In his view, there is no future for Islamism in Afghanistan: the fight for Kabul between Hezb and Jamiat from 1992 to 1995 has killed the idea of an 'Islamic state', and this failure of the

Islamist political model has led to a surge in ethnic division. The problem with the Taliban is that they mean what they say. However, their message is unlikely to spread: they represent a maverick fundamentalism, and cannot be easily manipulated by anyone. Finally, M. Nazif Shahrani explores the future of the state and community governance in Afghanistan. He adopts a political ecological approach, and argues that rather than take the state as 'given', we should question the adequacy and appropriateness of forms of post-colonial state, and examine whether these may actually breed communal violence and conflict. This leads to a detailed discussion of communities based on family and kin-based loyalties, and of ways in which such communities were challenged by the push to establish a strong, centralised, 'modern' state. He argues that it was such communities which provided the backbone of resistance to the Soviet invasion, and writes critically of the disposition of post-communist regimes to seek to rebuild the very kind of state structures which had served Afghanistan so poorly in the past. Rather than seeking ready-made models for political organisation from Western or Eastern precedents, one should instead seek to incorporate the strengths of Afghanistan's reemergent civil society into a state structure based on community governance. Afghanistan must not again become, in the words of Afghan poet and UN General Assembly President Abdul Rahman Pazwak, a land where the people are imprisoned and the country is free.

'A shame that nobody talks about', an Afghan once remarked to one of the contributors to this volume, Bernt Glatzer, 'is no shame'.[67] This unusually deep and subtle observation points to the high level of pragmatism in Afghan society, which fleeting visitors too often overlook. It illustrates an acute awareness that daily life in Afghanistan must be lived in a context richly endowed with potentially repressive codes of behaviour, and that life will be livable only if a way is found around them. The Taliban are notable for their avowed refusal to take this path–in this respect, they lend some credence to the late Ernest Gellner's claim that there is 'little or no populism in Islam'[68]–and time alone will tell whether their self-proclaimed purity will prove too rigid for them to be able to persist with their political experiment without provoking further backlashes. The Taliban 'system' provides no one to guard the guardians, no institutional protections against the abuses which constitute the core

67 Bernt Glatzer, *Nomaden von Gharjistan: Aspekte der wirtschaflichen, sozialen und politischen Organisation nomadischer Durrani-Paschtunen in Nordwestafghanistan* (Wiesbaden: Franz Steiner Verlag, 1977), p. 158.
68 Ernest Gellner, *Nationalism* (London: Weidenfeld & Nicolson, 1997), p. 82.

of tyranny;[69] and the corrupting influences of power, of which writers such as Lord Acton and George Orwell in their different ways warned, may prove hard to escape. Indeed, cynics would say that the Taliban succumbed to the temptation of power as early as September 1995, when in the name of 'peace' and 'order' they overthrew the administration in the notably peaceful and orderly city of Herat. The Taliban experience may well be a transient episode in the life of Afghanistan. It has touched fewer Afghan lives than is often realised, which is one reason why some Afghans have accepted it in good faith, hoping that something better would evolve from it. But many Afghan lives have nonetheless been scarred in the process. The whole case of the Taliban stands yet again as an example of the difficulties of realising a utopian vision amidst the complexities of the real world, in which one's building materials are limited to what Isaiah Berlin, quoting Kant, described as 'the crooked timber of humanity'.[70] The Holy Book of the Islamic faith, the Koran, itself contains a powerful warning against missionary utopianism, with the message that there shall be no compulsion in religion.[71] The utopian instinct, however, is difficult to suppress, and the simple wisdom of the Koran can easily be lost in the tumult created by its interpreters who believe that purity can be enforced, or that ritual without faith actually counts for something. But from the Taliban experience, we also find vindication of a truth which was noted long ago by Ralf Dahrendorf: 'Utopia is the home not of freedom, the for ever imperfect scheme for an uncertain future, but of the perfection either of terror or of absolute boredom'.[72] One hopes that the many ordinary Afghans who sacrificed so much in their war against the Soviets in order to live as they chose will soon have the freedom to do so.

[69] See Daniel Chirot, *Modern Tyrants: The Power and Prevalence of Evil in Our Age* (Princeton: Princeton University Press, 1994).

[70] Isaiah Berlin, *The Crooked Timber of Humanity: Chapters in the History of Ideas* (London: John Murray, 1990).

[71] *Sura al-Baqarah*, 2: 256. For a discussion of this and other passages which emphasise the liberal dimensions of Islam, see Mohammad Hashim Kamali, *Freedom of Expression in Islam* (Kuala Lumpur: Berita Publishing, 1994), pp. 85-102

[72] Ralf Dahrendorf, 'On the Origin of Social Inequality', in Peter Laslett and W.G. Runciman (eds.), *Philosophy, Politics and Society: Second Series* (Oxford: Basil Blackwell, 1962), pp. 88-109 at p. 109.

THE RABBANI GOVERNMENT, 1992-1996

Amin Saikal

In late April 1992, the disintegration of the Soviet-installed Najibullah government in Kabul and the success of the Mujahideen, led by Commander Ahmad Shah Massoud, in taking over the capital opened a euphoric yet painful phase in the historical evolution of Afghanistan. The removal of the dreaded Najibullah's regime finally vindicated the Afghans' popular resistance to the attempted imposition of Soviet-style socialism. The Mujahideen takeover was welcomed by many Afghans in the expectation of returning their war-ravaged country to peace and order. However, their expectations were soon to be confounded, for the Mujahideen victory quickly turned sour, making their rule a continuation of the warfare of the preceding thirteen years, with further tragic losses for the Afghans.

Although the factors which explain this phenomenon cannot be explored in isolation from one another, the objective of this chapter is very specific. It is to focus on what went wrong with the Islamic government of President Burhanuddin Rabbani, which assumed the reins of power in Kabul from June 1992 until it was forced by the Taliban militia to retreat north in September 1996. This chapter is thematic in approach, and argues its case by focussing on problems of political legitimacy, which dogged the Rabbani government from its inception; élite settlements, which failed to secure the position of the Rabbani government; party rule and intra-party conflict, which had few if any historical precedents in Afghanistan and which the Rabbani leadership could not master effectively; and foreign intervention, especially by Pakistan which from the start distrusted the Rabbani government and was determined to replace it with one which would be under the control of one of its protégés.

Political legitimacy

The process of legitimation on which the Rabbani government sought to ground its claim to power was forged under complex circumstances but was at best rudimentary. Political legitimation[1] has historically

---

[1] For background on political legitimation in Afghanistan, see William Maley, 'Political legitimation in contemporary Afghanistan', *Asian Survey*, vol. 27, no. 6, June 1987, pp. 705-725.

been an elusive process and a daunting objective to achieve in Afghanistan. No government since the foundation of modern Afghanistan in the mid-eighteenth century has come into existence on the basis of a direct popular mandate. Legal-rational frameworks and constitutional legitimacy marked Afghan politics only for a short time, from 1964 to 1973, and even then only in a very limited sense. In Afghanistan, political order and governance have always largely rested on a mixture of personalised, clientelistic politics, and élite alliance and élite settlement, legitimated through traditional mechanisms of consensus building and empowerment, such as the Loya Jirga (Grand Assembly)–but with the threat or actual use of force frequently deployed as means of rule enforcement and rule maintenance. Given the dearth of legitimised avenues for political expression, regime change and development has often proved arbitrary and violent. It was in this context that Najibullah's government faced severe legitimacy problems and the alternative Islamic resistance government sought legitimation and public acceptance.

As the collapse of the Najibullah government approached, the Mujahideen remained as fragmented along ethnolinguistic, tribal, sectarian and personality lines as ever. The leaders of the seven main Sunni Islamic Mujahideen groups, who were based in Pakistan, had failed to agree on a common political platform, and there was little cohesion among the leaders of the minority Shiite Islamic groups, who were based in Iran. Nor were there any effective links between the Shiite and Sunni groups. Not one of the groups or their respective leaders had managed to develop a national profile or a nation-wide following. Most groups functioned as fighting militias within specific localities from which their leaders originated, and enjoyed support substantially along lines of ethnic or tribal identification, although this does not imply that they pursued ethnically-exclusivist recruitment policies. The groups' leaders often exercised only nominal influence over their commanders and other autonomous resistance figures.[2]

These problems were exacerbated by the fact that most leaders had been either cultivated or adopted in one form or another by rival international patrons of the resistance. Gulbuddin Hekmatyar, who led the extremist Hezb-e Islami Afghanistan, was nurtured by Pakistan's military intelligence (ISI) with the view that he should head the post-communist government in Kabul in order to further Islamabad's wider regional interests; Abdul-Rab al-Rasul Sayyaf, the leader of another smaller Pushtun-dominated group, the Ittehad-e Islami, was strongly

---

[2] For a detailed discussion, see Oliver Roy, 'Afghanistan: Back to Tribalism or on to Lebanon?', *Third World Quarterly*, vol. 11, no. 4, October 1989, pp. 70-82; Amin Saikal and William Maley, *Regime Change in Afghanistan: Foreign Intervention and the Politics of Legitimacy* (Boulder: Westview Press, 1991), pp. 118-134.

backed by Saudi Arabia whose agenda was to disseminate its primarily anti-Iranian Wahhabi Islam; and Abdul Ali Mazari, who headed the pro-Iranian Hezb-e Wahdat, and who after his assassination by the Taliban in 1995 was replaced by Abdul Karim Khalili, acted very much at the behest of Tehran.

The two strongest groups–Jamiat-e Islami, led by Burhanuddin Rabbani and supported by Ahmad Shah Massoud, and Hekmatyar's Hezb-e Islami–were locked in a bloody power struggle. This was partly due to personality rivalries among the leadership and partly to traditional ethnolinguistic differences. The Jamiat was dominated by ethnic Tajiks, who have historically formed about 30 per cent of the Afghan population and provided the core of the Afghan intelligentsia, concentrated in Kabul, and northern and western Afghanistan. The Hezb consisted overwhelmingly of ethnic Pushtuns, who had reputedly constituted about 40-50 per cent of the Afghan population, inhabiting mainly south and southeastern Afghanistan, but with sizeable pockets scattered through the north. While Jamiat lacked the capacity to point to a substantial representation of other important non-Pushtun minorities, such as the Uzbeks, Turkmen, and Hazaras, the Hezb was in this respect in an even worse position. Its popular base of support was so narrow that it could not possibly act as the political spearhead of the highly-tribalised Pushtuns. It essentially represented a segment of the Ghilzais–a Pushtun tribe which had had no substantial share in the Afghan power structure since 1825 when the rival Durrani tribe, or more specifically its Mohammadzai clan, assumed the reins of power to rule the country almost uninterruptedly until the communist coup of April 1978. Furthermore, there were at least two other Mujahideen groups which also competed for support among Ghilzais.

The resistance was not in a position to invoke any legal or for that matter conventional processes of political change to create a broad-based and representative Islamic government to replace the regime of Najibullah. In this setting, no outside mediation could produce any desirable result either. The UN efforts to put together a transitional team, composed of 'neutral' Afghans, proved futile, although the inability of the Secretary-General's representative Benon Sevan to develop an appropriate understanding of the nature of the Afghan conflict also played its part in this respect.[3] The collapse of Najibullah's regime represented a political revolution, even if not a social one. As a consequence, the imminent fall of Najibullah's government provoked a scramble among the Mujahideen leaders for power.

---

3   See Amin Saikal, 'The UN and Afghanistan: A Case of Failed Peacemaking Intervention', *International Peacekeeping*, vol. 3, no. 1, Spring 1996, pp. 19-34.

In the process, the Mujahideen leader who found himself best positioned was Massoud. And it was his relatively better organised and disciplined forces that succeeded, in alliance with those of Najibullah's Uzbek general Abdul Rashid Dostum, who defected to Massoud's side, in seizing Kabul. Nonetheless, their control of the capital was by no means complete, as they were not able to prevent other Mujahideen groups, especially their main rivals, Hezb and Wahdat, from occupying the southern and western outskirts of Kabul, from where they could endanger the security of civilians in the city whenever they could not secure compliance from Massoud. This they proved more than willing to do.

Élite settlement

As he stood poised to enter Kabul, Massoud was acutely aware of two overarching imperatives. One was that the history of modern Afghanistan had shown that no single ethnic group could rule the country on its own, and that the best way to proceed was to secure a transitional coalition as the first step towards creating a legitimate national government. The other was that in order to achieve this objective, the Mujahideen leaders had to reach a power-sharing agreement among themselves. He thus called on the Pakistan-based Mujahideen leaders to work out such a deal. The only hope for stability lay in an élite settlement,[4] whereby various leaders, not only acting on behalf of their respective Mujahideen groups but also in effect claiming representation on behalf of different ethnolinguistic categories, would construct a power structure whose durability and effectiveness would rest solely on the goodwill of the individual signatories to respect each other's end of the bargain, as well as on their capacities to control their subordinate forces.

The result was the Peshawar Agreement of 24 April 1992, forged between the Pakistan-based Mujahideen leaders, but with the involvement of the Pakistani government of Prime Minister Nawaz Sharif.[5] It was essentially designed to provide a framework for an interim government, to be implemented in two stages. The first was to dispatch to Kabul the leader of a small Pushtun Mujahideen group, Sebghatullah Mojadiddi, as a compromise choice, to head a two-month transitional government. The second was to enable a longer term interim government, headed by Burhanuddin Rabbani, the leader

---

4   On elite settlements more generally, see Michael G. Burton and John Higley, 'Elite Settlements', *American Sociological Review*, vol. 52, no. 3, June 1987, pp. 295-307.
5   For the text of the Agreement, see Appendix I in *Situation of Human Rights in Afghanistan* (New York: United Nations, A/47/656, 17 November 1992).

of Jamiat—whose control of Kabul through Massoud provided him with extra political clout—to take over from the transitional government for a period of four months. This was to be followed by the holding of a 'Council of Solution and Pact' (*Shura-i ahl al-hal val-aqd*) to constitute an interim government for eighteen months as a prelude to an election. Amid some controversy over the representativeness of its membership, a shura was convoked in late 1992 which endorsed the continuation of the Rabbani administration for eighteen months.

However, the settlement's Achilles heel was that it only needed the disaffection of one key party to wreck the whole thing. And this was precisely what happened. Hekmatyar's power ambitions rapidly led him to work against the Peshawar Agreement, which he had not even signed. He argued that under the Agreement the position of prime minister (reserved by the signatories for the Hezb) should not be subordinated to that of the president; and that the position of defence minister, to which Massoud had been appointed by Mojadiddi, should function at the behest of the prime minister. Although Mojadiddi's efforts to prolong his interim presidency from two months to two years had created considerable difficulties between him and Massoud, who viewed the implementation of the Peshawar Agreement as the best course of action, ultimately it was Hekmatyar's obstructionism that rendered the Agreement totally ineffective.

Initially Hekmatyar nominated one of his aides, Abdul Saboor Farid, to assume the prime ministership, but he himself refused to enter Kabul and used every excuse possible to undermine the Rabbani government. In early August 1992, he launched a barrage of rockets against Kabul which killed over a thousand civilians. His aim was to weaken the dominance of Jamiat in the coalition which included Dostum and a formerly close Pushtun ally of Hekmatyar, Sayyaf. While ignoring his own alliance with former Pushtun Khalqi communist ministers, such as Shahnawaz Tanai and Aslam Watanjar, Hekmatyar attacked Massoud's alliance with Dostum and sought to catalyse conflict between Jamiat and Wahdat by encouraging Sayyaf to move against them forcefully, so that he could ally himself with them once they had left Rabbani's government. Even after he was named Prime Minister pursuant to an agreement signed in Islamabad in March 1993,[6] he remained outside Kabul, and in January 1994, in alliance with his erstwhile enemy Dostum and with Mojadiddi, he unleashed the most ferocious artillery and rocket attacks that the capital had ever experienced. By the end of 1994, Hekmatyar's indiscriminate bombardment of Kabul had managed to destroy half of the city and kill some 25,000 of its citizens. Numerous peace efforts,

---

6   *Afghan Peace Accord* (New York: United Nations, S/25435, 19 March 1993).

pursued by various Mujahideen leaders, the Organisation of the Islamic Conference (OIC) and the United Nations, produced no result. In all his operations, Hekmatyar had three objectives. The first was to make sure that Rabbani and Massoud were not allowed to consolidate power, build a credible administration, or expand their territorial control, so that the country would remain divided into small fiefdoms, run by various Mujahideen leaders and local warlords or a council of such elements, with only some of them allied to Kabul. The second was to ensure that the Rabbani government acquired no capacity to dispense patronage, and to dissuade the Kabul population from giving more than limited support to the government. The third was to make Kabul an unsafe city for representatives of the international community, and to prevent the Rabbani government from attracting the international support needed to begin the post-war reconstruction of Afghanistan and generate a level of economic activity which would enhance its credibility and popularity. His tactics proved highly successful in all these respects.

However, despite the carnage he engendered, Hekmatyar was unable to seize Kabul, and it was this which ultimately made him a liability for Pakistan. This prompted the ISI to shift support to a newly-created alternative: the Taliban militia, which had just taken over the southern city of Kandahar and was moving rapidly towards Kabul. This abundantly equipped and financed movement, composed of Pakistani and Afghan Pushtuns from both sides of the border, quickly overwhelmed Hekmatyar's forces and proved a formidable foe to Rabbani's government, fighting and buying their way to the southern gates of Kabul within just months of their emergence. Initially, Massoud's forces were able to defend Kabul effectively, especially when the Taliban in their anti-Shiite zeal killed the Wahdat leader Mazari, and thus freed government forces to concentrate on driving the Taliban from the vicinity of the city. This produced a welcome respite from conflict for the residents of Kabul. But it did not last long.

Intra-party difficulties

Jamiat originally splintered from Hezb when Hekmatyar went his own way in the wake of the Soviet invasion. Its structure and functions were very much defined under the leadership of Rabbani, shortly after he went into exile in Pakistan in 1979. Although it had its origins in the Islamic movement for reform of Afghanistan which was set up in Kabul University in the late 1960s, it was essentially reborn as an Islamic resistance coalition of non-Pushtun Mujahideen. While containing some Pushtun elements, especially from the north, it was dominated by Badakhshis and Panjsheris, who were kindred of and led by Rabbani and Massoud respectively.[7]

In this coalition, while Rabbani assumed the overall leadership and developed a party structure, with various committees to discharge different political, economic, military and sociocultural functions, Massoud built up a cluster of fighting groups, which were drawn mostly from the six northern and northeastern provinces and at the core of which lay his own ethnic Panjsheri devotees, to provide the armed resistance of the coalition inside Afghanistan. To place this cluster within a coherent military-political structure, Massoud set up the Supervisory Council (*Shura-i Nazar*), which grew into an almost self-contained entity, but with a shared ideological goal, as well as some political and military links with Jamiat.

Thus from the outset Jamiat developed an oddly bifurcated structure: a political wing, with only limited input in military operations, under Rabbani; and a military-political wing operating inside Afghanistan under the full–and charismatic–leadership of Massoud. During the years of resistance this bifurcation caused little friction, and the two wings worked together quite well, but the situation changed when Massoud's forces took over Kabul. The former division of military and political responsibilities complicated the daunting task of transforming resistance forces into a governing body, a situation aggravated by four specific factors.

The first was that it was now Massoud and his Supervisory Council who stood supreme, as the security of Kabul and other Jamiat-dominated areas rested in their hands,. Without them, the organisation's political wing could not have played a central role in establishing a government. The upshot of this was a desire by elements in the Supervisory Council to have a determining share in the power structure and substantial input in shaping the Rabbani government's policies. Yet those senior Jamiat functionaries who had returned with Rabbani from exile wanted their expertise to be recognised, and to fill most of the important governmental and bureaucratic posts.

The second arose from ethnicisation within each of the Jamiat's wings. Although the Supervisory Council and the political wing of Jamiat contained representation from a wide range of non-Pushtuns, in

---

[7] For background material, see Olivier Roy, *Islam and resistance in Afghanistan* (Cambridge: Cambridge University Press, 1990), pp. 69-138; Eden Naby, 'The Afghan Resistance Movement', in Ralph H. Magnus (ed.), *Afghan Alternatives: Issues, Options, and Policies* (New Brunswick: Transaction Books, 1985), pp. 59-81; Olivier Roy, *Afghanistan: From Holy War to Civil War* (Princeton: The Darwin Press, 1995); *Afghan Resistance: Achievements and Problems* (Peshawar: Jamiat-e Islami Afghanistan, 1986).

the growing atmosphere of distrust which had beset the Afghan nation
in general, and the Jamiat in particular, ethnic loyalty to both Massoud
and Rabbani rapidly came to take precedence over the need to develop
a multiethnic administration and military force. Whereas Massoud
became more and more reliant on his core Panjsheri supporters,
Rabbani surrounded himself largely with staff and armed personnel
who had come from his native Badakhshan province. This gave rise to
divisions even within the Supervisory Council and the Jamiat party, as
well as between them; and to plotting by factions against each other in
ways which served the interests only of those who resented any form
of Tajik rule. Jamiat members and supporters could be divided into
three broad categories: the core, who were ethnically loyal to either
Massoud or Rabbani; the middle circles, whose loyalty was
questionable but who, for reasons of political expediency, were
allowed to penetrate the administration at some strategic points; and
those who were ostensibly supportive of the Rabbani administration,
but mindful of maintaining the possibility of supporting Hekmatyar or
whoever else could triumph in the power struggle between the
Rabbani-Massoud camp and the Hezb. This was hardly a recipe for
stability.

The third concerned the relationship between the Jamiat-led
government and Governor Ismail Khan in Herat. On the one hand, the
governor's alliance with the government was a source of comfort to
Rabbani and Massoud. On the other, his growing stature and strength
as the Amir (ruler–as he was addressed) of all western Afghanistan
ultimately became disconcerting for some of the Kabul authorities.
This, together with the fact that Ismail Khan rapidly succeeded in
transforming Herat into a peaceful haven with a thriving social and
economic life, prompted some in the Rabbani-Massoud camp to view
the governor's power with a degree of disdain and jealousy. Jamiat's
clumsy attempts to gain a strong foothold in the running of Ismail
Khan's administration led to bad feelings between the two sides, thus
undermining the close cooperation which was required to enable them
to develop a national government. Although Ismail Khan faced his
own problems of internal dissension, mismanagement, and
administrative malpractice, which contributed to the demise of his
administration at the hands of the Taliban in mid-1995, the growing
differences between him and the Rabbani-Massoud administration
also played their part. The defeat of Ismail Khan, resulting in his flight
and that of his core supporters to Iran and in the fall to the Taliban of
the large Shindand air base with many of its jet fighters, as well as a
huge amount of other military equipment, proved very damaging to
Rabbani and Massoud. It had a serious psychological and material
impact on their forces, making their grip on Kabul increasingly
tenuous.

The fourth stemmed from the fact that, once Rabbani assumed the presidency, he formally resigned as the head of the Jamiat, in order to depoliticise the office of presidency and free himself from party restrictions and accusations of political bias. In reality, Rabbani still remained very closely attached to the Jamiat, and more specifically to his Badakhshi clique, for loyalty and support. As his power base remained confined to the Jamiat, he simply could not depoliticise his position. Thus his resignation as the head of Jamiat had two unforeseen consequences. On the one hand, since during the years of resistance he had grown to personify his party, it caused a great deal of confusion among those of his supporters who had little understanding of party politics and were traditionally accustomed to the personalisation of politics. On the other, it did nothing to reduce his vulnerability to accusations of political bias and ethnic cronyism–a fact which came rapidly to permeate Rabbani's administration at all levels.

Pakistan's interference

Pakistan's policy toward Afghanistan from the time of the Soviet invasion became one of 'cross-border ethnic clientelism'. Given Pakistan's own substantial Pushtun minority, the Mohammadzai clan's dominance of Afghan politics, and successive Afghan governments' support for the Pushtuns of Pakistan to gain independence within a 'Pushtunistan' entity,[8] Pakistan had always sought leverage in Afghan politics. The Soviet invasion provided President Zia al-Haq with a unique opportunity to achieve this objective. Islamabad increasingly adopted an approach which was pro-Pushtun. It gave the greatest assistance to those resistance groups which were predominantly Pushtun, above all to its own favourite, Hekmatyar's Hezb. The ISI gave the latter the lion's share of American arms and other foreign aid to the Mujahideen, and promoted Hekmatyar as the most powerful and legitimate resistance figure, a man capable of leading a post-communist Afghanistan.[9]

[8] For a detailed discussion of this issue, see Abdul Samad Ghaus, *The Fall of Afghanistan: An Insider's Account* (New York: Pergamon-Brassey's, 1988), pp. 109-147; S.A. Haqshenas, *Dasayis was junayat-e Rus dar Afghanistan: Az Amir Dost Mohammad Khan ta Babrak* (Tehran: Komiteh-i Farhangi Daftar-e Markazi Jamiat-e Islami Afghanistan, 1984); Amin Saikal, *The Rise and Fall of the Shah* (Princeton: Princeton University Press, 1980), pp. 171-172.

[9] See Olivier Roy, *The Lessons of the Soviet/Afghan War* (London: Brassey's, 1991), pp. 39-41; Mohammed Yousaf and Mark Adkin, *The Bear Trap: Afghanistan's Untold Story* (London: Leo Cooper, 1992), pp. 9-10; Barnett R. Rubin, *The*

Pakistan's objectives were twofold. The first was to secure a receptive leadership in Kabul which would ensure the transformation of Afghanistan into a Pakistan-dominated Pushtun-ruled enclave and assist Pakistan's goal of wider regional influence, and broader regional political, economic and strategic gains. The other was to enable Pakistan to enmesh the identity of Pakistan's and Afghanistan's Pushtuns into one and settle once and for all the longstanding Afghanistan-Pakistan border dispute in line with Pakistan's interests. These considerations assumed greater urgency after the collapse of the Soviet Union, which not only signalled the imminent end of communist rule in Kabul, but also opened up the potentially resource-rich Central Asian republics.

However, the Jamiat's domination of post-communist power in Kabul proved very unsettling for Pakistan. Islamabad could not possibly expect the new Islamic government leaders, especially Massoud (who had always maintained his independence from Pakistan and never visited the country during the Soviet occupation), to subordinate their own objectives in order to help Pakistan realise its regional ambitions. Although originally, at the political level, Islamabad had little choice but to recognise this reality, the ISI was given a free hand to do whatever was necessary to shift the balance of power in favour of Hekmatyar. Hence ISI's continued support for Hekmatyar's military actions against the Rabbani government.[10]

Rabbani's and Massoud's uneasiness and eventual public expression of concern about Pakistan's behaviour precipitated a sense of mutual distrust and recrimination. As Pakistan sidelined Hekmatyar in order to support the Taliban, and as the latter made rapid territorial gains, Rabbani and Massoud became increasingly vocal in their condemnation of Pakistan's interference in Afghanistan's internal affairs–a fact which the Afghan representative at the UN repeatedly aired in both the General Assembly and Security Council meetings from mid-1995. This coincided with anti-Pakistan demonstrations in Kabul, which led to the sacking of the Pakistani embassy and the death of one of its employees. Islamabad not only closed down its embassy, and demanded an official apology and compensation, but also dropped any pretence which it had so far exhibited of supporting Rabbani's government.

In early 1995, Prime Minister Benazir Bhutto publicly attacked Rabbani's policies and declared his government 'illegitimate'. She argued that Rabbani was supposed to step down from the presidency by mid-1994, and that his failure to do so was the main cause of the

Fragmentation of Afghanistan: State Formation and Collapse in the International System (New Haven: Yale University Press, 1995), p. 113.
10   Ahmed Rashid, 'Afghanistan: Apocalypse Now', *The Herald*, October 1995.

ongoing fighting in the country. Yet she ignored two key facts. First, the Peshawar Agreement, the basis for her claim, had been massively violated when Pakistan's client Hekmatyar mounted his coup attempt in January 1994; and to suggest that Rabbani remained bound by it when no other party treated it as meaningful was ludicrous. Second, UN mediation had not succeeded in putting in place any viable transitional mechanism which could allow Rabbani to step down, without jeopardising still further the security of thousands of people in areas under government control. Ms Bhutto also ignored fact that no Afghan government had ever come to power on a popular base of legitimacy, and that the question of what has historically constituted a legitimate government in Afghanistan is a highly academic one.

From then on it was clear that Pakistan would do everything possible to wreck Rabbani's government and its claim to any form of legitimacy in favour of a decisive tilt towards the Taliban. Furthermore, it paid little more than lip service to UN mediation efforts, and circumvented every gesture made by the Rabbani government in the hope of building a better working relationship. Although publicly maintaining a policy of denial of any support for the Taliban, Bhutto's government expanded its logistic and military assistance to the militia, as was subsequently confirmed by Pakistani officers, troopers and volunteers who were captured by anti-Taliban forces.[11] In the meantime, Islamabad launched a massive diplomatic and public relations campaign to promote the Taliban as the strongest and most popular force in Afghanistan. It spared no effort to sell the Taliban to Saudi Arabia and the United States as a player capable of not only bringing stability to Afghanistan, but also serving Saudi and American interests, especially against Iran, in the region. Pakistan argued forcefully that a stable Afghanistan under the Taliban could open up a valuable transit route to the Central Asian Muslim republics, and that at least two international consortia, one led by UNOCAL of the United States and Delta Oil of Saudi Arabia, and another comprising Bridas of Argentina, could compete for contracts to construct pipelines through Afghanistan for the import of gas from Turkmenistan to Pakistan and beyond.[12] The financial windfall for both the Taliban and Pakistan was considered to be critical for sustaining their operations in Afghanistan. Washington publicly denied any association with the Taliban, but in reality it maintained a conspicuous silence over their human rights violations, especially

---

11 Ishtiaq Ahmed, 'Options in Afghanistan', *The Nation*, 5 November 1996; Edward Barnes, 'Friends of the *Taliban*', *Time*, 4 November 1996.

12 For a discussion of the power game over the gas and oil resources of Central Asia and their possible export through Afghanistan, see Ahmed Rashid, 'Power Play, and "Pipe dreams"', *Far Eastern Economic Review*, 10 April 1997, pp. 22-28.

against women, their ultratraditionalist and theocratic approach to governance, and their tolerance of widespread opium poppy cultivation. The US also allowed senior officers from both the State Department and the CIA, including Assistant Secretary of State for South Asia Robin Raphel, to meet Taliban leaders on a regular basis inside and outside Afghanistan.[13]

This gave rise to a serious shift in the strategic picture in the region, alarming not only Rabbani and Massoud, but also Iran, the Central Asian republics, Russia and India. While Tehran viewed the whole development as one designed to enforce the American policy of containment of Iran,[14] the secularist Central Asian leaderships felt threatened by the possible spread of the Taliban's Islamic extremism. Moscow came to perceive the changing situation as threatening its vital strategic interests in its former Central Asian republics, and New Delhi found the changes upsetting the regional balance in favour of its arch enemy, Pakistan.[15]

Although thus far Rabbani and Massoud had refrained from being closely identified with the Iranian regime, they now found it necessary to seek assistance from wherever it could be found. However, Iran remained indecisive as to whether to increase its aid solely to Wahdat or also to provide some help to the Rabbani government; Uzbekistan persisted in channelling its logistic support exclusively to Dostum; Tajikistan could provide little help since it remained embroiled in the complications of its own civil war; and Russia and India were content to supply mostly political support for the Rabbani regime. Under the circumstances, Rabbani and Massoud made a last frantic effort to broaden the government's power base not only by making up with Wahdat, but also bringing Hekmatyar–a well-known but by 1996 essentially powerless Pushtun–into the government. This reconciliation with Hekmatyar, who joined the government in June 1996 as prime minister, was perhaps the worst strategic mistake that the Jamiat leaders committed, a severe miscalculation which badly backfired, subjecting the Jamiat to destructive internal and external pressures. His inclusion achieved the reverse of what was intended: it resulted in the government's power base contracting rather than expanding. There were many in the Rabbani and Massoud camp who were fiercely opposed to Hekmatyar, holding him responsible for the

---

13 John Jennings, 'The *Taliban* and Foggy Bottom', *The Washington Times*, 25 October 1996.

14 For the comments of Iran's Supreme leader, Ayatollah Khamanei, on the issue, see *Kayhan Havai*, 16 October 1996.

15 See O.N. Mehrotra, 'The Troubled CIS', in Sreedhar (ed.), *Taliban and the Afghan Turmoil: The Role of USA, Pakistan, Iran and China* (New Delhi: Himalayan Books, 1997) Chapter 6.

predicament in which the government was placed. They could not bring themselves to serve a prime minister who had done everything possible to destroy them.

This led to a profound collapse of morale within the government and its military defenders, and the end result was disastrous. As the Taliban launched their final assault on Kabul, it was Hekmatyar's commanders who surrendered one after another in eastern Afghanistan and *en route* from there to Kabul, and Massoud's forces could not hold the dam once it had burst. By September 1996, Kabul had become indefensible; Massoud found himself with little choice but to retreat to his native Panjsher Valley and to shift the government to the north in order to be able to fight the Taliban from a more secure base. The fall of Kabul to the Taliban without a fight opened a bloody new phase in the evolution of Afghan and regional politics. Pakistan 'won', but only to face bigger problems in Afghanistan and in the region[16]–a development too familiar to students of Afghan politics and history, who had witnessed similar Pyrrhic 'victories' for the British in Afghanistan in the nineteenth century and the Soviets in the 1980s.

The Pakistani action invited greater involvement on the part of those other regional actors which found both the politics of the Taliban and their patron repugnant to their individual national and regional interests. A reluctant Iran now found it imperative to enhance its assistance not only to Wahdat, but also to two other major anti-Taliban forces–Massoud and Dostum. Similarly, the Uzbek government of President Karimov found it necessary to augment its support for Dostum, and President Rakhmonov of Tajikistan felt sufficiently alarmed to invite Massoud, who had had a very good relationship with the Tajik Islamic opposition, to play an important role in speeding up a settlement of the Tajik civil war, and in return to receive growing logistic support from Tajikistan. Concerned about the implications of the fall of Kabul for its interests in Central Asia, Russia too began supplying some arms to the anti-Taliban forces, and India joined forces with Iran and Russia in turning up the diplomatic heat on Pakistan and in dissuading the international community from according recognition to the Taliban.

As the regional actors embarked on a mini cross-border ethnic 'great game', the scene was set for a prolongation of the Afghan conflict, with no side emerging as a clear winner, and with the Afghan people being those with most to lose from the conflict. Meanwhile, Pakistan could attract only Saudi Arabia and the United Arab Emirates to join it in according diplomatic recognition to the Taliban. The

---

16 For subsequent Pakistani setbacks, see Christopher Thomas, 'Taliban Rout ends Islamabad's dream', *The Australian*, 4 June 1997; M. Ilyas Khan, 'War Without End', *The Herald*, June 1997.

Rabbani government continued to staff most Afghan diplomatic posts, and to occupy the Afghan seat at the United Nations as the legitimate government of Afghanistan.

The dislodging of Rabbani's government from Kabul was grounded in both domestic and exogenous factors. Internally, it faced a problem of political legitimacy from the start. The Peshawar Agreement, based on the method of élite settlement, provided Rabbani with no broad power base or monopoly of force, on the basis of which his government could expand its rule beyond Kabul and a few ethnolinguistically affiliated provinces. At the same time Jamiat, which had functioned during the Soviet occupation as a combat and combat-support organisation, not only lacked the necessary experience in the art of governance, but also harboured many internal divisions. Often its political and military wings could not coordinate their activities in support of a single leadership and common policy objectives. Personal rivalries within the party and between it and its allies elsewhere in Afghanistan, especially in Herat, proved to be extremely debilitating. However, nothing undermined its position more than the acrimonious relationship which developed between Jamiat and Pakistan. Islamabad's rejection of the Rabbani government as one which was not prepared to subordinate itself to Pakistan's wider regional interests, and its persistent attempts to influence Afghan politics through cross-border ethnic clientelism, led to active Pakistani intervention in Afghanistan with Hekmatyar as the instrument. This deprived Rabbani's government of the opportunity that it needed to consolidate, and eventually exacerbated the conditions for its dislodgement from Kabul by the Taliban. Yet its shift from the capital to the north of Afghanistan has not meant its end; it has simply inaugurated a new phase in its struggle to gain wider legitimacy. The Afghan conflict continues, and so do the chances of the Rabbani government to play a role in determining the future of Afghanistan.

HOW THE TALIBAN BECAME A MILITARY FORCE

Anthony Davis

The military rise of the Taliban

Between their emergence in the summer of 1994 and the seizure of Kabul just two years later, the rise of the Taliban movement marked the most dramatic shift of forces in Afghanistan's recent history since the Soviet invasion of 1979. The speed with which the army of madrassa students erupted into southern Afghanistan spoke volumes for the political bankruptcy of their Mujahideen foes and the exhaustion of a population eager for peace at almost any cost. Less visibly, perhaps, it also said much about the bruised pride of Afghanistan's Pushtun community, whose political dominance of two and a half centuries had been rudely challenged by newly-assertive minorities. But beyond that, the rise of the Taliban was first and foremost an avowedly military enterprise, a crusade sworn to reunify the country by firepower as much as by exhortation. How that firepower was acquired and deployed is basic to an understanding of the Taliban phenomenon.

While the essential outlines of how the Taliban moved from the madrassas of Pakistani Baluchistan to the Presidential Palace in Kabul are clear enough, the origins of the movement are still confused. The Taliban themselves have, perhaps understandably, shown little interest in clarifying matters. The official Taliban version of history traces the genesis of the movement to a humble madrassa in Singesar village of Kandahar province's Maiwand district where Mohammad Omar, a former mujahid was studying. Long incensed by the excesses of predatory Mujahideen bands on the provincial highways where arbitrary 'taxation', robbery and rape had become a depressing norm, he and thirty comrades finally decided to take up arms in the summer of 1994. On a wave of popular anger, the movement grew from there.

But what is clear is that from the outset, Omar and his colleagues needed support to pursue their still limited objectives. Of the original

30 initially only 14 were armed.[1] At first some assistance in the form of money and weapons came from Haji Bashar of Maiwand, a commander of Mawlawi Younos Khalis's Hezb-i Islami, and Abdul Ghaffar Akhundzadeh, the major potentate in neighbouring Helmand province. In September, however, it appears that Mullah Mohammad Rabbani, a close associate of Omar's, travelled to Kabul with several companions, met President Rabbani and gained a level of endorsement and financial backing from Rabbani who appears to have seen in the Taliban a force that might be used against Gulbuddin Hekmatyar's Hezb-i Islami, which was rocketing Kabul.[2]

Whether the Taliban's first contacts with Pakistani authorities were made before or after this trip and exactly what authorities they were is obscure. The probability is that Pakistan was aware of the new movement before September and that various channels were at work in liaising with them. Pakistan's Inter Services Intelligence (ISI) had long-established networks in and around Kandahar, where Pakistan had a consulate and where ISI had its own close links with the so-called 'Airport Shura' of commanders. At around this time, other Taliban groups under Mohammad Ghaus, who was later to rise high in the movement's hierarchy, began operating near Kandahar airport. The Taliban themselves had their own long-established links with the madrassa network of the Jamiat-e Ulema-i Islam in Baluchistan where thousands of Afghan refugee youths and some students from inside Afghanistan were engaged in Koranic studies. As has been pointed out, the Jamiat-e Ulema-i Islam leader Fazlur Rahman served in the Benazir Bhutto government and worked with Interior Minister Major General (Retired) Naseerullah Babar.

A family friend and confidant of the Bhuttos, Babar had played a leading role in defining Afghan policy for Benazir's father Zulfiqar Ali Bhutto in the mid-1970s and enjoyed the reputation of being something of an expert in Afghan affairs. It was courtesy of Babar, himself a Pushtun with an extensive knowledge of the Frontier and taste for clandestine operations, that Afghanistan's Islamists-in-exile, Burhanuddin Rabbani, Gulbuddin Hekmatyar and Ahmad Shah Massoud had been granted asylum and secretly trained by élite Special Service Group instructors in the 1970s.[3] Back in the Great Game two decades later, Babar's overriding interest was developing for Pakistan a secure trade route to Central Asia, something which would boost the

---

[1] According to Mawlawi Abdul Hakim, quoted in 'Here Come the Taliban', *Newsline*, February 1995.

[2] Private communication from Steve LeVine of *The New York Times* to the author, July 1997.

[3] Author's interviews with Naseerullah Babar, Peshawar, June 1993.

country's flagging economy. With the Salang highway from Kabul north to Uzbekistan blocked by fighting, Babar had first announced the government's interest in an overland route from Quetta to Turkmenistan and Central Asia via Kandahar and Herat during a cabinet session in June 1994.[4] In September he visited Chaman on the Baluchistan-Afghan frontier where the Quetta-Kandahar road crosses the border, and then surveyed the highway inside Afghanistan. On his return to Islamabad in late September he announced that experimental use of the road by Pakistani traders would likely start in October (though neither then nor later was any clearance sought from the government in Kabul). Whether Babar met any Taliban leaders at this time is unclear; but he cannot have failed to have been briefed on the highway situation by intelligence officers of the Frontier Corps, subordinate to his Interior Ministry, and possibly by ISI officers also based in Quetta and Chaman.

One such ISI officer was 'Colonel Imam'. A Pushtun with extensive experience in cross-border liaison with southern Afghan Mujahideen, 'Imam' (the *nom de guerre* of Sultan Amir) was to play an important role in the rise of the Taliban and subsequently served as Pakistan's Consul-General in Herat. Interestingly, at an earlier stage in his career he had served with the élite Special Service Group and in 1982-83 had been based in Quetta training Afghan Mujahideen.[5] Among them had been groups of Talibs from the refugee community who on returning to fight in Afghanistan were generally affiliated with the Hezb-e Islami of Younos Khalis and the Harakat-e Enqelab of Nabi Mohammadi. In many cases, however, they operated in bands known specifically as 'Taliban', antecedents of the movement that was, under very different circumstances, to attempt the conquest of the country.[6]

The Taliban's first major military operation came between Babar's September visit to Afghanistan and the departure of the first 'experimental' convoy. On 12 October a force of some 200 Taliban, divided into three groups, assaulted the border district centre of Spin Boldak, a sprawling trucking stop-over point opposite Chaman. The rout of the Hezb-e Islami garrison under Mullah Akhtar Jan by reportedly well-organised and disciplined Taliban was all over in around two hours. According to one account only one Talib died in the fighting while seven Hezbis were killed and many wounded.[7] Diplomatic sources were also later to claim that the attackers were

---

4   'Afghanistan: La Vengeance de la CIA', *Le Figaro*, 21 February 1995.
5   On Imam's background, see Steve LeVine, 'Helping Hand', *Newsweek*, 14 October 1997.
6   Author's interview with Hamid Karzai, Islamabad, April 1997.
7   'Rout of the Warlords', *Newsline*, November 1994.

supported by artillery fire from across the border.[8] If true, this marked
a curious echo of a similar report of Pakistani cross-border artillery
support for the forces of Hekmatyar's Hezb when they first captured
Spin Boldak from Najibullah's communist garrison in September
1988.[9]

Around the same time they captured Spin Boldak, the Taliban also
seized the Pasha arms depot, an extremely large munitions dump that
had been moved across the border from Pakistan in 1991. As one
source later put it to the author: 'The Hezb-e Islami dump was a huge
dump, a central dump with rockets, artillery ammunition, tank
ammunition, and small arms–both captured from the (pre-1992)
Afghan government and Western supplied ammo. I believe they have
sufficient stocks to run their affairs for quite some time. For years
even.'[10]

Not surprisingly, no independent observers were on hand to
witness the Taliban seizure of either Spin Boldak or the arms dump.
But the seizure of the Pasha depot has since gone down in what might
be termed the semi-official history of the Taliban: by December the
Western press was quoting Western diplomats as confirming it.[11]
However, it says something for the opaque nature of events on the
border at the time that some independent analysts question whether the
Taliban did actually capture such stocks there, arguing that the Pasha
dump had been systematically looted long before.[12] The implication of
such doubts is clear enough: the purported seizure of the dump
established a strong case for the Taliban's subsequent campaign being
conducted without their depending on external sources, and also
provided a thick smoke-screen behind which such supplies might flow.

The seizure of Spin Boldak was the first real sign of an impending
shift of forces in Afghanistan. In the wider context of the Kabul
government's struggle to survive the attacks of Hekmatyar and his
allies of the Supreme Coordination Council–Uzbek warlord Abdul
Rashid Dostum and the Shiite Hezb-e Wahdat-e Islami (Islamic Unity
Party)–the fall of the southern district attracted little attention. But for
the clutch of squabbling Mujahideen warlords who had misruled
Kandahar city since the fall of Najibullah it came as a clarion alarm.
Most powerful was Mullah Naqib, a Jamiat loyalist appointed Corps
commander by the Rabbani government who was in effect Kabul's

8 Author's interviews with Western diplomats, Islamabad, January 1995.
9 Author's interview, Western intelligence source, Islamabad, October 1988.
10 Author's interview with Pakistani intelligence officer, Chaman, March 1995.
11 See, for example, Oxford Analytica, *Asia Pacific Daily Brief*, 16 December 1994.
12 Private communication to author from Steve LeVine of *The New York Times*, July
    1997.

senior figure in Kandahar. There was also Amir Lalai who had inherited the base of the former 15th Division and its cantonment at Keshlai-e Jadid. The Hezb-e Islami's local strongman, Sarkateb, had earlier controlled part of the Corps Headquarters but had subsequently been ousted by Naqib and pushed out of the city to his base at Bagh-e Pul on the highway to the west. The road to the airport and the Pakistan border was controlled by Mansur Achakzai, a cousin of the former communist militia leader, Esmat Achakzai whose 'chains' or road blocks on the Kandahar-Spin Boldak road were notorious. Nominally presiding over the anarchy was Kandahar's governor, Gul Agha, ostensibly loyal to Gailani's NIFA and son of Haji Latif, the late 'Lion of Kandahar'. No lion himself, Gul Agha had never been a military player and was to flee Kandahar even before the Taliban arrived.

Following the fall of Spin Boldak, tensions rose immediately between the Taliban and the Kandahar commanders. The latter maintained that the Taliban were being supported by the Pakistani authorities and evidently feared the Koranic students had bigger things in mind, specifically the city itself. But characteristically they made no attempt to sink their differences and present a united front. Despite attempts by Ghaffar Akhundzadeh of Helmand to mediate between the two sides, tension finally led to open conflict over the celebrated convoy incident that, like the humble madrassa of Singesar village, has become an essential part of Taliban lore.

On 29 October, a 30-vehicle convoy loaded with medicines, consumer goods, and foodstuffs left Quetta *en route* for Turkmenistan via Kandahar and Herat. This marked the first practical manifestation of the Central Asian land-route policy Pakistan had been pursuing diplomatically since September. In an October visit to Ashgabat, Benazir Bhutto had met both Herati strongman Ismail Khan and northwestern warlord, Abdul Rashid Dostum, and had secured from both promises of cooperation in safeguarding the road link. Then on 20 October, just one week after the fall of Spin Boldak, Babar headed a group of Islamabad-based ambassadors from the United States, the United Kingdom, China, Italy, and Korea on a flight from Quetta to Kandahar and Herat. This effort to drum up support for a US$300 million project to upgrade the trans-Afghan highway further underscored Babar's foreign policy concerns and his very personal commitment to Central Asian trade. At the foot of the Khojak Pass where the mountains of Baluchistan rise up from the southern deserts of Afghanistan, the convoy halted at Chaman. By the time it ground out across the wide expanse of desert north of Spin Boldak, at least two ISI officers, Colonels Imam and 'Gul' (another *nom de guerre*) were aboard, and Taliban commanders Borjan and Turabi with some of their men were riding shotgun.[13] But the convoy's arrival in Kandahar was delayed: on 2 November it was halted by the fighters of Mansur Achakzai at his base at Takht-e Pul, 35 kilometres outside Kandahar. The incident was not the usual casual banditry: this was rather political ransom on the part of commanders angry over what they understood to be Pakistani backing for the new force. Conditions for the convoy's release–put forward to the Pakistani authorities by Mansur, Amir Lalai and a Sayyaf commander, Ustaz Halim–were that permits should be issued permitting free movement across the frontier by their supporters; and that the ISI and the Frontier Corps should cease supporting the Taliban.[14]

Following an attempt at negotiation through a tribal jirga dispatched to Takht-e Pul by the Taliban, matters were resolved violently. Taliban reinforcements from Pakistan freed the convoy on 3 November. Then, abruptly, they swept on into Kandahar city, Afghanistan's traditional royal capital, to rout the warlord forces. Crucially, Naqib, who commanded an estimated 2,500 men did not resist. Those who did–Mansur, Lalai, Halim and Sarkateb–were swept away in two days of fighting. According to Taliban accounts they lost only nine killed. But total casualties were heavier, totalling in all some 50 or more.[15] While this much is broadly clear, what is far from resolved is the vital question of who gave the order to move from freeing a convoy to seizing a city–Borjan and Turabi? Imam and Gul? Or a third party across the Pakistani border?

In addition to the ammunition that may–or may not–have been captured at Pasha, in Kandahar the Taliban seized the real sinews of war for continued advance. At the airport they inherited six MiG-21 fighters (of which only one was still operational) and four Mi-17 transport helicopters. At Sarkateb's base, 20 tanks and two additional Mi-17s were seized.[16] From both Lalai and Naqib they inherited additional armour, including tanks and BMP armoured fighting vehicles. Thus in the space of less than three weeks a hitherto unknown force had seized control of the country's second city and was

---

13   Ibid. Details on the Taliban escort for the convoy are from LeVine's later interview with Gul Agha in Quetta.

14   'Rout of the Warlords', *Newsline*, November 1994.

15   Anthony Davis, 'Afghanistan's Taliban', *Jane's Intelligence Review*, vol. 7, no. 7, July 1995, pp. 315-321.

16   Author's interview with Pakistan intelligence officer, Chaman, March 1995. *AFGHANews*, vol. 11, no. 2, February 1995, reported seven helicopters and eight jets at Kandahar airport.

estimated to have grown from several hundred to some 2,500-3,000 disciplined and motivated fighters.

To suggest, as senior Islamabad officials including the Prime Minister were later to do, that Pakistan had no hand in facilitating, if not actually planning, these events is to beggar belief. Reports of artillery support and cross-border assistance in the capture of Spin Boldak were accorded considerable credibility by Western diplomats in Quetta and Islamabad. These suspicions were shared by the warlords themselves, who were convinced of official Pakistani involvement soon after Spin Boldak fell, unsurprisingly given the position of the town on the border itself and the size of the operation. 'You don't mount a military operation of that size without some assistance from somebody', was how one Western diplomat later put it.[17] Beyond Spin Boldak, the presence of ISI officers and senior Taliban commanders in the Pakistani convoy indicates clearly enough the degree of coordination between the two parties.

Critical to the Taliban success was the fact that Naqib, arguably the most powerful force in the city, did not oppose the Taliban militarily. Some reports suggest that Colonel Imam–who was evidently active in the city before its fall–was personally involved in preparing the political ground. In late October or early November he met the corps commander in a closed door session. Naqib's deputy, Khan Mohammad, and one of his principal advisers, Moallem Akbar, were subsequently informed by Naqib that he had decided to hand over his weapons. Senior officials of the Rabbani government are convinced that Naqib accepted money from either the Pakistanis or Taliban emissaries on the understanding that after the Taliban takeover he would be permitted retain his position.[18] One figure cited is a total of US$1.5 million spent in the taking of Kandahar, a massive figure in the context of Afghanistan today.[19] Given his cooperation with the Taliban it seems likely a substantial proportion of any such sum went to Naqib. In the upshot, the Taliban kept their side of the bargain, at least for some two months. After that Naqib was persuaded to leave Kandahar for his home district of Arghandab to avoid the wrath of the populace; his residual force was later disarmed. History has yet to relate how much of the money, if any, he got to keep.

Interestingly, it also seems clear that even at this late hour President Rabbani continued to regard the Taliban with favour and endorsed Naqib's decision to cooperate with them. Following Naqib's

---

[17] Author's interview with Western diplomat, Islamabad, January 1995.
[18] Information from Ahmad Shah Massoud's personal secretary, Dr Abdullah: author's interview in the Panjsher Valley, April 1997.
[19] Oxford Analytica, *Asia Pacific Daily Brief*, 16 December 1994.

meeting with Imam and announcement to his deputy that his men should give up their weapons, an incredulous Khan Mohammad contacted Kabul by radio, spoke to Rabbani directly and queried Naqib's instructions. The message he heard was apparently unambiguous: obey Naqib and cooperate with the Taliban.[20] The extent to which Rabbani was aware of the Taliban's cross-border links and the fact that Naqib may have accepted payment for cooperating with the Taliban remains, like much else during these days, unclear.

It also bears noting that many of the Taliban who participated in the seizure of Kandahar were armed with brand new weapons, in particular Kalashnikov-type assault rifles. Foreign aid officials leaving the city as or shortly before fighting broke out reported to one Western correspondent seeing several hundred Taliban reinforcements who had crossed the border grouped on the Spin Boldak-Kandahar road. Grease paper, said the foreigners, was everywhere as the madrassa students removed new weapons from their wrappings.[21] While it is conceivable these weapons had been brought from the Pasha depot to be distributed to the students, it is just as likely that they were shipped from ISI warehouses inside Pakistan to be handed over to the combatants as they moved into Afghanistan. Either way, there is no question that large numbers of Taliban fighters were bussed across the border with the full concurrence of Pakistani border officials.[22]

The south

The second phase of the Taliban's rise involved the extension of their power both north and east. As increasing numbers of Talibs were trucked across the border from the Jamiat-e Ulema-i Islam madrassas of Baluchistan, Kandahar-based units moved into Uruzgan province to the north and Zabul to the northeast. Feelers had already been extended to local commanders and where the new movement's moral and religious standing failed to carry the day, generous disbursement of cash usually

---

[20] Information from Ahmad Shah Massoud's personal secretary, Dr Abdullah: author's interview in the Panjsher Valley, April 1997.

[21] Private communication to author from Steve LeVine of *The New York Times*, July 1997.

[22] Free movement of Taliban across the border has been substantially documented in Pakistani press reports. In the July 1997 issue of *Newsline* magazine, p. 63, Shahzada Zulfiqar noted 'Pakistani buses carrying thousands of religious students continue to enter ... Afghanistan from the legal entry point of Chaman without any check or hindrance by the Pakistani immigration personnel at the check post. According to some estimates, over 60,000 Taliban, both Afghan and Pakistani have entered the country through this porous border'.

succeeded. The two provinces joined the Taliban with scarcely a shot fired. Their biggest catch was Mullah Salaam 'Roketi', a warlord affiliated to Sayyaf's Ittehad-e Islami who had earlier in the summer distinguished himself by kidnapping two Chinese engineers and nine Pakistanis in an effort to retrieve Stinger missiles that had been confiscated by Pakistani authorities from his house in Baluchistan. As 'divisional commander' of Zabul, Roketi's allegiance brought with it hundreds of new adherents to the cause.

Neither moral authority nor cash counted for much, however, in Helmand province to the west. Traditionally the breadbasket of the south and by the late 1980s Afghanistan's foremost opium-producing province, Helmand was the fiefdom of the Akhundzadeh family who had earlier been affiliated to Harakat-e Enqelab but more recently allied with the Rabbani government. It was ruled by Ghaffar who had assumed the governorship on the death from cancer of his elder brother Rasul Akhundzadeh earlier in the year, and who had no particular quarrel with the Taliban. What precipitated the conflict was the long-standing feud between the Akhundzadeh clan and Abdul Wahid, the self-styled 'rais' (director) of Helmand's northernmost district, Baghran. Since fighting had broken out between them in the 1980s, hundreds had died in a vicious but largely unnoticed local war. Traditionally weaker, Abdul Wahid saw in the Taliban capture of Kandahar an opportunity finally to even scores.

In November, soon after the fall of Kandahar, he held meetings with Omar and the Taliban's ruling shura, offering his loyalty and urging on them the strategic importance of Helmand and the need to supplant Ghaffar. A 60-man Taliban delegation subsequently visited the provincial capital Lashkargah and held discussions with Ghaffar in the main mosque. Any illusions Akhundzadeh might have entertained that his earlier contacts with Taliban leaders would allow for coexistence were soon shattered. Following a thinly-veiled ultimatum, he was persuaded to withdraw his forces from the town and retreat north to the family stronghold in Musa Qala and Kajaki districts. Less than two weeks later he was ordered to surrender his weapons.

The Akhundzadeh clan of the Alizai tribe were of a different calibre to Naqib: the ultimatum was a declaration of war and the battle for Helmand lasted much of December and early January 1995. The first real military challenge the Taliban had yet faced, it pitted Ghaffar and his allies from Girishk–Abdul Rahman Jan and Moallem Mir Wali, former militia commanders who had joined the Hezb-e Islami–against the Taliban and Abdul Wahid. The fighting was bitter, with casualties running into the hundreds.[23] But Ghaffar was caught in a strategic pincer between the Taliban in the south and Rais-e Baghran to the north. Musa Qala was finally occupied in mid-January and Ghaffar fled into the mountains of Ghor, later to link up with the Kabul government forces of Ismail Khan. On the national highway, the Taliban secured Girishk and by late January had reached Delaram on the borders of Ismail's western domain.

On their eastern front they had already moved into Ghazni where a thoroughly-alarmed Hekmatyar precipitated hostilities by attacking Ghazni city and Kabul's provincial governor Taj Mohammad, better known as Qari Baba, a former Harakat-e Enqelab commander. The governor, who had earlier refused Taliban demands that he disarm, was then obliged to call on them for assistance. The Taliban swiftly entered the fray, driving out the Hezbis and finally securing an agreement from Qari Baba that he, like Mullah Naqib, would surrender all powers to them.

In one crucial respect Ghazni marked a watershed. Reports from Radio Kabul asserted that the Taliban were intervening in support of government forces and there were some reports of government air strikes on the Hezb. But for their part, the Taliban abruptly dismissed any suggestion of an alliance with Kabul against Hekmatyar. 'We are neutral in the power struggle between Rabbani and Hekmatyar', announced Khairullah Khairkhwa (later to become the Taliban interior minister).[24] The subtext was unambiguous: regardless of any earlier dealings with Kabul or attempts by Kabul's representatives like Naqib and Qari Baba to cooperate with them, the Taliban were now openly denouncing all Mujahideen factions as being as bad as each other. Between December and mid-January, the movement had thus undergone a fundamental shift. From an essentially provincial force that had successfully imposed peace and security on the anarchy of Kandahar, it had now become a crusade committed to establishing Sharia law and disarming of Mujahideen 'criminals' across the country. Abruptly all Afghanistan was in its sights.

Exactly what decisions lay behind this shift, who made them and when, remains, like so much else about the Taliban, obscured in the secrecy surrounding the 22-member ruling shura. But significantly, at around this time the weight of opinion within the upper echelons of the ISI–whose traditional Pushtun candidate for the throne of Kabul had long been Hekmatyar–now began to swing towards the Taliban. While in late 1994 Babar's appears to have been the leading voice in

---

[23] Information from Pakistani intelligence sources, Chaman, March 1995; Economist Intelligence Unit, *Report on Afghanistan*, First Quarter 1995.

[24] *United Press International,* 27 January 1995.

the Islamabad establishment propounding the students' cause, by January the ISI was taking a growing interest.[25] By then it was entirely clear that the Durrani-dominated Taliban had succeeded in achieving a legitimacy, popularity and a momentum of victory in the heartlands of Pushtun Afghanistan far beyond anything Hekmatyar, a Ghilzai Pushtun from northern Afghanistan, could ever have hoped to achieve.

With Ghazni behind them, the Taliban advanced into Wardak at the end of January. The target of their advance was again the Hezb-e Islami, whose forces were ranged in a wide arc around southern Kabul. On 30 January 1995 clashes broke out with Hezb forces at Saydabad on the main highway. On 31 January fighting in Wardak reportedly resulted in 80 Hezbis killed, 250 captured and 12 tanks and multiple-barrelled rocket launchers seized along with three D-30 122mm artillery pieces. Two days later the Taliban asserted control over Saydabad and Shaikhabad on the highway. On 5 February fighting broke out for control of the provincial seat of Maidanshahr, and resulted in over 200 killed on both sides in four days, with a massive Taliban assault repulsed on the 7th. Both sides reinforced the next day and on the night of 9-10 February the Taliban launched a concerted attack on Maidanshahr, overrunning it in several hours' fighting.[26]

This marked the Taliban's most telling victory to date, bringing them within striking distance of both Hekmatyar's Charasyab base in the Logar valley to the east, and Kabul itself, 35 kilometres up the highway. It might have marked a pause for consolidation and negotiations; but there was none. On the same day they secured Maidanshahr, Taliban forces drove Hezb out of Chak district in Wardak and Baraki Barak in Logar and on 13 February entered Pul-e Alam in the main Logar Valley. With his position in Charasyab wedged between the government and the Taliban now untenable, Hekmatyar completed an ignominious evacuation to Sarobi the next day. He left behind him significant stocks of artillery (including powerful 220mm. 'Uragan' multiple rocket systems), ammunition and one Mi-17 transport helicopter.

By now, the Taliban had mushroomed to an army of at least 10,000 fighters backed by perhaps as many as 100 operational tanks and AFVs.[27] While they were to be refined over the campaigns of 1995 and 1996, their military characteristics were in several essentials

25 Western diplomatic sources, interviewed in Islamabad, March 1995.
26 Economist Intelligence Unit, *Report on Afghanistan*, First Quarter 1995; *AFGHANews*, vol. 11, no. 3, March 1995.
27 Information from Pakistani intelligence sources, Chaman; Kabul Defence Ministry sources, March 1995.

already apparent. They marked a significant break with anything seen earlier on the Afghan battlefield. Tactically the Taliban operated with a flexibility that hinged on a notably efficient communications and command-and-control network. There was also an unusual readiness to undertake night operations. These frequently involved repeated attacks against an enemy position in the space of a single night–despite sometimes high casualties.[28] While such attacks were far from the massed human-wave assaults typical of Iran's 'Baseej' infantry in the Iran-Iraq conflict, they were sufficiently unusual on the Afghan battlefield to give rise to a powerful and growing mythology of Taliban invincibility. Strategically, meanwhile, the student-led army displayed an unwavering direction combined with disconcerting speed and mobility. All this was at startling variance with the Jihad-era warfare of Afghanistan's tribal south in which the Taliban chiefs had cut their teeth: a conflict of hit-and-run skirmishing, organisationally fragmented and seldom if ever fought to conclusion.

This may have been partly due to the fact that as early as January 1995, technical functions required for mobile warfare in artillery and armour were being filled by ex-communist regime officers with specialised training. Noticeable by early 1995, for example, was the impressive accuracy of Taliban mortar and artillery fire.[29] Many of these officers–once more receiving salaries–were former members of the largely Pushtun Khalq wing of the People's Democratic Party of Afghanistan; and some were loyal to former Defence Minister General Shahnawaz Tanai who, following his abortive bid to topple Najibullah in March 1990, had been resident in Pakistan as a guest of the ISI. The evidence points strongly towards Tanai's reactivating his own networks and filling key gaps in the fighting capability of the Taliban. None of this could have been done without permission, if not active encouragement, from the ISI itself. In a February interview with the Pakistani newspaper *The Frontier Post*, Hekmatyar was to claim that 1,600 communist officers were serving in Taliban ranks.[30] Given the overall size of Taliban forces then, this must be seen as an exaggeration. Nevertheless that there were even half that number is a telling reflection on the speed with which the Taliban were being organised as a military force.

In January, training camps were established at Spin Boldak and Kandahar. Fresh recruits from Pakistani madrassas were inducted for

---

28 Defence Ministry sources, Kabul, March and November 1995.
29 Author's interviews with government troops, southern Kabul lines, March 1995; Economist Intelligence Unit, *Report on Afghanistan*, First Quarter 1995.
30 *Agence France Presse*, 22 February 1995.

training courses lasting two months.[31] Training over such a period can be assumed to have involved courses not only in field craft and small arms but also support weaponry such as rocket propelled grenades, mortars and recoilless rifles. Whether instructors were former Afghan Army personnel, or Pakistanis from the Pakistan Army, or Babar's Frontier Corps is unclear. However, the ease with which ethnic Pushtun Pakistanis, bearded and in local 'shalwar kameez', might have blended into a force that was in any event a thoroughly cross-border phenomenon hardly requires comment. At the same time, informed western sources were convinced that before long Taliban training was also been undertaken by Pakistan army instructors on Pakistani soil as during the anti-communist Jihad.[32]

By early 1995 the Taliban army had thus established the three-legged structure that was to characterise its subsequent growth. The forces were composed of madrassa youth, the real Taliban; former Jihadi fighters whose commanders found it expedient or profitable to climb aboard the bandwagon; and former communist regime officers. Hardly surprisingly, these disparate backgrounds were to give rise to a degree of friction. But such tensions have undoubtedly been played up by Rabbani government critics of the Taliban, and what is perhaps remarkable is that the militia was to prove itself as well-integrated militarily as it did.

It is also worth noting two factors evident in late 1994 and early 1995 that Taliban mythology has since largely obscured. First, with the exception of Zabul and Uruzgan, the takeover of other provinces involved hostilities and occasionally substantial human losses. That the fighting was not more protracted was indeed due to the Taliban tactics, ample supplies of cash and an aura of invincibility. But the later tendency to portray the religious students as having swept the south on a wave of popular adulation with scarcely a shot fired has strayed from the factual record.

Another more pervasive myth is that the areas they conquered were racked by lawlessness and anarchy. One most certainly was: Kandahar and its environs. But in most other areas the Taliban laid down ultimata and fought their way into regions that were at peace and in many instances–Qari Baba's Ghazni and before long, Ismail Khan's Herat–recognised as being relatively well administered. Ironically, administration, services and schooling in these regions were far in advance of anything delivered by the Taliban. Their energies were focused almost exclusively on war.

---

[31] *AFGHANews*, vol. 11, no. 2, February 1995, p.5.

[32] Information communicated to the author by Steve LeVine of *The New York Times*, who interviewed Islamabad-based western military and intelligence officials.

Kabul

Kabul was to mark the Taliban's first major setback, and for reasons that are not difficult to discern. Most strikingly, Taliban field commanders, Mullahs Rabbani, Borjan and Ghaus, evidently had very little understanding of the military and political situation in the city. Unsophisticated men with little or no formal education beyond Koranic studies, they appear to have made the mistake of transposing their experiences in Kandahar and the south to the altogether different climate of Kabul. Many believed the popular disgust with the Mujahideen and support for their moral authority that they had encountered in Kandahar would be mirrored in the capital.[33]

This was a total misreading of the situation. Kabul is a Persian-speaking city and many residents viewed Massoud–who is no petty warlord–as having defended the city over three years from Hekmatyar's ruthless attacks. Many too were decidedly–and, as events later proved, justifiably–concerned over the imposition of Taliban-style fundamentalist strictures. Massoud's troops, some of the most battle-tested units in the country, had nothing in common with Taliban foes to that date. Despite the belief among some western diplomats in Islamabad that they might be reluctant to open fire on the Taliban, most of Massoud's front-line Panjsheris saw the students less as Islamic crusaders than as Pushtun provincials with inflated expectations stiffened by a good sprinkling of 'Khalqis'.[34]

Nevertheless it was clear that Massoud himself had no immediate interest in confrontation provided the Taliban stayed outside Kabul. By late February his concern was to play for enough time to deal with his remaining enemies inside Kabul–specifically the Shiite Hezb-e Wahdat of Mazari and the remnants of Dostum's Kabul contingent, dug into the southwest of the city and now vulnerable after Hekmatyar's departure. With this in view, Massoud adopted a pointedly conciliatory attitude towards the Taliban. Hekmatyar's flight from Charasyab had been followed by its swift occupation by government forces. But at the demand of the Taliban, the base was handed over to them along with several nearby mountain-top positions. Government mechanics from Bagram even reportedly assisted in repair work on the Mi-17.[35]

The following weeks were marked by a three-way stand-off. On the one hand, negotiations opened between the Taliban and the Wahdat

33 Author's interviews with Taliban commanders and troops, Charasyab, March 1995.

34 Author's interviews with government troops Sang-e Nevishta and Bini Hissar, March 1995.

35 Witnessed by western journalists, Charasyab, February 1995.

chief Mazari, raising the possibility of an entente at the government's expense. Giving credence to this was the fact that during their advance into Uruzgan and Ghazni–both provinces with significant Shiite minorities–the Taliban had been noticeably conciliatory in their dealings to the point of not disarming Shiite Mujahideen when they did disarm fellow Sunnis.[36] At the same time negotiations also opened between the Taliban and the government. Massoud met leading Taliban commanders twice, once in Maidanshahr and once in Kabul. The talks only underscored to both sides the yawning differences in world view that divided them. Nor did they serve to mitigate government fears that the Taliban were the latest vehicle for Pakistani interference in Afghanistan.[37]

The lull was abruptly broken when on 6 March Massoud opened a full-scale offensive against Wahdat. Two days and several hundred casualties later, Mazari turned to the Taliban in desperation and struck a fateful deal. The agreement stipulated that Wahdat would surrender its heavy weapons to the Taliban who would take up positions along the western Kabul front line as a buffer force. For the Taliban this appeared to promise a foothold inside the capital as the 'neutral' force they insistently proclaimed themselves to be. Mazari, for his part, was almost certainly calculating on the Taliban being drawn into the battle against Massoud's forces. Lightly-armed Taliban troops began moving into the Deh Murad Khan quarter on the afternoon of the same day, 8 March.

The atmosphere of hair-trigger tension on the frontline all but guaranteed things would go wrong. First, government troops opened fire on the advancing Taliban; whether deliberately or by mistake remains unclear. The religious students lost several armoured vehicles and some men before the situation was stabilised. The situation again slid out of control when Wahdat troops, holed up in the ruins of the former Soviet and Polish embassies on Darulaman Avenue, refused to surrender their weapons and defected to join the pro-government forces of the Wahdat splinter faction led by Akbari. They then turned their guns on the Taliban.

The defection of Wahdat troops to Akbari was clearly not part of Mazari's original calculation. Nevertheless, it was interpreted by Taliban chiefs as a betrayal. As an aggrieved Mullah Mohammad Ghaus complained a few days later: 'During the first two days of fighting (6-7 March), both Massoud and Wahdat sent delegations to

---

36 Interview with western diplomat, Islamabad, March 1995; Rahimullah Yusufzai, 'The New Mujahids', *Newsline*, February 1995.
37 Interviews with Ahmad Shah Massoud's personal secretary, Dr Abdullah, March 1995; 'Showdown in Kabul', *Asiaweek*, 28 April 1995.

us. As a result we came in with no intention of fighting. But in the end both sides attacked us'.[38] The naivete behind this move was remarkable. But it was to be repeated just over two years later when another Taliban force–this time in Mazar-e Sharif–again walked calmly into the lion's den and set about attempting to disarm the Shia with even more disastrous consequences.

Whether Massoud did actually agree to the Taliban moving into southwest Kabul remains a moot point. But whatever the Taliban may have believed, he had no intention of permitting them to remain. Having pushed one enemy to the wall, he was not about to allow another to step in as a 'neutral' force and pursue its stated goals of ruling in Kabul. After a brief lull, he struck again on the late morning of Saturday 11 March in an offensive that unleashed the full panoply of government military might. With blocking points at the Soviet and Polish embassies now turned by the Wahdat defectors, government armour punched down the main axis of Darulaman Avenue as Mi-35 helicopter gunships and Su-22 jets provided close air support. Wild retaliatory rocket barrages on the city centre from both Taliban and Wahdat meanwhile inflicted scores of casualties. By late afternoon however, government troops had pushed south to the battered shell of the Darulaman Palace on the city's outer edge and, amid considerable looting of Shiite quarters,[39] were mopping up resistance in the suburbs behind them.

Mazari paid for his miscalculations with his life. Taken bound to Charasyab he was later killed–purportedly after an attempt to seize a guard's rifle during a helicopter flight to Kandahar. His death effectively buried the Taliban attempts to maintain good relations with the Shia, as well as further stoking growing alarm in Tehran over the movement's advances and its alleged links to Saudi Arabia and the United States. After a week of scattered fighting in the hills beyond Darulaman, the final act in the battle for Kabul came on 19 March. A coordinated government offensive struck at Charasyab and Rishkor, south of the city, and along the Maidanshahr road to the southwest. In a dawn rout of ill-prepared Taliban forces, Charasyab was taken by 7 a.m., government forces pushing on to establish a new defence perimeter overlooking the Taliban-held district centre of Mohammad Agha, 32 kilometres south of Kabul. The former Afghan Army base at Rishkor fell the same morning while in the afternoon, fighting in thick snowfalls, government armoured forces made some ground along

[38] Author's interview with Mullah Ghaus, Charasyab, 18 March 1995.
[39] Government spokesmen angrily denied BBC reports of the looting of Shiite quarters; nevertheless, scenes of unchecked and often brutal pillage were witnessed by several foreign journalists.

the Maidanshahr road. By evening, Massoud was for the first time in complete control of the capital with all his enemies pushed back beyond rocket range.[40]

The west

By the time the Taliban were driven from Kabul, they had already made striking gains in the west. Following heavy fighting around Delaram on the Kandahar-Herat highway, they had by mid-March swept up much of Nimroz and most of Farah, both part of Ismail Khan's western fiefdom. By late March it had become apparent that despite doubts in Pakistani intelligence circles over the wisdom of the offensive,[41] Taliban leaders had decided to exploit gains in the west rather than reinforce failure around Kabul. The objective was Herat.

The defection and defeat of Pushtun allies of Ismail Khan in Nimroz and Farah proved nearly disastrous, permitting a rapid Taliban advance. And even as the Taliban attacked from the southwest, Dostum's forces arrayed on Ismail Khan's northwestern front moved to attack in Badghis in the last days of March. In response, Kabul reacted by airlifting 2,000 troops of the Central Corps west to Herat–the first airlift of its kind since 1992 and one which involved the induction of Ariana Airline jets as well as military Antonov transports.

By 4 April the Taliban were announcing–prematurely as it transpired–the capture of four districts in Herat province itself. But when the government did succeed in holding a line it was within sight of Shindand Airbase, a mere 95 kilometres south of Herat city. The Taliban were pushed back to a shifting front some 30 kilometres east of Shindand which saw probably the heaviest fighting in the Afghan civil war since the spring 1989 battle for Jalalabad. Involving up to 6,000 men, the Taliban advance was stemmed in a series of battles which took hundreds of casualties on both sides and in which unchallenged government air power played a decisive role. Taliban wounded in Kandahar spoke of facing 10-15 airstrikes a day and later more still–remarkably high figures by the standards of post-1992 Afghanistan and a clear indication of the government's desperate determination to prevent the fall of Herat. By late April, hindered by poor logistics, and ammunition shortages, the student-led army had

---

40 'Showdown in Kabul', *Asiaweek*, 28 April 1995.

41 Author's interviews with Pakistani intelligence officers, Quetta and Chaman, March 1995: they believed, correctly, that the Taliban would find the going tougher in the west which they recognised was well-administered. The Taliban decision to advance on Herat was an early indication that the movement's leaders were scarcely ISI puppets.

run out of steam. On 20 April they pulled back from Shindand after a blistering three-day battle. One week later government forces retook Farah, claiming to have killed another 200 Taliban troops in a engagement on 28-29 April and pushing their enemies back towards Delaram.

The severe set-backs suffered outside Kabul and Shindand prompted some analysts to predict the end of Taliban expansion and even their demise under the pressure of Pushtun tribal loyalties.[42] This did not happen. The summer of 1995 brought a lull in military operations. But rather than a prelude to collapse it was a breathing space that allowed for consolidation and a marked improvement in the Taliban's capacity to wage war. Training was stepped up with a greater emphasis on mobility, while logistics, which had been revealed as seriously inadequate in the western campaign, were improved by the acquisition of large numbers of new pick-up trucks from across the Pakistan border.[43] At the same time the quasi-alliance with Dostum took a step forward with the arrival in July of airforce technicians. Having come to Kandahar from Mazar-e Sharif via Peshawar and Quetta–an itinerary that pointed strongly towards official Pakistani brokering of the arrangement–they set about restoring Taliban MiG-21 fighters to air worthiness.[44] The results were palpable: on 3 August one MiG forced down a chartered Russian Il-76 transport aircraft carrying Albanian ammunition to Kabul; and in September the exercise was repeated with an Ariana Boeing-727 returning from the Gulf to Jalalabad with commercial goods.

Recruitment too was stepped up sharply during the summer. A force which in the spring was estimated to number 15,000 was 25,000-strong by the end of the year.[45] New forces were coming both from the Taliban's main recruitment base in the madrassas of Baluchistan and the Frontier Province as well as from Mujahideen groups from Paktia and Logar where a major recruitment drive was launched in September. Under the auspices of Mawlawi Ehsanullah, Taliban commander of Khost, and veteran Mujahideen chief Jalaluddin Haqqani, who had thrown in his lot with the Taliban, a force of some 2,000 was raised and dispatched to Kabul with suitable exhortations over the patriotic role of the border tribes in ousting Tajik usurpers from the capital in 1929![46] Similarly, Pakistani Talib volunteers,

---

[42] Davis, 'Afghanistan's Taliban'; 'Grinding Halt', *Far Eastern Economic Review*, 18 May 1995.

[43] Interviews with Defence Ministry sources, Kabul, October 1995.

[44] *AFGHANews*, vol. 11, no. 9, August 1995, p.7.

[45] Interviews with Defence Ministry sources, Kabul, November 1995.

[46] *AFGHANews*, vol. 11, no. 10, September 1995, p. 8.

whose numbers increased markedly in 1996 and 1997 to over 3,000, were beginning to make their presence felt.

In August the government, in need of some victories and eager to relieve the pressure around Kabul, ordered a western offensive. Ismail Khan's troops, backed by exiled Helmandi and Kandahari forces and the Central Corps troops under Najim Khan, pushed south along the highway, scoring a series of successes against largely unprepared Taliban fighters. On 23 August, backed by airstrikes and artillery, they swept into Delaram, capturing armour and trucks. A mere three days later they had overrun large areas of Helmand, seizing Musa Qala, Now Zad and parts of Girishk and threatening Kandahar itself.

At this critical juncture, many foreign analysts are convinced the ISI intervened decisively and rapidly with logistics support rather than see the Taliban driven back to Kandahar. Western intelligence sources in Islamabad reported that the dramatic turnaround in Taliban fortunes that followed these setbacks owed not a little to infusions of well-trained reinforcements and new weapons–now supported by a functioning logistics machine.[47]

Rapid Taliban reinforcement compounded serious mistakes on the part of Ismail Khan. Army officers by background, he and his deputy, Alauddin Khan, had embarked on an ambitious but premature attempt to establish regular army formations, rather than maintain the voluntary and irregular structures built up during the Jihad. But after years of communist press-ganging, renewed conscription was not greeted with enthusiasm by the populace of Herat. At the same time, dragooning reluctant youths into regular units was evidently easier than establishing a proper logistics infrastructure to support them.[48] As a result, even before government forces reached Girishk, they were severely over-stretched logistically. Raw hunger and indifferent motivation made for a disastrous combination.

At Girishk, government forces advanced on three axes, the main road and two flanks. As a result of inadequate reconnaissance the road force blundered into a large-scale and evidently well-prepared Taliban ambush in which Commander Nasir Ahmad of Shindand was killed along with scores of troops. Ismail Khan, himself some way behind the government vanguard, promptly ordered a general retreat. But this was thrown into disarray when pick-up mounted Taliban units began cutting the main road behind it. An attempt to establish a defensive line near Delaram collapsed due to mobile flank attacks and on 29

---

[47] Economist Intelligence Unit, *Report on Afghanistan*, Fourth Quarter 1995.
[48] Interview with Dr Abdullah, personal secretary to Ahmad Shah Massoud: Kabul, October 1995.

August, less than a week after they had lost it, the Taliban recaptured the town.[49]

Ismail Khan's forces again fell back towards a frontline some 60 kilometres beyond Shindand. The line itself might have been defensible but when a senior Massoud envoy arrived from Kabul, he found a logistics system which had collapsed and troops who had not eaten for 36 hours. Morale was low with Helmandis and Kandahari commanders voicing open criticism of Ismail's leadership. Even more seriously, Ismail failed to establish fall-back positions outside Shindand. The Taliban exploited these weakness with an adroitness and a speed that was impressive—maintaining the momentum of the offensive in company-sized units of one or two hundred men, moving fast and light off the main and anticipated axes of advance in pick-ups with truck-mounted ZU-2 anti-aircraft cannon and BM-21 multiple-barrelled rocket launchers. These Blitzkrieg tactics proved strikingly successful and again it bears emphasising, marked a sudden shift to mobile warfare that caught the government completely off balance.

In the early hours of Sunday 3 September, against the protestations of Kandahari and Helmandi commanders, Ismail Khan gave the order to abandon Shindand without a fight. It ranked as one of the most surprising and controversial decisions of the Taliban war and gave rise to a storm of accusation and innuendo that Rabbani's western supremo had sold out for Taliban gold. Nothing has ever been produced to substantiate these allegations, least of all in Ismail Khan's subsequent military service and personal commitment to leading his men back to Herat. The truth is almost certainly that, exhausted by lack of sleep and dispirited by the relentless Taliban advance, he staked his hopes on further reinforcements from the Central Corps and a chance to reestablish a line nearer Herat. But by then it was too late for Massoud to bail him out. As dawn broke on 3 September, government forces were streaming north on foot and in vehicles in a ragged retreat that verged on a rout.

Dostum meanwhile had apparently been prevailed on by Pakistan to provide air support: the 17th Division headquarters in Herat and the airport (to which some assets from Shindand had been flown) was bombed on 4 September. But there was no attempt to fight for Herat: finally, early on Tuesday 5 September, Ismail Khan and his commanders fled towards Islam Qala and the Iranian border. The retreat from the city was so poorly undertaken that some units were not even aware that they were supposed to flee. One group that had arrived from the south in darkness slept by its vehicles in one of the main city squares. They awoke to find Taliban fighters moving into the area and

---

[49] Ibid.

were all killed in the shoot-out that followed–the only real military action in the city itself.[50]

The loss of Herat came as an immense blow to government morale. Both in Kabul and at the United Nations, government spokesmen found it convenient to blame the incompetence and cowardice of their forces on the hand of Islamabad. But while Pakistan's alleged role in resupplying and reinforcing the Taliban may well have proved decisive in turning the tide at Girishk, there has never been anything to show for the more hysterical accusations that Pakistani ground troops, armour and airstrikes were committed to the Blitzkrieg on Herat: they were scarcely necessary. None of that, however, was to prevent Pakistan's Embassy in Kabul being sacked the next day while government security men stood and watched. Relations between Kabul and Islamabad plunged to their lowest point since the 1991 fall of Khost in the days of Najibullah.[51]

Kabul again

With the west in their hands, the Taliban moved swiftly to exploit their advantage and increase the pressure on Kabul before the onset of winter. Indeed, in the autumn of 1995, against a backdrop of sustained Pakistani efforts to broker a united opposition front that would include other key anti-Kabul forces, they clearly hoped to capture the city by continuing to hammer harder on its southern and western gates.

The first serious push in mid-October won significant ground south of Kabul and recaptured the base at Charasyab lost in March. However, as with many Taliban successes, the advance owed as much to political subversion as to military punch: the breakthrough began as a result of treachery by a government commander. It cost Massoud ground he could ill afford to lose and tested government nerves to the edge: some well-to-do Panjsheris were quick to flee Kabul for the valley, cars piled high with belongings.

On the night of 25 October heavy fighting again erupted on the Charasyab front as armour-backed Taliban forces tried to overrun positions screening the gorge at Sang-e Nevishta. This near-suicidal assault was repulsed after the attackers lost over 90 dead in a minefield along with two T-62 tanks and several trucks. A third push in the second week of November saw the capture of several villages on the southwestern Maidanshahr front, but within three days the irregulars

---

[50] Ibid.

[51] The fall of Khost to Mujahideen commanded by Jalaluddin Haqqani was another operation in which the involvement of the ISI has been extensively documented. The ISI's relationship with Haqqani goes back to the early 1980s.

had been forced to surrender their gains along with ground earlier held. The clashes triggered a vicious rocketing of Kabul that on 10-11 November killed 36 and wounded nearly 60.[52]

The main Taliban thrust, however, came on 16 November with a strong offensive on the city's eastern flank. The direction of the attack was no surprise to Massoud's commanders but its intensity caught them off guard. Between 16-23 November, Taliban infantry backed by some (but insufficient) armour and intense artillery barrages captured the villages of Band-e Ghazi and Khord Kabul, pushing over 15 kilometres to overrun a base at Pul-e Charkhi. This dramatic advance brought them to within three kilometres of the main Kabul-Jalalabad highway, the cutting of which would have been a serious setback for the government. However by 24 November, reinforced Kabul troops had stabilised the line and on 28 November launched a counter-offensive that negated Taliban gains.[53]

These autumn offensives cost the Taliban disproportionately high casualties–estimated at several hundred dead–and exhausted their capacity for further serious ground offensives before the onset of winter. They also underscored the difficulties for irregulars of achieving a breakthrough by purely military means against well-entrenched defenders operating on short interior lines. By January, the Taliban were contenting themselves with a daily rocket bombardment of the city. In the course of the month, 287 rockets were fired into Kabul, killing 44 civilians and wounding 167[54]–precisely the random terror tactics employed by Hekmatyar between 1992 and 1995. Long gone were the days of the Taliban's moral ascendancy when their leaders had vowed they would never rocket civilian populations. But killing luckless Kabulis was likely to prove as militarily futile as Hekmatyar had found it. New strategies were called for.

The campaign in the east and the seizure of Kabul

With the benefit of hindsight, it can be argued that one of Ahmad Shah Massoud's greatest mistakes as a general was his failure to launch a major winter offensive in the first quarter of 1996 to break up Taliban main forces grouped around the capital.[55] Even before the

[52] Author's interviews with government commanders, October-November 1995.

[53] 'Winter Set to Join ranks with Kabul's Defenders', *Jane's Intelligence Review Pointer*, January 1996, p. 3.

[54] *AFGHANews*, vol. 12, no. 1, January 1996, p. 8.

[55] In discussions with the author Massoud has conceded there should have been a winter offensive; he argued it was continally postponed owing to political developments and Hekmatyar's joining the government.

onset of winter, his Central Corps was arguably in better shape than at any time since the beginning of the post-1992 civil war: Numbers were up to between 20,000-25,000; resupply from both Russia and Iran in 1995 had provided reserves of ammunition; morale had recovered from the débâcle in Herat and the effectiveness of his better Panjsheri units against Taliban forces around the city had been amply demonstrated in March 1995. His troops, moreover, were operating on interior lines from a secure base. The Taliban, by contrast, were exhausted by their failed offensives of October and November, and sitting out a bitter winter in a wide arc around southern Kabul with some 7000-8000 men. Many tribal elements had filtered away.

As it was, Massoud, ever cautious, did not move in the winter; and then delayed long into the spring. When it came on 10 May, the first offensive was relatively limited in scope. It aimed at moving through Khord Kabul in the southwest and taking the Ainak copper mines in Logar, thus threatening the Taliban base at Charasyab from the east. Some advances were made around Band-e Ghazi by government troops supported by gunships and jets; Taliban casualties were claimed to be heavy. But the offensive did nothing to alter the overall strategic situation around the capital, in particular the capacity of the Taliban to rain rockets in from the south.

The worst rocket and artillery attack came on 26 June, when following a May accord with the government, Gulbuddin Hekmatyar entered Kabul to take up the prime ministership. His arrival triggered a blistering barrage of some 300 rockets that killed 64 and wounded 138.[56] From then on military strategy became inextricably caught up in the political compulsions of the new government in Kabul. And this proved disastrous.

In August Taliban forces defeated Hekmatyar's forces in Paktia, capturing his main base at Spin Shighar near the Pakistan border. Massoud was under immediate pressure to extend his defences from fortress Kabul–which arguably might have been held indefinitely–out to Laghman, and Nangarhar to defend Hezb-e Islami bases. 'We came out [from a defensive position around Kabul], we didn't pay attention to the defensive line', Massoud later reflected. 'Every day Hekmatyar was worried [saying]: "They're working to a plan. They've taken Paktia, they've taken Paktika, and you've done nothing, you're not cooperating, you're not fighting". Every day the talk was of this, and every day Ustaz [Rabbani] was pressuring me, saying "Well, maybe Hekmatyar's right".'[57] Fatefully, Massoud thus fell between two stools: between January and August 1996, he failed to break the

---

56 *Associated Press,* 26 June 1996.
57 Interview with the author, Panjsher Valley, April 1997.

Taliban outside Kabul, and then, against his better judgement, he allowed himself to be cajoled into over-extending himself defensively. Step by step, the ground for the débâcle of September and the fall of Kabul was laid.

From Paktia, the Taliban pushed on directly into Nangarhar where a sudden upsurge of lawlessness suggested that their gold had already been at work. In the first week of September they seized Azra on the Logar-Nangarhar border, despite government reinforcements being dispatched from Kabul and Sarobi. From there they advanced east to Hisarak where the local commander, Haji Daoud, joined them. As the fractious Nangarhar Shura splintered into pro- and anti-Taliban groups, its leader Haji Qadir, who belatedly had thrown in his lot with the Kabul government, fled Jalalabad for Pakistan. On 11 September a Taliban column commanded by Mullah Borjan reached Jalalabad and had secured the city by the next day in fighting that left some 70 dead.[58]

The speed of this offensive, the political groundwork in Jalalabad and all that followed suggest strongly that both the capture of the city and what followed were indeed part of an integrated and carefully-planned strategy, rather than merely a series of tactical successes following haphazardly one upon another. Involving what government intelligence estimated to number some 8,000-10,000 troops, the eastern campaign of 1996 may well go down as the high point of Taliban military endeavour.

Without pausing for breath, flying columns then drove on into Laghman and Kunar provinces north of Nangarhar. But as both sides knew, the real target was Sarobi. A district centre on the Kabul-Jalalabad highway 75 kilometres east of Kabul, and traditionally a Hezb-e Islami stronghold, Sarobi had been chosen by Massoud as the new linchpin of Kabul's defences on the eastern front. He had reinforced the town and the long Tangi Abreshom Gorge that leads up to it from the Vale of Jalalabad with infantry, armour and artillery. Situated at the western end of the Tangi Abreshom defile, where the Kabul river and the highway are forced into a narrow defile, the town was, in theory, easily defensible. But politically Massoud was on dangerous ground. In addition to his own Tajik forces under General Fahim, Sarobi was garrisoned by Pushtun Hezb-e Islami forces of the local Ahmadzai commander, Zardad, whose relations with Hekmatyar were in any event badly strained. Moreover, Massoud and his commanders were largely unfamiliar with the topography of the surrounding area. One aide who spent 12 September with Massoud on

---

[58] *Associated Press*, 12 September 1996.

a tour of inspection in and around Sarobi noted that they spent much of the time studying the map.[59]

But before all else it was the sheer speed of the Taliban advance that caught government commanders by surprise. The push from Jalalabad towards Sarobi that many had thought would be weeks in preparation flowed on from Jalalabad in days. Nor did it confine itself to a single axis of advance. As with the advance on Shindand one year earlier, the Taliban exploited mobility to the full, advancing not only along the highway but also from the south on the dirt road from Hisarak to the south and across the hills from Laghman north of the highway. The defence of the gorge itself was thrown into confusion by the defection and desertion of many Hezb-e Islami fighters in their rear as well as by a massive explosion of an ammunition dump in Sarobi, apparently the work of Taliban sympathisers. When finally on the night of 24 September the militia assaulted the town in a three-pronged attack the battle rapidly became a rout, as scores of fleeing government troops were cut down.[60]

Any hopes Kabul commanders might have entertained that the Taliban would halt to regroup before a battle for the capital were promptly shattered. Without pausing, their advance swept on relentlessly both down the axis of the main highway as well as across the Lataband Pass that opens onto the Kabul plain and leads to Bagrami. The government suffered more heavy casualties in an unsuccessful bid to hold the pass. Simultaneously, another axis of advance was opened northwards from Sarobi into the Tagab Valley, threatening Bagram Airbase and beyond it the highway north from Kabul to Jabal Saraj. On the Maidanshahr and Rishkor fronts to the south and southwest of Kabul respectively, other government units were tied down by Taliban probing attacks that had been stepped up earlier.

Massoud's forces never recovered from the débâcle at Sarobi. On 25 September they attempted to establish a last-ditch line of defence at Pul-e Charkhi on the eastern edge of the Kabul plain where the highway emerges from the arc of mountains east of the city and where ten months before they had stemmed Taliban advances. But airstrikes and helicopter gunships could not compensate for the confusion and despair at ground level. A situation slipping rapidly out of control was only aggravated by the multi-pronged probing of the Taliban across the plain south of the highway into Kabul and along the heights screening the highway from Dehsabz to the north.

---

[59] Interview with Massoud Khalili, Kabul government Ambassador to India, October 1996.

[60] Author's visit to Sarobi and interviews, 28 September 1996.

By 4 p.m. on the afternoon of Thursday 26 September, the last government armour laden with troops was roaring east along the highway out of the city towards Pul-e Charkhi even as Taliban artillery rounds impacted along the road behind them. Whether they knew it or not, their task was now less to defend Kabul than to buy time to abandon it. At around 3 p.m. Massoud, in council with senior commanders at the Armoured Division headquarters at Khair Khanah, on the northern edge of Kabul, gave the order for a general withdrawal from the capital.[61] Rather than allow his forces to be destroyed in an ultimately futile battle, he had decided to gamble on perhaps the riskiest manoeuvre any army can attempt–an orderly retreat in darkness through an urban area with an enemy at its heels.

In the event it was remarkably successful. While stay-behind groups covered the retreat and maintained the fiction of a defence, most forces pulled back from the Maidanshahr, Rishkor and Sang-e Nevishta fronts to designated assembly points in the city in the early evening; and then began moving by different roads to the Khair Khanah Pass out of town. Some equipment–trucks, and BM-21 multiple rocket systems–was abandoned on the pass; several ammunition dumps were blown in the city. But the bulk of the army's armoured and artillery inventory was successfully evacuated.

A range of factors have been cited to explain the Taliban seizure of Kabul. Massoud's troops were clearly weary and in some cases demoralised by the alliance with Hekmatyar's Hezb, which for four bitter years they had regarded as an implacable enemy. Tactically, moreover, they were disorientated by Taliban infiltration and fifth column activities in a region in which neither they nor their commanders had much operational experience. By contrast, their opponents were fresh, fired with religious zeal, and propelled by a seemingly irresistible momentum of victory.

But the most decisive elements of the Taliban triumph went far beyond morale. These were planning; impressive command-and-control and intelligence in a fluid tactical situation; unfailing logistics support; and unrelenting, overwhelming speed. Indeed, it is a significant reflection on this campaign that in 17 years of war no Afghan force, either government or opposition, had ever carried out such a swift and complex series of operations over such a wide operation area. This was mobile warfare at its most effective. To suggest that semi-literate Taliban commanders whose military experience had never extended beyond the hit-and-run attacks of

---

[61] The author was on the highway into Kabul on the afternoon of 26 September 1996. Other details are from the author's interviews with Massoud aides, November 1996 and April 1997.

guerrilla warfare could have risen to this level of planning and execution defies belief.

It has become fashionable to portray the meteoric rise of the Taliban as stemming from the complex interplay of social and political conditions prevailing in southern Afghanistan. Popular war-weariness; an acceptance of any force that could guarantee peace and security; and an exhaustion with the political and moral bankruptcy of petty Mujahideen commanders have all been cited as underlying the movement's rapid growth. And all undoubtedly served to prepare the ground in which the student-led crusade with its simple prescriptions and transparent moral certitudes could grow rapidly.

But none of this should be permitted to obscure the fact that the Taliban were pre-eminently a military organisation rather than a political movement. In the short space of two years, their numbers multiplied rapidly from a force of less than 100 men, to one of several thousand and finally to one estimated in late 1996 to number at least 30,000-35,000 troops with a functioning brigade and divisional structure.[62] It was equipped with armour, a notably effective artillery arm, a small air force, an impressive communications network and an intelligence system. The organisational skills and logistical wherewithal required to assemble from scratch, expand, and maintain such an integrated fighting machine during a period of continuous hostilities are simply not to be found in Pakistani madrassas or Afghan villages.

Covert Pakistani support for the Taliban can thus be inferred to have been fundamental if not to the movement's political inception then at least to its expansion as a regional and then national force. The evidence, fragmentary and inconclusive as it is, suggests that while various players in Pakistan, official and non-official, have been involved in backing the Taliban, the pre-eminent role has been played by ISI's Afghan Bureau. The Bureau appears to have been active in three distinct areas.

Logistically, aid has involved expediting supplies of motor and aviation fuel, ammunition, spare parts and new vehicles to the Taliban. Given the scale and scope of Taliban operations it is ridiculous to suggest that such supplies are carried across obscure desert and mountain trails on the backs of donkeys: They are trucked down a few highways and secondary roads in convoys with the full concurrence of border authorities.

---

[62] Late 1996 figure from UN military observers, Islamabad. See also *Jane's Sentinel*, South Asia binder, September 1997 for detailed military break-down of Taliban and other Afghan factions.

Logistics support has been crucially complemented by the ISI's brokering of alliances with other key players on the Afghan chequer-board. Unquestionably the most important has been the large cadre of former regime officers, many of them like General Shahnawaz Tanai resident in Pakistan, who have joined the Taliban and provided its military machine with vital technical skills. It also appears likely that the ISI has assisted in the induction of certain key Jihadi commanders such as Jalaluddin Haqqani and their followings into Taliban ranks. As with Shahnawaz Tanai, Haqqani's links with the ISI go back a long way. Equally, Taliban links with Dostum and the technical assistance extended in 1995 to the Taliban air force clearly involved Pakistan in a brokering role.

Third, the evidence suggests that support has also come in the areas of training and operational planning. As we have seen, the Taliban style of rapid, mobile warfare has marked a sharp break with anything hitherto seen in modern Afghanistan and has been an important factor in their successes. Nor, as the eastern campaign of August-September 1996 clearly demonstrates, has this simply been a case of 'Allahu Akbar!' zeal and a wild rush forward. Painstaking planning, both political and military, has been basic to success.

That officers of the ISI could have been involved in any of the above areas is scarcely surprising. As has been extensively documented in a range of foreign and Pakistani publications, since as early as 1974 Pakistan's military intelligence has been deeply and aggressively embroiled in covert support to armed Afghan opposition movements.[63] Such support has involved all the areas noted above—and more. What is perhaps surprising is the extent to which Pakistan's military establishment has been transfixed by the conviction that in some obscure manner Pakistan's role in aiding the victory of the Mujahideen over Moscow's placemen has earned Islamabad the right to decide who should or should not rule in Kabul. Afghanistan, it seems, is far too important to be left to the Afghans.

To single out Pakistan for its interference in Afghanistan's affairs would hardly be just. Over recent years, Iran, Uzbekistan, Russia, and (to a very minor extent) India have all played their part backing Afghan factions and contributing to the destruction of a nation in pursuit of their own interests. But Pakistan's support for the Taliban has unquestionably been broader in its scope and ultimately far more ambitious in its goals than that of other regional powers for their

---

[63] Most revealing has been Mohammad Yousaf and Mark Adkin, *The Bear Trap: Afghanistan's Untold Story* (London: Leo Cooper, 1992); also 'Afghanistan-past, present and future', *Jane's Intelligence Review*, vol. 8, no. 4, April 1996, pp. 181-185.

Afghan candidates. It has been fundamental rather than incidental to the rise of the movement as a military power; and unwisely it has sought to aid the Taliban in imposing themselves militarily on the nation as a whole.

But while they have benefited from Pakistani aid and advice, the Taliban are anything but Pakistani puppets. Between early 1995 and the summer of 1997, their leadership has on numerous occasions displayed a pointed disinterest in advice that has not been to its taste. In early 1995 their campaign against Ismail Khan came initially at least against the advice of ISI. The detention of a Russian aircrew captured in August 1995 was prolonged for one year against the exasperated advice of Pakistani officials. And the Taliban's consistent intransigence over the social and gender strictures they have enforced has flown in the face of the better judgment of their Pakistani interlocutors.

Nevertheless, despite the unblinking rigidity of the Taliban, Islamabad has been content to remain a hostage to a policy of its own making. The *enfants terribles* of Islamic politics have been permitted, and indeed encouraged, to pursue their own agenda without sanction or criticism worth the name. And in May 1997, Islamabad was rash enough to reward their military adventures with the prize of diplomatic recognition. But the rise of the Taliban has dealt a heavy, perhaps even fatal, blow to the unity of Afghanistan as a multiethnic state. For Pakistan to hope to remain immune from the consequences of the events it has set in motion would be wishful thinking in the extreme.

PAKISTAN AND THE TALIBAN

Ahmed Rashid

Just hours after they seized Kandahar on 4 November 1994, the Taliban were accused of being mere surrogates of Pakistan's Inter Services Intelligence Directorate (ISI). Other Afghan warlords, regional countries, Western wire services and the Pakistani press suggested strongly that the Taliban had been created, launched and armed by Pakistan in order to fulfil the government's 'manifest destiny' of opening up trade routes to Central Asia via Afghanistan.

However the truth was and remains far more complicated than that. The Taliban have never been anyone's puppets and their strings are certainly not pulled in Islamabad. Yet their links to Pakistan are all-encompassing, forged through nearly two decades of war, devastation and life as refugees. The fact that the Taliban leadership is entirely indigenous to Afghanistan and fiercely independent does not detract from their social, economic and political links to Pakistan's own tribal milieu on the Pakistani-Afghanistan border. The shared Pushtun culture of this border region has never been better reflected than in the phenomenon of the Taliban.

Since 1994 Pakistan has rarely defined its Afghan policy–a reflection of the confusion, conflicting interests and rivalries of the various factions in government–but in a speech at the United Nations in November 1996, Foreign Secretary Najmuddin Sheikh spelt out the government's analysis of the Taliban's success. The Taliban phenomenon was a reaction to the state of anarchy in Afghanistan. It was neither the ideology the Taliban propounded, nor the religious fervour of the people that accounted for their subsequent success. Rather it was the war weariness of the populace which stood ready to welcome any force that promised the disarming of the local brigands, the restoration of peace, the semblance of an honest administration, no matter how rough and ready its system of justice.[1]

Most of the Taliban are the children of the Jihad against the Soviet Union. Many were born in Pakistani refugee camps, educated in

---

[1] Sheikh delivered this speech at a special meeting at the UN called by UN Secretary General Boutros Boutros-Ghali on 18 November 1996 of those countries involved with the Afghan crisis. The private meeting was the direct result of the capture of Kabul by the Taliban two months earlier.

Pakistani madrassas and learnt their fighting skills from Afghan Mujahideen parties based in Pakistan. Their families continued to live in Pakistan as refugees even after the fall of Kabul to the Mujahideen in 1992. While all Taliban speak their mother tongue Pushto, for many their second language is not Persian, the lingua franca of Afghanistan, but Urdu, the language of Pakistan.

Many Taliban carry Pakistani identity cards, as they spent years in refugee camps in Pakistan, and thousands voted in the 1997 elections in Baluchistan for their favourite Pakistani party–the Jamiat-e Ulema-i Islam. Moreover the Taliban recruited hundreds of Pakistani Islamic fundamentalist students to fight for their cause and were closely linked to Pakistan's fundamentalist Islamic parties such as the Jamiat-e Ulema-i Islam led by Maulana Fazlur Rahman. None of these links made them Pakistani; instead they contributed to the Taliban's unique interpretation of being Afghan. Nevertheless, the rootlessness of the Taliban and the ease with which they cross two cultures could become a troubling factor for Pakistan in the future. As children of the Jihad their emergence stemmed from their deep disillusionment with the factionalism and criminal activities of the once Islamically-pure Mujahideen. They saw themselves as the cleansers and purifiers of a social system gone wrong.

Their social history also allowed them to be extremely well connected to many Pakistani state institutions, political parties and business groups in what was already an extremely fragmented Pakistani power structure. Thus the Taliban were never beholden to one exclusive Pakistani lobby. Whereas in the 1980s Gulbuddin Hekmatyar and other Afghan Mujahideen leaders had exclusive relationships with the ISI and the Jamaat-e Islami, they had few linkages with other powerful political, economic or social groups in Pakistan.

The Taliban's unprecedented depth of contacts and support in Pakistan enabled them at times to defy the ISI, by enlisting the help of government ministers or the transport mafia. At other times the Taliban could defy the federal government by enlisting the support of the provincial governments in Baluchistan and the North West Frontier Province. Thus the Taliban's main advantage was that they never depended upon an exclusive relationship with just one Pakistani lobby. They had access to more influential lobbies and groups in the border regions than most Pakistanis. The Taliban's linkages with these groups are what constitute the nature of their 'support' from Pakistan.

The Taliban and the Jamiat-e Ulema-i Islam

Many of today's Taliban warriors were too young to fight against the Soviet occupation of their country. Instead they grew up in Afghan refugee camps in Baluchistan and the North West Frontier Province. Several Taliban leaders, such as Mohammad Omar, fought in the latter stages of the war against the regime of President Najibullah. But after Kabul fell to the Mujahideen in April 1992, these warriors expected the war to be over and went back to their families who were living in refugees camps in Baluchistan, or to the southern Afghan provinces of Kandahar, Helmand and Uruzgan.

Remaining in Baluchistan after 1992 had an added attraction. Dozens of madrassas run by the Jamiat-e Ulema-i Islam offered young Afghans the chance of a free education, studying the Holy Koran and Islamic Law. Thus for thousands of young Afghans, home became Pakistan rather than Afghanistan. It was here that their families lived, their children were educated, and they received international refugee assistance or worked as day labourers. Moreover, many had leased land in Baluchistan to grow fodder for their flocks and herds.

In this Pakistani tribal milieu there were several major influences on the Taliban. The primary religious and ideological influence was the Jamiat-e Ulema-i Islam, even though during the previous decade of Jihad the Jamiat-e Ulema-i Islam had played virtually no role. In the 1980s Pakistan's Afghan policy was conducted with the help of the Jamaat-e Islami, the main rival of the Jamiat-e Ulema-i Islam inside Pakistan, and the Afghan Hezb-e Islami, led by Gulbuddin Hekmatyar. For a decade the ISI's connection with Jamaat-e Islami and Hezb were the government's main instruments of policy, which for example ensured that armaments from the US and Arab countries went largely to the Ghilzai Pushtun warlords, who lived in central and north eastern Afghanistan. In comparison, the Durrani Pushtuns, who dominated the south and Kandahar and who generally backed the return of the former Afghan monarch Zahir Shah, were largely ignored by the ISI and the American CIA.

After 1992 Pakistan continued to back Hekmatyar, first in his refusal to legitimise the Kabul regime and then his strategic alliance with General Rashid Dostum in 1993, that led to the bloody two-year-long assault on Kabul which virtually destroyed the city. However by 1994 it was self-evident that Hekmatyar had failed not only to conquer the capital but also to unite the Ghilzai Pushtuns against the Tajik dominated regime of President Burhanuddin Rabbani. The majority of Pushtuns loathed Hekmatyar as much as they disliked Rabbani. Thus for much of 1994, Pakistan's Afghan policy was stranded like a beached whale, directionless and without powerful surrogates in Afghanistan.

Throughout the war in the 1980s the Jamiat-e Ulema-i Islam had quietly built up a support base amongst the Durrani Pushtuns living in Baluchistan and the North West Frontier Province, opening up madrassas and carrying out relief work in the refugee camps. In contrast the Jamaat-e Islami had little leverage in Baluchistan. The Pushtuns that belong to the Jamiat-e Ulema-i Islam have a great deal in common with the Taliban. Both come from the Durrani tribes that straddle the porous border between Afghanistan and Baluchistan. The activists of the Jamiat-e Ulema-i Islam are Deobandis, followers of a fundamentalist reformist sect which interprets Islam, particular its injunctions against women, extremely strictly. The Deobandi tradition is also opposed to the tribal and feudal structures of Pakistani society and there is a strong belief in egalitarianism. Moreover there is a deep-seated Deobandi antipathy to Shiite Muslims, who are viewed as unbelievers, and consequently to Iran. The Taliban, with their limited exposure to the world and arriving in the Jamiat-e Ulema-i Islam madrassas with only the imparted knowledge of the narrow-minded village mullahs at home, were soon turned into ardent Deobandis.

Thus the Taliban's interpretation of Islam, tempered as it was with Pushtunwali--the tribal code of the Pushtuns–was primitive in the extreme. While the Jamiat-e Ulema-i Islam forbade any political role for women, the Taliban were to ban women from both education and work. And whereas the Jamiat-e Ulema-i Islam was to rail against Iran and Shias, the Taliban were to kill Abdul Ali Mazari, the principal Shiite leader in Afghanistan, and in June 1997 close down the Iranian embassy in Kabul.

In the late 1980s the Jamiat-e Ulema-i Islam's influence over the southern Durrani Pushtuns was ignored by the ISI. Kandahar remained a backwater for Pakistani policy makers, allowing for the mushrooming of dozens of petty Afghan warlords in the region. Moreover the Jamiat-e Ulema-i Islam was politically isolated at home, remaining in opposition to the first Benazir Bhutto government (1988-90) and the first Nawaz Sharif government (1990-93). But in 1993 a new political situation arose for the Jamiat-e Ulema-i Islam. For the first time the party allied itself with the winning Pakistan People's Party led by Benazir Bhutto, so becoming a part of the ruling coalition.[2] The Jamiat-e Ulema-i Islam's newfound access to the

---

2   The Jamiat-e Ulema-i Islam have consistently won only a small number of seats in the National Assembly and the Baluchistan Provincial Assembly. They won 10 seats in the Baluchistan Provincial Assembly in the 1988 elections, 6 seats in the 1990 elections, 3 seats in the 1993 elections and 7 seats in the 1997 elections with the help of Taliban votes. In the National Assembly the Jamiat-e Ulema-i Islam

corridors of power allowed it to establish close links with the army, the ISI and the Interior Ministry under retired General Naseerullah Babar. Thus the Jamiat-e Ulema-i Islam could influence the central government's attitudes towards the Durranis and the Taliban. Meanwhile Bhutto had gained a useful 'Islamic' ally in combating the Jamaat-e Islami and the Muslim League, which were now in opposition.

Maulana Fazlur Rahman was made Chairman of the National Assembly's Standing Committee for Foreign Affairs–a position that enabled him to influence foreign policy. After 1994 Maulana Rahman visited Washington and European capitals to lobby for support for the Taliban. More importantly he went often to Saudi Arabia and the Gulf states to enlist their financial and military help for the Taliban, which was forthcoming. After Prince Turki al-Faisal Saud, head of the Saudi General Intelligence Agency, visited Pakistan secretly in July 1996, Saudi Arabia was to become the principal financial backer of the Taliban.

Fazlur Rahman organised the first bustard hunting trips for Gulf Arab princes to Kandahar in January and February 1995, thereby creating the first contacts between the Taliban and Arab rulers. The Arab hunting parties flew into Kandahar on huge transport planes bringing dozens of luxury jeeps, many of which they left behind for their Taliban hosts. The Jamiat-e Ulema-i Islam remained the most vocal advocate for the Taliban even after the fall of the Bhutto government in November 1996 and continued to exert pressure on Prime Minister Nawaz Sharif to recognise the Taliban as the legitimate government of Afghanistan.

The Jamiat-e Ulema-i Islam also benefited from the Taliban. Camps used for military training of non-Afghan Mujahideen inside Afghanistan (particularly Arab radicals) and which were run by either Pakistan's Jamaat-e Islami or Hekmatyar, were taken over by the Taliban and handed over to Jamiat-e Ulema-i Islam fringe groups. Thus Harakat ul Ansar, led by Fazlur Rahman Khalil, a Jamiat-e Ulema-i Islam ally and a key Pakistani Islamic militant group sending recruits to Kashmir, Chechnya and Yugoslavia was given Camp Badr near Khost on the Pakistan-Afghanistan border.

The Taliban and the transport mafia

Another major Pakistani influence on the Taliban was the truck-transport smuggling mafia based in Quetta and Chaman in

---

won 4 seats from Baluchistan in 1988, and 2 seats in the elections in 1990, 1993 and 1997.

Baluchistan. Made up largely of Pakistani but some Afghan Pushtuns, drawn from the same tribes as the Taliban leadership and closely knitted to them through business interests and intermarriage, this mafia had become frustrated by the warring warlords around Kandahar, who prevented the expansion of their traditional smuggling between Pakistan and Afghanistan further afield into Iran and Central Asia. By contrast, the transport mafia based in Peshawar had been relatively successful in being able to trade between Pakistan, northern Afghanistan and Uzbekistan, despite the continuing war around Kabul.

The Quetta-Chaman mafia funded the Taliban handsomely. Initially the mafia gave the Taliban a monthly retainer, but as the Taliban expanded westwards they demanded more and more funds–and received them. In March 1995 witnesses said the Taliban collected 6 million rupees (US$150,000) from transporters in Chaman in a single day and twice that amount the next day in Quetta as they prepared for an attack on Herat. Meanwhile the one-time, all-inclusive customs duty the Taliban charged trucks crossing into Afghanistan from Pakistan became the Taliban's major source of official income.[3]

The cross-border smuggling trade has a long history, but never has it played such an important strategic role as under the Taliban. In 1950 Pakistan gave landlocked Afghanistan permission to import duty free goods through the port of Karachi under an Afghan Transit Trade agreement. For decades Afghan truckers would drive their sealed goods up to Jalalabad or Kandahar and then turn around some of the goods to re-enter Pakistan, where they were sold in smugglers' markets. However, after the fall of Kabul in 1992, the smuggling of foodstuffs, fuel, building materials and other goods into Afghanistan began to cripple Pakistan's own economy as Afghanistan became virtually a fifth province for Pakistan in economic terms. In Pushtun tribal terms this form of commerce is legitimate 'trade and business', even though it is completely out of any government's jurisdiction.

The Central Board of Revenue estimated that Pakistan lost 3.5 billion rupees (US$87.5 million) in customs revenue in the financial year 1992-93, 11 billion rupees (US$275 million) during 1993-94 and 20 billion rupees (US$500 million) during 1994-95–a staggering increase. However these figures appear to be only the tip of the iceberg. In a 1995 study the Pakistan Institute of Development Economics estimated that the smuggling trade had an annual turnover of 100 billion rupees (US$2.5 billion) or almost one third of Pakistan's estimated black economy of 350 billion rupees (US$8.75

---

[3]   Ahmed Rashid, 'Nothing to Declare', *Far Eastern Economic Review*, 11 May 1995. The next few paragraphs are based on material collected for this article.

billion).[4] A 1995 UN study estimated that Afghanistan-Pakistan's total illicit drugs exports, which use the same routes and carriers as the Afghan Transit Trade, were worth another 50 billion rupees (US$1.25 billion) per annum.

Within a few weeks of the Taliban takeover of Kandahar, not only had the volume of smuggling expanded dramatically but also the area. From Quetta, truck convoys were travelling to Kandahar and then southwards to Iran, westwards to Turkmenistan and from there onwards to other Central Asian republics and even Russia. Within a few months the Quetta transporters were urging the Taliban to capture Herat in order to take full control of the road to Turkmenistan. Ismail Khan, the warlord who controlled Herat and was allied to the Kabul regime was charging exorbitant customs fees, having raised his customs duty from 5000 rupees (US$125) to 10,000 rupees (US$250) per truck for onward movement to Turkmenistan.

The ISI advised the Taliban not to attack Herat, because Pakistan had developed close relations with Ismail Khan and hoped that he might soon rebel against the Kabul government. Moreover the ISI's own assessment was that the Taliban were unprepared militarily to meet the trained forces of Ismail Khan. Nevertheless the Taliban rejected the ISI's advice and under the influence of the Jamiat-e Ulema-i Islam and the transport mafia launched a major attack on Herat in May 1995. The attack turned into a rout. It was the Taliban's first military defeat and they were pushed back all the way to Kandahar with over 3,000 casualties.[5]

Despite this setback, as business opportunities grew for Taliban families, so did the clout of the transport mafia that now expanded in Spin Boldak, Kandahar and Herat. Many Taliban bought trucks themselves or had a relative who was directly involved in trucking. Moreover, by 1996 influential heroin smugglers also began willingly to pay a 'zakat' tax of 10 per cent to the Taliban exchequer for permission to transport heroin out of the region. The heroin trade was officially condoned by the Taliban in contrast to the hashish trade, which they banned. With heroin traders now contributing substantially to the Taliban via the transport mafia, the influence of the Pakistan-based transport mafia became enormous.[6]

---

[4] Ibid.
[5] Ahmed Rashid, 'Grinding Halt', *Far Eastern Economic Review*, 18 May 1995. Interviews at this time with senior Pakistani military officials and diplomats brought out the conflicts that were going on within the Pakistani establishment over support for the Taliban.
[6] Ahmed Rashid, 'Drug the Infidels', *Far Eastern Economic Review*, 1 May 1997.

The Taliban and the Bhutto government

Ever since the Soviet invasion of Afghanistan, Pakistan's natural allies inside Afghanistan had been the Pushtuns who made up 40-45 per cent of the population, rather than the non-Pushtun minorities. This was largely because of their ethnic affinity with their own Pushtuns, the influence of Pushtuns in the upper echelons of the Pakistan army and bureaucracy, and General Zia ul Haq's conviction that the Jamaat-e Islami would eliminate the appeal of a 'Greater Pushtunistan' advocated by traditional Pushtun nationalists such as Wali Khan. But after the collapse of the Soviet Union in 1991, successive Pakistani governments were desperately keen to open up direct land links for trade and business with the five Central Asian republics of Kazakhstan, Uzbekistan, Kyrgyzstan, Turkmenistan and Tajikistan. The only hindrance to this was the continuing civil war in Afghanistan. Pakistan's policy makers were thus faced with a strategic dilemma. Either Pakistan could carry on backing one or the other Pushtun Afghan factions in its continued strategy of trying to bring to power in Kabul a Pushtun group which would be pro-Pakistan. Or Pakistan could radically alter its former policies and pursue a power-sharing agreement between all the Afghan factions at whatever the price for the Pushtuns, so that relative stability would allow the opening of the northern land route to Tashkent via Peshawar, Kabul and Mazar-e-Sharif.

This stark and simple strategic choice–in effect a policy reversal to sacrifice a pure Pushtun government in Kabul in favour of a broad based government that would allow greater trade and goodwill in Central Asia–did not appear attractive enough for the Pakistani military in 1992, which first backed Hekmatyar in his bid to capture Kabul and later the Taliban. As an alternative, and well before the advent of the Taliban, Pushtun elements in the Bhutto government and the military mooted the idea of securing a southern trade route to Central Asia via Quetta, Kandahar and Herat. Later the Taliban would become the guarantors of this route along which Pakistan planned to build oil and gas pipelines and a railway line to Central Asia.

In October 1994, one month before the Taliban captured Kandahar, Bhutto's Interior Minister Naseerullah Babar took a party of six Western ambassadors to Kandahar and Herat.[7] The delegation included senior officials of the Departments of Railways, Highways, Telephones and Electricity. Babar said he wanted to raise US$300

---

[7] The Ambassadors were from the US, UK, Spain, Italy, China, and South Korea. The delegation included officials from the United Nations. See *Dawn*, 21 October 1994.

million from international agencies to rebuild the highway from Quetta to Herat and another US$800 million for a railway track and satellite phone system linking 100 towns. Ismail Khan assured the delegation that work could start as soon as there was peace and security.

However in Kandahar, where nearly a dozen petty warlords competed for influence, the situation was much more complex and difficult. Warlord Amir Lalai, who on 2 November 1994 would lead the gang that stopped a Pakistani truck convoy outside Kandahar, issued a blunt warning to Babar. 'Pakistan is offering to reconstruct our roads, but I do not think that by fixing our roads, peace would automatically follow. As long as neighbouring countries continue to interfere in our internal affairs, we should not expect peace', said Lalai. Nevertheless Babar urged Bhutto to push ahead. On 28 October, Bhutto met with both Ismail Khan and General Rashid Dostum in Ashgabat, Turkmenistan. Along with President Saparmurad Niyazov she urged them to come to a settlement so that Pakistan could implement these projects.[8]

By then Pakistan, determined to bulldoze its policy through, was already planning to send a 30 truck convoy of goods through Kandahar to Turkmenistan. The story of that convoy is now a critical part of both the legend and history that surrounds the origins of the Taliban. The advance of the Taliban from Spin Boldak to Takht-e Pul outside Kandahar, where the Pakistani convoy had been halted by Amir Lalai, its subsequent release by the Taliban and the Taliban's capture of Kandahar were to change the political map of Afghanistan. Just before he was hanged by the Taliban, Amir Lalai told people that Jamiat-e Ulema-i Islam students were behind the attack on the city.

The Taliban were prompted to move at that moment by Pakistan. A small group of Taliban led by Mullah Mohammad Omar were already preparing to attack the Kandahar warlords because of the breakdown of law and order in the province. The fact that the Taliban would not just free the convoy but then capture Kandahar within 24 hours was beyond any Pakistani or even Afghan expectation. Subsequently Taliban leaders have expressed surprise at their own initial success, which was achieved with so little bloodshed.[9]

Within days the Taliban demonstrated their independence from Pakistan, as well as their willingness to deal with the Rabbani regime in Kabul. A Taliban founder member and later Foreign Minister,

---

[8] *Dawn*, 4 November 1994.

[9] In interviews, subsequently prominent Taliban leaders–such as Foreign Minister Mohammad Ghaus and Governor of Kandahar Mohammad Hassan–all admitted to being surprised as to how easily Kandahar fell to them.

Mullah Mohammad Ghaus, said on 16 November that Pakistan should not bypass the governments in either Kabul or Kandahar by trying to send convoys in future and should not cut deals with individual warlords. He also warned that the Taliban would not allow goods bound for Afghanistan to be carried by Pakistani trucks.[10]

Nevertheless the Taliban capture of Kandahar was wildly celebrated by the Jamiat-e Ulema-i Islam and the Bhutto government, but created an uproar amongst other political parties who felt directly threatened. Mehmood Khan Achakzai, head of the Pushtoonkhwa Milli Awami Party in Baluchistan publicly warned Bhutto and the ISI not to interfere in Afghanistan by trying to promote the Jamiat-e Ulema-i Islam. Other Baluch and Pushtun politicians issued similar warnings. Qazi Hussain Ahmad, leader of the Jamaat-e Islami, suggested an imperialist plot was underway as the United States and Britain were backing the Taliban.

But the Taliban were now unstoppable. By 7 December, just four weeks after taking Kandahar, they had captured the provinces of Helmand and Uruzgan and were advancing on Farah in the west and Zabul and Ghazni to the north. In Helmand they pushed out drug traffickers and for a few weeks declared opium growing to be illegal–a declaration that led to a flurry of activity and excitement at the US Embassy in Islamabad, followed by clear signals that US diplomats were supportive of the Taliban.

Meanwhile thousands of young Pushtun Afghans studying in madrassas in Baluchistan and the North West Frontier Province rushed to Kandahar in trucks and coaches to join up with the Taliban. They were soon followed by Pakistani volunteers from madrassas in all four provinces. By early January 1995, some 12,000 madrassa-educated Afghan and Pakistani students had joined the Taliban in Kandahar. Trade now flourished. In December the first regular Pakistani convoy of fifty trucks carrying raw cotton from Turkmenistan arrived in Quetta, after paying the Taliban over 200,000 rupees (US$5,000) in customs duties.

Pakistan had helped the Taliban decisively by allowing them to capture a crucial arms dump outside Spin Boldak. The dump previously belonged to Hekmatyar, but was guarded by troops of Pakistan's Frontier Corps who were under the command of the Interior Ministry rather than the regular army. These soldiers were ordered to walk away when the Taliban arrived. The Taliban took control of some 18,000 Kalashnikov rifles and 120 artillery pieces as well as large quantities of ammunition.[11]

---

10 *The Muslim*, 17 November 1994.
11 Interviews with senior Pakistani military officials and diplomats.

As international and domestic pressure mounted on Pakistan to explain its position, Ms Bhutto issued the first formal denial of any Pakistani backing for the Taliban in February 1995. 'We have no favourites in Afghanistan and we do not interfere in Afghanistan', she said while visiting Manila.[12] Later she said Pakistan could not stop new recruits from crossing the border to join the Taliban. 'I cannot fight Mr Rabbani's war for him. If Afghans want to cross the border, I do not stop them. I can stop them from re-entering but most of them have families here', she said. 'We can't just shut down the schools [madrassas] and allow these people to spread all across the country. We would rather they be confined. Because of the Afghan war, people were taught that to be a Muslim means to spread Islam by armed struggle', she added.[13]

Pakistan then tried for several months to broker an agreement between the Taliban and General Dostum. After the Taliban finally captured Herat in September 1995, General Dostum sent down Uzbek technicians to help the Taliban repair the ten MiG aircraft and helicopters they had captured. But these efforts never led to an agreement. Pakistan was still trying in February 1996 when Islamabad hosted a meeting between Hekmatyar, General Dostum and the Taliban in Islamabad in order to try to forge an alliance. At the same time Foreign Minister Sardar Aseef Ali was in Washington trying to persuade the United States to put its weight behind the Taliban. Pakistan failed to persuade the Taliban that if they linked up with Dostum, their credibility would be much higher in Western capitals; even at this stage the Taliban refused to share power with their rivals.

By now it was clear to everyone except the Pakistan government that the Taliban movement as a whole would not be consistently manipulated or guided by Pakistan. Thus when the Taliban captured a seven-man Russia aircrew in August 1995, they refused to release them despite considerable pressure from Islamabad. After Kabul fell to the Taliban in September 1996, Pakistan's attempts at shuttle diplomacy to persuade the Taliban to link up with Dostum also failed.

The Taliban and Pakistan's provincial governments

During the 1980s Pakistan's military regime had widened the scope of an already well-established system of patronage for the Pushtun tribal chiefs, politicians and mullahs living on the Pakistan side of the border in Baluchistan and the North West Frontier Province. It was prompted to ensure the loyalty of the Pushtun tribes straddling the

12   'Benazir Bhutto denies support to the Taliban', *The Nation*, 18 February 1995.
13   'Pakistan not backing Taliban says Bhutto', *Dawn*, 18 March 1995

border, because there were similar overtures of money, weapons and bribes coming from the Kabul regime and the Soviet occupation forces in Afghanistan.

The British Raj began the system of paying stipends to the tribal chiefs or maliks along the border to keep their loyalty. Pakistan had continued this practice after 1947. But under General Zia ul Haq the system became much more extensive. Maliks received payments and weapons from the ISI, the provincial governments and Mujahideen parties for granting permission to Mujahideen fighters to cross their territory to carry supplies for those fighting inside Afghanistan. The maliks also received payment for hiring out their pack animals, guides and manpower. The North West Frontier Province and Baluchistan provincial governments received a windfall as they were authorised to issue permits to the maliks to buy foodstuffs on the Pakistani market and then supply the Mujahideen inside Afghanistan. With the end of the war against the Soviets in 1989, these sources of income dried up for the maliks, but the permit system boomed as Afghans cities were liberated, tens of thousands of refugees returned to Afghanistan and the need for food supplies increased dramatically.

In 1994 the Pakistan People's Party government in the North West Frontier Province, established under Chief Minister Aftab Sherpao, remained politically fragile. Sherpao used the permit system as a major source of patronage to retain the loyalty of MPs, politicians and tribal chiefs. Moreover Sherpao was often in competition with the Governor of the North West Frontier Province who had the power to issue his own permits to maliks in the Federal Administered Tribal Areas–the no man's land of Pushtun tribes that straddle the border. Those around the governor and the chief minister made a bonanza in the permit business and they were often supplying goods to rival warlords or in opposition to the declared policy emanating from Islamabad. Thus Sherpao continued to issue permits for the supply of food to the Rabbani regime, even though Pakistan was trying to isolate it internationally.

In Baluchistan the provincial government under Chief Minister Zulfiqar Ali Magsi was a complex coalition of political parties, which was largely in opposition to the federal Pakistan People's Party government. Here there was a constant tussle over who benefited from permits. This infighting allowed the Taliban to gain the maximum advantage from the permit system, by playing off one Pakistani faction against another.

The Taliban were part of this lucrative system of patronage. With their own deep links with the border tribes, the Jamiat-e Ulema-i Islam, the maliks, refugee camp officials and the transport mafia, the Taliban had an enormous advantage over other Afghan factions. Their ties with the provincial governments were closer than those of any

Afghan faction that preceded them. And the Taliban soon developed close relations with several businessmen close to Asif Ali Zardari, the husband of Benazir Bhutto, who in turn were given the highly lucrative permits to export fuel to Afghanistan. As the Taliban's war machine expanded, permits for fuel supplies from Pakistan became a major money earner for Pakistani politicians and the Taliban, and a key element in the Taliban's military successes.

The permit system thus created a stratum of Pakistani politicians and middlemen who had a vested interest in backing the Taliban and ensuring that the Taliban were able to conquer other cities. As the Taliban expanded, the greater the demand for Pakistani food and fuel in Afghanistan. The role of provincial governments only further fragmented Pakistan's policy debate on Afghanistan. The permit issue also created periodic shortages of key foodstuffs in Pakistan and contributed to the rise in inflation. In February 1997, the Nawaz Sharif government faced a crisis over wheat shortages, because of excessive wheat smuggling to the Taliban. Provincial governments thus played a major role in actually blocking the peace process and influencing the Bhutto government and the military to back the Taliban. 'There is a vested interest now amongst the leaders of the two provinces to maintain the present status quo and block the peace process in Afghanistan because there is so much money to be made', said the former Afghan Minister of State for Foreign Affairs Dr Najibullah Lafraie in 1996.[14]

The Taliban and the ISI

Before the Taliban's capture of Kandahar in 1994, Pakistan and in particular the ISI's Afghan policy were facing serious problems. The ISI's main protégés, Hekmatyar and Dostum, had failed to capture Kabul and unlimited support for them was proving to be too expensive. Rabbani could not be ousted from Kabul, but he could not be trusted by Islamabad either as he expanded his links with Iran, Russia and India. Moreover, since the end of the Cold War, the ISI, due to the severe economic crisis in Pakistan, had been stripped of the substantial funds to which it had access in the 1980s. Most significantly, the ISI's resources were directed towards another war of attrition–this one against India for the hearts and minds of the Kashmiris.

After 1992 the ISI chief Lieutenant-General Javed Nasir, appointed by Nawaz Sharif and an advocate of Jihad, had continued the agency's

---

[14] In an interview with the author.

backing of Hekmatyar while trying to micro-manage other warlords. The agency's operatives in Afghanistan were Pushtun and Islamic fundamentalist officers–a leftover from the military regime of General Zia ul Haq. After Sharif's dismissal by President Ghulam Ishaq Khan in 1993, the army under considerable American pressure cleaned up the ISI. General Nasir was retired and dozens of Zia era officers were removed from the agency in July 1993. The ISI's new chief Lieutenant-General Javed Ashraf Qazi was more cautious than his predecessors. For much of 1994 the ISI had retreated into a shell as far as Afghanistan was concerned. The military stalemate inside Afghanistan explains the ISI's reluctance to start any new policy initiatives.

When the Taliban captured Kandahar, the ISI were initially more sceptical than the government about their chances of further success. While General Babar and the Jamiat-e Ulema-i Islam pushed for support to the Taliban, the ISI took a back seat, preferring to watch developments rather than act prematurely in giving the Taliban military backing.[15] Thus Babar had a free hand in 'civilianising' the initial support to the Taliban. He created an Afghan Trade Development Cell in the Interior Ministry, which ostensibly had the task of coordinating ministries to facilitate a trade route to Central Asia. The principal spinoff was considerable logistical and infrastructure support for the Taliban. Thus Pakistan Telecom set up a microwave telephone network for the Taliban in Kandahar, which became part of the Pakistan telephone grid. Kandahar could be dialled from Pakistan as a local call using the prefix 081–the same prefix as that for Quetta. Civilian engineers from the Public Works Department and the Water and Power Development Authority carried out feasibility studies for road repairs and electricity supply in Kandahar city. The paramilitary Frontier Corps were used to help the Taliban set up an internal wireless network for their commanders in the field. Pakistan International Airlines (PIA) and the air force sent in technicians to repair Kandahar airport and the MiG fighter jets and helicopters the Taliban had captured.

After the capture of Herat, Pakistani efforts intensified. In January 1996, a ten-man team led by the Director-General of the Afghan Trade Development Cell travelled by road from Quetta to Turkmenistan. Those who accompanied him included officials from civil aviation, Pakistan Telecom, PIA, Pakistan Railways, Radio Pakistan and the National Bank of Pakistan. These ministries and government corporations were encouraged to help the Taliban from their own

---

[15] Interviews with senior Pakistani military officers and diplomats.

ministerial budgets.[16] After Kabul fell to the Taliban in 1996, Pakistan said it would start building the first 100 kilometres of the Chaman-Kandahar road at a cost of US$2.5 million. Pakistan estimated the total cost of a new road to Torgundi, on the Turkmenistan border, at US$10 million. Pakistan's infrastructural support to the Taliban was farmed out to various government departments.

During 1995 the ISI continued to debate the issue of greater support for the Taliban. The debate centred around those largely Pushtun officers involved in covert operations on the ground, who wanted greater support for the Taliban, and other officers who were involved in longer term intelligence gathering and strategic planning, who wished to keep Pakistan's support to the minimum so as not to worsen tensions with Central Asia and Iran.

The Pushtun grid in the army high command eventually played a major role in determining the military and ISI's decision to give greater support to the Taliban. Both the army chief General Abdul Waheed and the head of Military Intelligence Lieutenant-General Ali Kuli Khan were Pushtuns, as were all operational ISI field officers involved with the Taliban. The military appear to have decided by the summer of 1995 that the Taliban were the only possible alternative for Pakistan's own strategic interests in Afghanistan, especially as President Rabbani appeared to be getting too close to Pakistan's rivals–Russia, Iran and India. Another major factor was the ISI's reluctance to trust Rabbani's commander Ahmad Shah Massoud, who had had a running battle with the ISI since the 1980s.

When the Taliban launched their second attack on Herat, the ISI weighed in with a limited amount of military support. This included providing ammunition for large-calibre machine guns and artillery shells, of which the Taliban were short; extending their military wireless network; and helping the fledgling Taliban air force, which doubled in size after the capture of Herat. But the ISI's ability to provide sustained military support was severely hampered by serious financial and logistical restraints and a continuing debate within the ISI and between the army and the ISI as to the benefits of long term support to the Taliban.

The ISI also helped the Taliban by providing them with hundreds of ex-Afghan army officers and technicians who had sought shelter in Pakistan after 1992. Many of these officers were linked to General Shahnawaz Tanai, the former second-in-command of President Najibullah's armed forces, who led an abortive coup attempt against

[16] Mariana Babar, 'Battle for economic gains in Afghanistan', *The News,* 15 January 1996.

him in March 1990. Tanai's coup was backed by Gulbuddin Hekmatyar and the ISI, but its failure forced Tanai and his men to flee to Pakistan where they were given refuge. Tanai belonged to the Khalq faction of the People's Democratic Party of Afghanistan. Khalq was predominantly Pushtun and many of its officers were ardent Pushtun nationalists. These officers saw the Taliban as a possible vehicle for a Pushtun resurgence in Afghanistan and thus were willing to join up with the students, even though they had little else in common with them. By the time the Taliban captured Kabul, their entire air force and a large section of their armour and heavy artillery were being manned by former Khalqis. By then Hekmatyar had fallen out with Tanai and in a bitter rebuttal of his former ally, Hekmatyar claimed that over 1,600 Khalqis were now working for the Taliban.

In Islamabad the involvement of several ministries, corporations, provincial governments and the ISI effectively sidelined the Pakistan Foreign Ministry, which had less and less to do with policy formulation towards the Taliban. The competition within the government only further fragmented Pakistan's decision making on Afghanistan. The Foreign Ministry's ineffectiveness reduced Pakistan's ability to counter the hostile criticism from neighbouring countries of Islamabad's support for the Taliban. After the capture of Herat by the Taliban, Iran, Russia and the Central Asian Republics became openly hostile to Pakistan. And after Kabul fell to the Taliban in 1996 all the regional states again made it clear to Pakistan how they opposed the Taliban's expansionist aims.

The ISI played a leading role in helping the Taliban's capture of Jalalabad and Kabul, by first helping subvert the Jalalabad Shura and offering its members sanctuary in Pakistan and then allowing the Taliban to reinforce their assault on Kabul by fresh troops drawn from Afghan refugee camps on the border. Pakistani diplomats and ISI officials arrived in Kabul promising all-out support to the Taliban and the Jamiat-e Ulema-i Islam sent a delegation to help the Taliban write a new Afghan Constitution.

The ISI had became deeply concerned that an unholy alliance had sprung up between the regional states that would soon include India. But efforts to defuse the tension, such as the secret visit to Moscow in November by ISI chief Lieutenant-General Naseem Rana and the Prime Minister's Special Envoy Ijlal Zaidi's visits to Iran and Central Asia, did little to defuse regional tensions. The more Pakistan demonstrated its support to the Taliban, the greater the anger and frustration amongst the regional states.

By May 1997, when the Taliban launched their abortive bid to take over Mazar-e Sharif, the military and the ISI had calculated that a recognised Taliban government which controlled the entire country would be easier to deal with than a Taliban movement. Moreover the

ISI estimated that all the regional states would then have to deal with
the Taliban reality and these states would look to Islamabad to
demonstrate leverage over the Taliban and improve their own
relationships with them. It was a gamble that seriously misfired when
the Taliban were pushed back from Mazar-e Sharif after suffering
thousands of casualties.

For many experts in and out of government, especially for
Pakistan's frustrated diplomatic corps, it was another classic example
of Pakistan's overreaching foreign policy aims and ambitions, which
were set in the Zia era when the country could at least claim lavish
support from the USA, China and Saudi Arabia. But in the post-Cold
War era, Pakistan had neither the resources, nor the domestic economic
and political stability, to sustain such an ambitious foreign policy.
Yet the fact remains that with the constant infighting and overlap on
Afghan policy within the Pakistani establishment and the lack of any
serious attempt to create a high-level decision making body that could
make and implement policy, Pakistan's strategy towards the Taliban
was characterised as much by drift as by determination. Islamabad's
policy was as much driven by corruption, infighting and inefficiency
as it was a concerted attempt to push forward a Pushtun agenda in
Afghanistan.

And the Taliban had become masters at using these differences
within the Pakistani establishment to their advantage, extracting the
maximum benefits from Pakistan without giving any political
concessions in return. Thus instead of using its clout with the Taliban
to exert leverage on them on key political and social issues, Pakistan
appeared to fritter away its authority and respect amongst many
Afghans–a respect that had been built up over two decades of support
for the Afghan Mujahideen and the Afghan nation.

The Taliban movement has extremely serious political implications
for Pakistan, which the military and the political élite in the country
first ignored and only began to grasp after the battle for Mazar-e
Sharif. The Taliban's close links with Pakistani society, their
uncompromising stance on their version of Islamic values and the fact
that they represent a new form of Islamic radicalism which is admired
by a younger generation of Pakistani madrassa students, give them far
more clout inside Pakistan than other Afghan Mujahideen groups. For
many Pakistanis the Taliban are an inspiration.

Moreover, after the battle for Mazar, the Taliban had virtually won
over all those more traditional Islamic parties in Pakistan such as the
Jamaat-e Islami, who had at first viewed them with suspicion. As
Nawaz Sharif's government slipped into inertia six months after being
voted into power in February 1997, most major Islamic parties
publicly declared that they had lost faith in parliamentary politics and

aimed to mobilise a mass movement for an Islamic revolution by the end of the year. Any such movement will almost certainly be joined by the thousands of Pakistani madrassa students who have fought alongside the Taliban in Afghanistan. Armed, trained and motivated, these students would be a formidable force for any state apparatus to encounter.

With Pakistan's civil state machinery eaten away by corruption and ineffectiveness and growing public disillusionment with the political system, the law and order agencies would be unable to cope with an Islamic movement which would be violent and self-sacrificing. Almost immediately, such a movement would come up against the army. But the middle and lower echelons of the army's officer corps are themselves now full of fervent fundamentalist officers, many of them having graduated from a madrassa-style education rather than the public schools of the ruling élite. In any future prolonged confrontation with Koran-waving Islamic youths, the army's more secular high command would be hard-pressed to order their troops to open fire. The threat of an Islamic revolution in Pakistan has never been greater.

THE UNITED STATES AND THE TALIBAN

Richard Mackenzie

Herself a former refugee, once from the Nazis and once from communism, US Secretary of State Madeleine Albright on 18 November 1997 went down on her hands and knees to greet a group of Afghan children in a mud-walled school at a desolate refugee camp in Nasir Bagh, Pakistan. She listened intently as six Afghan refugee women recounted the horrors of their young lives. 'I'll never forget you–being here with you,' Albright said. 'I will do everything to help you to help your country'.[1]

In a full day of statements and appearances during a fast-paced but important visit to Pakistan, the highest-ranking US official in the sphere of foreign policy took a rigorous stand against the Taliban movement. In words and deeds, Albright was adamant in her disdain for the faction. All this occurred in front of embarrassed–if not irate— officials of Pakistan, one of only three nations in the world to recognise the Taliban formally as the legitimate government of Afghanistan. Asked by a local reporter why the United States did not recognise the Taliban, Dr Albright offered the strongest criticism of the group ever by a senior US official: 'I think it is very clear why we are opposed to the Taliban. Because of their approach to human rights, their despicable treatment of women and children and their general lack of respect for human dignity ... that is more reminiscent of the past than of the future'.[2]

Citing the concern of American women for the plight of their Afghan 'sisters', Albright urged the Afghans to demand education for themselves and seek equality–opportunities denied them thus far by the Taliban's draconian version of Islamic law. 'It is impossible to modernise a nation if half or more of the population is left behind', Albright said. 'If a society is to move forward, women and girls must have access to schools and health care. They should be able to participate in the economy. And they should be protected from

---

[1] *Associated Press*, 18 November 1997.
[2] *Reuters*, 18 November 1997. See also Ian Brodie, 'Albright attacks Taleban oppression of women', *The Times*, 19 November 1997.

physical exploitation and abuse'.[3] Apart from being 'backward and harsh'[4] toward women, the Taliban did not have much chance of extending their control over any more territory than they now occupy, she said. 'Let me say too that we do not believe that the Taliban are in a position to occupy all of Afghanistan. There are other parties who need to be recognised and there needs to be a government that is composed of them'.[5] According to her aides, she encouraged Pakistan to use its relationship with the Taliban to push the movement into negotiations with the anti-Taliban forces.

Could this be the same US government that spoke with such optimism when the Taliban rolled into Kabul? With what a British commentator, Tim McGirk, called 'unseemly haste', the Clinton Administration 'rushed to give support to the Taliban'.[6] US officials spoke of seeking early talks with the Taliban leaders and even discussed re-opening the US Embassy in Kabul when the dust settled. Hours after the Taliban took Kabul in September 1996, Acting State Department Spokesman Glyn Davies said the United States could see 'nothing objectionable'[7] about the version of Islamic law the Taliban had imposed in the areas they then controlled. In an address to the United Nations two months later, the then Assistant Secretary of State for South Asian Affairs, Robin L. Raphel, conceded international 'misgivings' about the Taliban, but insisted the Taliban had to be 'acknowledged' as an 'indigenous' movement that had 'demonstrated staying power'.[8] Such statements only exacerbated the growing belief in Afghanistan and beyond that the United States–specifically the Central Intelligence Agency (CIA) in collaboration with Pakistan's military intelligence service, ISI–was behind the creation and growth of the Taliban.

On the dusty floor of Bibi Mariam School in the refugee camp near Peshawar, Madeleine Albright left no doubt that, whatever might have taken place before then, a shift was under way. 'The sight of Albright on her hands and knees showed how much attitudes in Washington have changed', wrote Thomas W. Lippman in *The Washington Post*.[9]

---

3   'Albright visits refugee school in Peshawar' (Washington DC: US Information Agency, 25 November 1997).

4   *Reuters,* 18 November 1997.

5   *Voice of America*, 18 November 1997.

6   *The Washington Times*, 5 October 1996.

7   *Voice of America*, 27 September 1996.

8   Statement by Robin L. Raphel, Head of US Delegation, United Nations Meeting on Afghanistan, 18 November 1996.

9   Thomas W. Lippman, 'U.S. Plans More Active S. Asia Role: Albright's Trip Signals New Interest in Region', *The Washington Post,* 19 November 1997.

Newspaper Editor and Pakistan's former Ambassador to the United States Maleeha Lodhi told *The Sydney Morning Herald*: 'There is a very clear perception that the US is reweighing its relations in this part of the world towards India'.[10]

Shaping US policy

Only the most naive would believe, however, that Albright's personal compassion or some form of altruistic contemplation by bureaucrats at the State Department led to the new approach. In fact this was the latest course Washington would take–some might say stumble into–in a twentieth century version of the Great Game, the diplomatic and military contest acted out in the last century between Russia and Britain. This time, the players are drug barons and international oil conglomerates, modern-day terrorists and travellers on ancient trade routes. And the United States has finally realised that it has a role to play.

Afghans observing the roles which the United States has played over the years in Afghanistan have every reason to feel perplexed, even bewildered, by the turns which US policy has taken. One of the reasons for this is that the processes by which US foreign policy is determined are complex and obscure. Within the constraints imposed by law, the President of the United States enjoys great freedom to set foreign policy objectives, but it is by no means the case that all presidents will have a great interest in foreign affairs, or that those who do will be equally interested in all parts of the globe. The attention which a particular issue receives depends in part upon a president's choice of key foreign policy actors–the Secretary of State (and the senior staff of the State Department), the director of the CIA, and the senior staff of the National Security Council–and whether the issue engages *their* attention. But much also depends upon the pressure of other issues at any given time, and whether the issue gives rise to a crisis in which an immediate and decisive US response is unavoidable. The United States may, in the words of one prominent commentator and participant, be 'bound to lead'[11]–but this does not guarantee that it is *equipped* to lead.

---

10 Christopher Kremmer, 'Taliban policies despicable, says US Secretary of State', *The Sydney Morning Herald*, 19 November 1997.

11 See Joseph S. Nye, Jr., *Bound to Lead: The Changing Nature of American Power* (New York: Basic Books, 1990).

The situation is further complicated by the role of Congress and pressure groups in setting broader foreign policy agendas.[12] While Congress's formal powers in the area of foreign relations are quite considerable, it is perhaps even more significant as a venue in which alternative foreign policy options can be canvassed. A number of former or current members of Congress–notably Senator Gordon Humphrey of New Hampshire, Congressman Charles Wilson of Texas, Senator Hank Brown of Colorado, and Congressman Dana Rohrabacher of California–have at different times taken a serious interest in the Afghanistan issue. An energetic congressional advocate can keep options 'on the table' which might otherwise be discarded by professional diplomats. This is not to say that diplomats are necessarily better informed than their congressional counterparts: the processes by which officers are selected for particular positions in the State Department do not guarantee that those selected will be experts on the countries or regions for which they are responsible, although some may well be. Pressure groups and corporate interests may also play some role in shaping the approach to particular issues, either by direct lobbying, or by supplying personnel for particular administrations.

A consequence of this multiplicity of influences is that there is rarely a 'mastermind' behind US foreign policy steps, let alone a 'master plan'. Occasionally an exceptionally influential individual such as Henry Kissinger may leave a distinctive stamp on policy, but policy makers of his ilk are few and far between. Odd as it may seem to Afghans–for whom the US appears as an almost omnipotent superpower–the US may face great difficulty in crafting informed and appropriate policy responses to developments in a country as remote and apparently inscrutable as Afghanistan.

The evolution of US policy

All that said, America's understanding of Afghanistan is perhaps best illustrated by a moment during the taping of a television interview in 1993. Robert Gates, a former director of the CIA, was sitting at a long, polished conference table in a suite of luxurious offices atop a high-rise building in downtown Washington. The normal serenity of the meeting room was disrupted by a CNN crew that had come to interview him–their cameras, strewn equipment and blazing lights dominating the room. At the centre of the controlled chaos, Gates was answering questions from Peter Arnett, the renowned and tenacious

---

[12] For a classic discussion, see Robert A. Dahl, *Congress and Foreign Policy* (New York: W.W. Norton & Co., 1964).

international correspondent. Mr Arnett and this writer were working on a documentary investigating unintended consequences of the Afghan War–and how they were linked to the bombing of the World Trade Center and other terrorism.[13] As the former CIA chief spoke of the Afghans who had led the jihad against the Soviet invasion of their nation, he quipped, 'A lot of them weren't people you'd invite home to dinner. The reality is you had to make do with the strategic situation you found in Afghanistan'. Setting aside the gratuitous and ironic remark about an hospitable people, Gates well described Washington's Afghan *modus operandi*: 'making do'. As a policy, 'making do' proved less than adequate. Today, the US Embassy in Kabul is padlocked and forgotten, a symbol of the American experience in Afghanistan. Surprisingly, while most of the city lies in ruins, the embassy building is largely intact–rusting basketball hoops and a vintage gasoline pump bearing testimony to the passage of time. A pedestal with a brass plate commemorates the last US Ambassador to Kabul, Adolph 'Spike' Dubs, who was kidnapped and slain under mysterious circumstances in the early days of communism, shortly before the Soviet invasion.[14] During his time in the chair in Kabul, Ambassador Dubs was frustrated by the difficulty in gathering information, particularly because he had no access to Afghan government officials. The ambassador's monument is slowly wearing away through neglect.

From the moment of the Soviet invasion, Washington was caught flat-footed, even after the administrations of Presidents Jimmy Carter and then Ronald Reagan assigned the CIA to spend what became $3 billion to support the Afghan resistance.[15] The agency quickly delegated important decision-making to Pakistan, often neglecting the fact that Pakistan might have interests that did not necessarily coincide with those of either Washington or the Afghan people. Prime facie evidence of that failure was the 'creation' of Gulbuddin Hekmatyar, who gained notoriety in Afghanistan for killing more fellow Mujahideen than he did communists. Despite repeated warnings from

---

13 *Terror Nation: US Creation?* ('CNN Presents', 16 January 1993. Produced by Peter Bergen and Richard Mackenzie).

14 See Henry S. Bradsher, *Afghanistan and the Soviet Union* (Durham: Duke University Press, 1985), pp. 98-100.

15 For details of the tortuous evolution of the policies of successive administrations, see Charles G. Cogan, 'Partners in Time: The CIA and Afghanistan since 1979', *World Policy Journal*, vol. 10, no. 2, Summer 1993, pp. 73-82; Minton F. Goldman, 'President Bush and Afghanistan: A Turning Point in American Policy', *Comparative Strategy*, vol. 11, no. 2, 1992, pp. 177-193; James M. Scott, *Deciding to Intervene: The Reagan Doctrine and American Foreign Policy* (Durham: Duke University Press, 1996), pp. 40-81.

human rights groups and Western journalists over several years,[16] US government officials rarely deviated from the Pakistani line that Hekmatyar was the most effective and representative Mujahideen leader.

By 1992, America's main motivation for close attention to Afghanistan–the existence and threat of the Soviet Union–had passed. Both Washington and Moscow cut off supplies to their clients at the end of 1991 and, by April 1992, the Mujahideen had entered Kabul. During the first few months following the Mujahideen victory, while Sebghatullah Mojadiddi briefly held the presidency, the US Ambassador to the Afghan Resistance, Peter Tomsen, and his deputy, Richard Hoagland, made the last significant visit of a US official to Kabul. As Barnett R. Rubin noted in an insightful paper for *Muslim Politics Report*, a publication of the Council on Foreign Relations, the entire international community had no political strategy for Afghanistan from 1992 to 1994. This was widely noted at the time, most frequently by aid agencies.[17] It was only in 1994 that the United Nations revived its involvement through travel to the region of a Special Mission led by a nominee of the Secretary General. 'But', adds Rubin, 'the regional powers who voted for the mission in the UN continued to undermine it through their policies of covert aid to the warring factions'.[18] At that time, the evolution of the Taliban was already under way. The group's mysterious emergence in southern Afghanistan is by now the stuff of legend. At the time, American officials professed general ignorance of the identity and origin of the group, obfuscating any suggestion that the Taliban were financed and backed by Pakistan–a US position that today appears ludicrous.

---

[16] See Richard Mackenzie, 'When Policy Tolls in Fool's Paradise', *Insight*, 11 September 1989; *By All Parties to the Conflict: Violations of the Laws of War in Afghanistan* (New York: Helsinki Watch/Asia Watch, 1988), pp. 35-42; *Afghanistan: The Forgotten War* (New York: Asia Watch, 1991), pp. 54-55; Ted Galen Carpenter, 'The Unintended Consequences of Afghanistan', *World Policy Journal*, vol. 11, no. 1, Spring 1994, pp. 76-87.

[17] See, for example, Hiram A. Ruiz, *Left Out in the Cold: The Perilous Homecoming of Afghan Refugees* (Washington DC: US Committee for Refugees, 1992); 'Afghanistan: Off the Agenda', in *Life, Death and Aid: The Médecins Sans Frontières Report on World Crisis Intervention* (London: Routledge, 1993), pp. 27-32.

[18] Barnett R. Rubin, 'U.S. Policy in Afghanistan', *Muslim Politics Report*, no. 11, January-February 1997, pp. 1-2, 6, at p. 2.

US interests and the Taliban

Behind the scenes in the United States, however, there were even then some fairly obvious clues. Long before the Taliban began to thrust toward Kabul, US officials had high aspirations for the 'students'. US federal narcotics agents based in Pakistan privately expressed strong hope that the Taliban would bring an end to the booming opium trade out of Afghanistan. That was just one of several reasons that Washington thought the Taliban would serve its purposes. Along with the wish that the Taliban would clean up drugs, Americans then also thought they would (1) serve as a bulwark against Russian and Iranian interests in Afghanistan; (2) restore order to all of Afghanistan as they had done in Kandahar and other corners of the south; (3) get rid of terrorist training camps; (4) pave the way for the return of the former king, Zahir Shah; and (5) provide a US ally, Pakistan, an overland link to the immense profits to be made from trade with the new Central Asian republics. Most importantly, and unrecognised at the time, the Taliban promised to open doors for the construction of giant gas and oil pipelines from Central Asia down through Afghanistan to Pakistan. The main contender for that pipeline was an American-Saudi coalition of UNOCAL and Delta oil companies. As Rubin stated, the Taliban's 'most important function [...] was to provide security for roads and, potentially, oil and gas pipelines that would link the states of Central Asia to the international market through Pakistan rather than through Iran'.[19]

It would be some years before the full impact of UNOCAL-Delta would become publicly obvious. In the summer of 1996, US Senator Hank Brown from Colorado chaired hearings on Afghanistan. The most memorable presentation was not by an Afghan but by Marty Miller, the UNOCAL Vice President in charge of the proposed Afghan pipeline project. With a slick, Madison Avenue-style presentation, Miller explained and displayed the routes for both the gas and oil pipelines. As he spoke, the situation quickly became clear to even the most obtuse. The oil route through Afghanistan, could, on Day One, start pumping a million barrels of oil per day. In a few years, once linked with other oil fields in Central Asia, the pipeline could pump 5 million barrels a day.

If it took a while for some in the West to catch on, some of those inside Afghanistan were already aware of the implications of these commercial interests. In a conversation in Kabul in the summer of 1996 not long before the Taliban reached the capital, Ahmad Shah Massoud was pensive. Beyond anything else, he wanted to know about

[19]   Ibid., p. 6.

UNOCAL, its motives, its methods and its ties to the US Government. The fall of Kabul to a well-financed Taliban would follow shortly thereafter. In a statement that the oil company would spend months trying to retract, another UNOCAL official would applaud the arrival of the Taliban in Kabul and speak glowingly about the immediate prospects of doing business with them.[20] In light of such blunders and of the high stakes involved, it is easy to understand how it became accepted wisdom in Afghanistan that the United States backed, supported or even financed the Taliban.

In fact, there is no real evidence thus far that the Clinton Administration implemented a policy to establish the Taliban. CIA officials cringed at the idea of getting reinvolved with Afghanistan. As the backwash from the Afghan war continued–a heavily-armed nation in chaos, regional instability, a booming narcotics trade and terrorist training camps–personnel at CIA headquarters reacted to any mention of Afghanistan with something close to a shudder. At the State Department, there was no real policy in existence, other than the perennial call for a 'broad-based government' for Afghanistan. In a recent *Newsweek* report, Steve LeVine writes that until Kabul fell, the US administration seemed 'unconcerned about the Taliban's growth'. He added, 'Some midlevel State Department officials applauded the movement's campaign for law and order, despite the mullahs' knuckle-dragging views on women's rights'.[21] Certainly what one staunch critic (in an interview with the author) called a 'cabal' at the State Department was not as enlightened as their brothers and sisters at the CIA. Assistant Secretary Robin Raphel and two of her staff gave good impressions of being at least occasional cheer leaders for the Taliban. In one encounter a few months before the Taliban entered Kabul, a mid-level bureaucrat at the State Department claimed to this writer that 'You get to know them and you find they really have a great sense of humour', apparently believing the words he was uttering.

Building support for pipelines

The driving force behind such US toleration of the Taliban–an attempt, to use Anthony Davis's words, to install in Afghanistan a Pax Talibana–was the UNOCAL game plan. Officials say that, while the CIA did not embark on a new Afghan operation of its own, UNOCAL officials were briefed extensively by US intelligence analysts. Equally importantly, UNOCAL and its partner Delta hired as

---

[20] *Reuters,* 1 October 1996.
[21] Steve LeVine, 'Helping Hand', *Newsweek,* 14 October 1997.

consultants every available member of the inner circle of those Americans involved in Afghan operations during the jihad years. The former US Ambassador to Pakistan, Robert Oakley, was one, as were other 'think tank' analysts across the United States. A former official of the UN Secretary General's mission to Afghanistan, Charles Santos, was given a far more delicate and unobservable position, working on the payroll of UNOCAL's partner, the Saudi firm Delta. One of the best pieces of reporting on the role of the American oil companies was done by the *Omaha World-Herald* in Nebraska.[22] That story centred on Thomas E. Gouttierre's Center for Afghanistan Studies at the University of Nebraska. A former Peace Corps worker in Afghanistan and a veteran academic visitor to Peshawar, Gouttierre heads a body which is reportedly to receive as much as $1.8 million from 1997-99 to complement UNOCAL in its Afghan operations. The university's role is to create goodwill in Afghanistan by establishing vocational and educational training programs, the paper said. Gouttierre was quoted as commenting of the Taliban that 'The fact is, they are not out there oppressing people'. He reportedly conceded to the paper that UNOCAL's primary motive in the $1.8 million programme was to help get the pipeline built: 'The priorities are seen in the language of the 13-page contract', the paper said. Of 14 skills to be taught by the University of Nebraska in Afghanistan, at least nine are peculiar to the building of a pipeline. The remainder are more general but apply to administrative and support services. Only marginal provisions are made for training teachers and establishing general education programs. Here one finds interesting resonances with earlier US commercial involvements in Afghanistan, such as those associated decades ago with the activities of the Helmand Valley Authority, modelled on the Tennessee Valley Authority of 'New Deal' days, which stood as a monument to the difficulties of exporting to one country a set of institutional arrangements designed for the peculiarities of another.[23]

The dangers are high, of course. But off-setting the risks is the enormous potential for profit. The reason for the oil companies' largesse was simple. Analysts believe that Central Asia may be the next Middle East.[24] One country alone, Turkmenistan, has 21,000

22 'Odd Partners in UNO's Afghan Project', *Omaha World-Herald*, 26 October 1997.

23 See Louis Dupree, *Afghanistan* (Princeton: Princeton University Press, 1980), pp. 482-485, 499-507.

24 For background on the politics and economics of energy resources in Central Asia, see Rosemarie Forsythe, *The Politics of Oil in The Caucasus and Central Asia* (Oxford: Oxford University Press, Adelphi Paper no. 300, International

billion cubic metres of gas, the third largest reserve in the world. Neighbouring Uzbekistan has comparable amounts of gas. The prospective reserves of oil in Kazakhstan and Azerbaijan are what have been called 'legends in the industry'. The problem was that UNOCAL placed itself in the same position the CIA fell into during the jihad. Relying heavily on the Taliban's backers in Pakistan, UNOCAL executives did good imitations of CIA officials who bought the Pakistani line that Gulbuddin Hekmatyar was the most effective anti-communist Mujahideen leader. As in the days of the jihad, UNOCAL's day-to-day policy was often crafted in cooperation with the US embassy in Islamabad, where officials hosted functions and other gatherings on UNOCAL's behalf.

To experienced observers of Afghanistan, the proposal to build oil or gas pipelines might well seem quite bizarre in present circumstances: pipelines, and the expatriate staff involved in their operation, would be attractively 'soft' targets for disgruntled groups who saw their opponents benefiting disproportionately from the companies' activities. But to the United States, a key appeal of the pipeline proposal has been a simple one, unrelated to Afghanistan: *the isolation of Iran*. Pipelines through Afghanistan would exclude the possibility of direct supply by Iran of resources to meet Pakistan's energy needs, and the consequent flow of foreign exchange earnings into Iran's coffers. The isolation of Iran is not especially an obsession of the State Department, but there are such strongly anti-Iranian attitudes in sections of Congress, reinforced by the lobbying of pressure groups such as the America-Israel Public Affairs Committee (AIPAC), that a president has little incentive to take his political life in his hands by exploring the possibility of a less antagonistic relationship with Iran. This may change over time given the recent election to the Iranian presidency of the moderate cleric Mohammad Khatemi: the policy of 'dual containment' of Iran and Iraq, initially articulated on behalf of the Clinton Administration by the Australian-born former lobbyist Martin Indyk, is proving increasingly creaky.[25] The irony in the case of Afghanistan is that the attempt to exclude Iran by means of the expansion of Taliban power has had the opposite effect: Iranian involvement in Afghanistan, which was at something of an impasse following the murder of their favoured client Abdul Ali

Institute for Strategic Studies, 1996); Ahmed Rashid, *The Turkmenistan-Afghanistan-Pakistan Pipeline: Company-Government Relations and Regional Politics* (Washington DC: Focus on Current Issues, The Petroleum Finance Company, October 1997).

25 See Zbigniew Brzezinski, Brent Scowcroft and Richard Murphy, 'Differentiated Containment', *Foreign Affairs*, vol. 76, no. 3, May-June 1997, pp. 20-30.

Mazari of Hezb-e Wahdat in February 1995, has escalated since the Taliban takeover of Herat in September 1995, the fall of Kabul in September 1996, and the intrusion into the north in May 1997, largely as a result of the heightened fears in Tehran for the safety of Afghanistan's vulnerable Shiite minority. This should come as no surprise to anyone.

The breakdown of US policy

The policy of 'making do' with the Taliban appears to have broken down under the weight of its own contradictions. The process actually began shortly after the seizure of Kabul,[26] but gathered pace as the flaws in the reasoning of those who foresaw a swift Taliban victory became more and more obvious. Five factors in particular contributed to the shift in policy, four related to developments in Afghanistan, and the last related to personnel turnover in Washington.

Internally, the Taliban proved a sad disappointment to their Western supporters. First, the Taliban proved incapable of rapidly extending their control over Afghanistan. While Washington had hoped for nationwide 'peace', the Taliban takeover of Kabul resulted in the establishment of an obvious police state in the capital, ethnic cleansing of the areas to its immediate north, and the spread of violence in areas which had long been relatively quiet. The argument that the Taliban were the bearers of stability for the country as a whole simply failed to ring true. Second, the hope that the Taliban would put an end to the cultivation of the opium poppy in Afghanistan predictably proved to be an illusion. Far from being partners in a 'war against drugs', the Taliban were revealed to be beneficiaries of the poppy. By late 1997, 7.5 per cent of the estimated nationwide opium crop of 2,500 tonnes was reported to be coming from the Taliban heartland of Kandahar,[27] with over 90 per cent of the crop originating in areas over which the Taliban claimed control. Third, the Taliban proved markedly less sensitive to US political interests than some in Washington had hoped. The most mortifying example of this was the hospitality which the Taliban provided to the Saudi billionaire Osama Bin Laden, who was suspected by US agencies of having financed anti-American outrages such as the bombing of a barracks in Saudi Arabia, in which US military personnel were killed. The report by Steve LeVine that Bin Laden had been a significant source of the monies

---

[26] See Elaine Sciolino, 'U.S. to Distance Itself From New Kabul Regime', *The New York Times*, 23 October 1996.

[27] *Associated Press*, 27 November 1997.

which funded the Taliban's final thrust to Kabul[28] helped explain the hospitality, but did not lessen the American mortification, given Washington's strong stance against sponsors of terrorism. More seriously, some of the Taliban's powerful Pakistani supporters also adopted a hostile stance towards Washington, notably Maulana Fazlur Rahman of the Jamiat-e Ulema-i Islam, who made a vituperatively anti-American speech following the murder in Karachi in mid-November 1997 of four staff of a US oil company. Fourth, and probably most importantly, the Taliban's treatment of women, widely publicised following the fall of Kabul, was an affront to key values for which the United States avowedly stood. Women's groups which previously had not been involved with the Afghanistan issue voiced their solidarity with Afghan women, and in the run-up to a presidential election, this effectively blocked any rapprochement with the Taliban for which the oil companies and their bureaucratic sympathisers might have hoped.[29]

Furthermore, in early 1997, with the appointment of Dr Albright as Secretary of State to replace Warren Christopher, there were important changes in the rank and file in Washington. The new Under Secretary of State, Thomas Pickering, took an interest in the Afghanistan situation, and the entire chain of command on Afghanistan (from the Assistant Secretary for South Asian Affairs down to the Afghan desk officer) all retired or were reassigned in the summer of 1997. Robin L. Raphel was succeeded as Assistant Secretary of State for South Asian Affairs by Karl F. ('Rick') Inderfurth, who reportedly enjoyed a significantly closer relationship with the new Secretary of State than had Ms Raphel with Secretary Christopher.[30] Once welcomed and heralded by the State Department's Afghan Desk, the Taliban movement came to be seen as Untouchables. Rather than being staffed by someone who appreciated the Taliban's 'sense of humour', the office now contained a seasoned and pragmatic veteran of Afghanistan's troubles, the former US Consul to Peshawar, Michael Malinowski. The new team brought with it a new outlook and a new vocabulary. What had once been vague references to international 'misgivings' about the Taliban's human rights violations became unapologetic condemnations. Coinciding with the arrival of new staff, the Taliban made the first of their abortive attempts to take over the north of Afghanistan. It was

---

28 LeVine, 'Helping Hand'.

29 See Dan Morgan and David B. Ottaway, 'Women's Fury Toward Taliban Stalls Pipeline', *The Washington Post,* 11 January 1998.

30 Lippman, 'U.S. Plans More Active S. Asia Role: Albright's Trip Signals New Interest in Region'.

there they proved to Washington they could not deliver, that they could not occupy the entire country and provide the type of nationwide security their Pakistani friends had promised and the international oil companies had hoped for.

In testimony to the Senate Foreign Relations Subcommittee on Near East and South Asia on 22 October 1997,[31] Assistant Secretary Inderfurth gave a clear statement of official US policy towards Afghanistan which showed a more nuanced grasp of Afghan complexities than a simple policy of 'making do' could embody. He argued that the Taliban's attempt to take Mazar-e Sharif appeared 'stymied', and voiced disbelief that any side could 'win a military victory resulting in a peaceful and stable Afghanistan'. In a comment which appeared particularly threatening to the Taliban's aims and practices, he identified as Washington's objective 'an Afghan government that is multi-ethnic, broad-based, and that observes international norms of behavior'. The Taliban's restrictions on women, he stated, 'have justifiably shocked the world'. Those in Pakistan who were staggered by Secretary Albright's remarks less than a month later had no reason to be: the signs of a sea change in US policy were already to be found in Mr Inderfurth's testimony.

Notwithstanding such strong words, UNOCAL continues to show no hesitation in reaching out to the Taliban. A couple of weeks before Christmas 1997, the oil company hosted a trip to the United States for a delegation of Taliban officials, led by Acting Minister of Mines and Industry Ahmad Jan. The group met with Assistant Secretary Inderfurth at the State Department in Washington, a conference at which Ahmad Jan tried valiantly to prove the Taliban had much to deliver to the United States. In particular, the delegation stressed what it called its efforts to combat narcotics production, including an agreement with the United Nations. A US official later told the press: 'We welcomed that but noted we wanted to see results'.[32] Throughout the meeting, US officials stressed human rights were first and foremost on Washington's agenda. The Taliban men in turned spoke of Afghan 'traditions', but were unable to convince Inderfurth who 'made it clear the world had a different view and their ability to develop a healthy relationship with the outside world depended on how they treated people'. Nor, said the US officials at the meetings, was a pipeline across Afghanistan a realistic possibility without a political solution to the war. At a daily press briefing on December 8, State Department spokesman James B. Foley voiced US motives that were a

[31] 'Inderfurth Details US Policy on Afghanistan in Senate' (Washington DC: US Information Agency, 22 October 1997).
[32] *Reuters*, 8 December 1997.

far cry indeed from opinions stated at the briefing when the Taliban took Kabul. The meeting with the Taliban was merely part of Washington's policy of being in contact with all Afghan factions, Foley said. 'The meeting ... provide[d] us with the opportunity to reinforce our message of concern over Taliban behaviour, particularly on human rights and the treatment of women and girls'.[33]

Thus, more than a year after their seizure of Kabul, Taliban hopes for US recognition seem to be in vain. The US had suspended the operations of the Afghan Embassy in Washington rather than risk its falling into the hands of a Taliban supporter. And as Madeleine Albright demonstrated with her verbal attack at the refugee camp, the US State Department is at least superficially sensitive to the plight of women in Afghanistan–even if there are financial forces that would point it elsewhere. This is perhaps the key constraint now faced by US policy makers. As a senior Washington official said a few days before Albright's harsh words: 'With their attitude toward women, we couldn't reach out to those guys if we wanted to'.

[33] U.S. Department of State, *Daily Press Briefing* (Washington DC: Office of the Spokesman, 8 December 1997).

RUSSIA, CENTRAL ASIA AND THE TALIBAN

Anthony Hyman

The policies followed by Russia and the five Central Asian states towards Afghanistan since 1994 reflect a common preference for the *status quo*, with all its inherent instability, over the prospect of outright victory for the Taliban movement. Naturally, though, there are considerable differences in the respective governments' appreciations of trends and political developments, reflected in their various actions as well as nuance of statements issued.

Following their emergence as independent states at the end of 1991 the former Soviet republics of Central Asia developed formal links with Afghanistan within the loose framework of the Economic Cooperation Organisation, a greatly-expanded regional grouping of states taking in also Turkey, Iran and Pakistan. However, their relations with Afghanistan remained difficult and even problematic after the fall of the Najibullah government in 1992, with no government worth the name in existence and continuing civil war raging in many areas.[1]

Although the Afghan war and that in Tajikistan (which started in 1992) have many differences, it has been argued stridently and frequently in Central Asia as well as in Moscow that Tajikistan's civil war originated and continued so long basically because of interference from Afghanistan. This common assumption by Central Asian governments, and the associated blame given to the Kabul government, have coloured and distorted relations with Afghanistan. Likewise, the forced flight from Tajikistan into northern provinces of Afghanistan of Tajik refugees and also elements of the defeated Tajik

---

[1] Some recent analyses of regional foreign policies and rivalries with a bearing on Afghanistan are to be found in Adeed Dawisha and Karen Dawisha (eds.), *The Making of Foreign Policy in Russia and the New States of Eurasia* (New York: M.E. Sharpe, 1995); Alvin Rubinstein and Oleg Smolansky (eds.), *Regional Power Rivalries in the New Eurasia: Russia, Turkey and Iran* (New York: M.E. Sharpe, 1995); and Anthony Hyman, 'Central Asia's Relations with Afghanistan and South Asia', in Peter Ferdinand (ed.), *The New Central Asia and its Neighbours* (London: Royal Institute of International Affairs and Pinter Publishers, 1994), pp. 75-94.

opposition forces determined to carry on their struggle constituted a permanent source of tension.

It has been argued cogently by Mohiaddin Mesbahi that:

Afghanistan provided both the Russian and the Uzbek governments with the justification for their regional and extraregional security concerns and their military and political intervention in Tajikistan and in Afghanistan itself. The entire political logic behind the Islamic threat, in Russia's current threat perception and foreign policy formulation, has focused on the Tajik post-Soviet experience and the assertion that the Tajik opposition is fundamentally externally inspired and sustained.[2]

From a geopolitical point of view, Afghanistan forms a potential 'land-bridge' for bulk trade or oil and gas pipelines to be constructed from the Central Asian states to markets in Pakistan, India and elsewhere in the world via Karachi or another Pakistani port on the Arabian Sea. Irrespective of which government was in place in Kabul, Afghanistan's territory could provide access to world markets and an alternative to total dependence upon Russia's monopoly on trade routes.

Responding to disintegration

The steady fragmentation of Afghanistan along with what many observers saw as the possible or imminent breakup of the country along ethnic lines was not welcomed by any of the governments of Central Asia. Such a development would inevitably call into question their own borders, drawn up in arbitrary fashion in the 1920s-30s. However, in nationalist circles in some republics there was keen excitement over the prospect of a drastic reorganisation of territories inhabited by their kinsmen, or related ethnic groups, through revision of borders frozen since the nineteenth century. Afghanistan's seemingly endless cycle of fighting and apparent disintegration served to feed the hopes of some nationalists, notably of Tajikistan and Uzbekistan, who wished to expand the existing state borders to include ethnic kinsmen in the provinces of northern Afghanistan.

2   Mohiaddin Mesbahi, 'Regional and Global Powers and the International Relations of Central Asia', in Adeed Dawisha and Karen Dawisha (eds.), *The Making of Foreign Policy in Russia and the New States of Eurasia* (New York: M.E. Sharpe, 1995), pp. 215-245 at p. 228; and see further for complexities of the Tajikistan conflict, 'Le Tajikistan existe-t-il? Destins politiques d'une "nation imparfaite"', *Cahiers d'études sur la Méditerranée orientale et le monde turco-iranien*, no. 18, 1994, pp. 1-198.

An explicit challenge to the *status quo* on state borders of the region came from Tajikistan, in the form of a speech of June 1995 by a maverick official minister, filled with political irredentist hopes. Tajikistan's Minister for the Interior Yaqubjan Salimov openly demanded the political unification of all ethnic Tajiks, whether living currently in Afghanistan or Uzbekistan:

I call on all those Tajiks, citizens of Tajikistan who have a drop of young blood and manliness, a little Tajik shame and honour: let us brothers unite together! Let us try to regain the land of the Tajiks, the land of the Samanids, in order to be able to hold our heads up high and say we are Tajiks! [...] There are six million (Tajiks) in the fraternal republic of Uzbekistan–six million. And there are 7.5 million in the republic of the Islamic state of Afghanistan. But because we are not united, are not like-minded, (only) three million of us live in the state of the Tajiks, in the country in which we want to unite all Tajiks today.[3]

This remarkable statement by a man who was at the time a senior official of the Tajikistan regime was, admittedly, repudiated promptly by the government, which clearly could not afford to antagonise its vital backers or patrons, Uzbekistan and Russia. However, the tenor of Salimov's speech is a good indication of populist nationalist undercurrents in Tajikistan.

Initial reactions to the dramatic Taliban capture of Kabul at the end of September 1996 were unambiguous. There was consternation and dismay as well as frank alarm at the rise to power of a movement about which little certain was known beyond its puritanical creed and retrograde social ideas. At an emergency meeting called in Almaty from 4 October, and attended by four Central Asian presidents, Russia's Prime Minister Viktor Chernomyrdin, and their security staffs, a stern warning was issued to the Taliban not to invade Commonwealth of Independent States (CIS) borders north of Afghanistan. In a joint communiqué it was declared:

The flame of war is approaching the borders of the CIS states, and this creates a direct threat to the national interests and security of these states and of the CIS in general and destabilizes the regional and international situation. We declare that any activity which undermines stability on the borders with Afghanistan is unacceptable. Such activity, no matter who is responsible or it, will be regarded as a threat to common interests and [...] will meet with an appropriate response.[4]

---

[3] BBC *Summary of World Broadcasts*, SU/2329/G/1, 14 June 1995.
[4] *Inside Central Asia*, no. 141 (30 September-6 October 1996).

Though this communiqué went on to rule out military intervention in Afghanistan's internal affairs, it called on the CIS Collective Security Council to 'examine urgently the situation which is developing on the southern borders of the CIS and to take necessary measures to strengthen the security of the CIS external borders'. While any military aid to the anti-Taliban forces inside Afghanistan was specifically denied in the meeting's conclusion, provision was made for what was called, 'humanitarian assistance, including supplies of flour and electricity [which] will be given to the inhabitants of Afghanistan's northern regions and to refugees'.

On behalf of Uzbekistan, Karimov pointedly denied that General Rashid Dostum was receiving any military assistance via Termez or other Uzbek military bases. However, Karimov chose to underline how vital was the role of Dostum's forces in northern Afghanistan at this juncture. In a speech broadcast on Uzbekistan TV, Karimov declared:

He defends a very important sector which in essence defends the north of Afghanistan from the arrival of the Taliban. If we really want to prevent a further escalation of the war, if we want the war currently under way to end, for the parties to the conflict to sit down at the negotiating table–including the Taliban–then we must do everything possible so that Mr Dostum can hold on to the Salang (tunnel).[5]

Turkmenistan for its part abstained from the Almaty meeting (and later such meetings) on the grounds that it was not party to the Collective Security Treaty of CIS states, having its own separate bilateral treaty with Russia. From Moscow there were influential voices which argued for much more vigorous action against the perceived threat of the Taliban.

President Yeltsin's own security adviser at the time, General Lebed, urged Russia to intervene decisively in support of the ousted regime of President Rabbani and to help all those organised military forces in Afghanistan opposed to the Taliban movement. In an alarmist, even apocalyptic speech, Lebed expressed the alarm or panic felt widely in Moscow. Lebed conjured up the bogey of Islamic fanaticism, and went on to assert a simplistic domino theory of imminent state collapse throughout the Central Asia region–unless, that is, Russia acted with decisive force to stem the Islamic tide. He declared of the Taliban:

5   Report on Uzbek TV, quoted in *Inside Central Asia*, no. 141 (30 September–6 October 1996).

Their plans include making part of Uzbekistan including Bukhara–one of Islam's holy places–part of the Afghan state. They will join with detachments of the Tajik opposition leader, Sayid Nuri. They share the same faith. They will then sweep away our border posts.[6]

Lebed actually stated that the problem of Chechnya would 'look like nothing in comparison' to Afghanistan, unless the Taliban challenge was crushed. As a populist politician and a former Soviet general, it was quite natural if Lebed wished to be seen standing up bravely to a resurgent Islam. It was on a par with his vigorous opposition to NATO's expansion of membership into central Europe. Yet it was uncertain exactly how far this populist and alarmist reaction was shared in the country outside nationalist circles in Moscow.

For all the rhetoric, no one in Moscow seriously anticipated the despatch of another army to invade Afghanistan, as the Soviet Union had done in December 1979. Not only was the débâcle suffered then a strong basis for caution, but the shocks from the Chechen war had recently exposed just how low morale and discipline had sunk within the Russian armed forces. Although there was an undeniable debate going on in the Duma and outside over Russia's role in Afghanistan, it was arguable as to whether or not Russia had a clear policy. Rather than direct military involvement in Afghanistan, it was probable that increased military supplies to Afghan opponents of the Taliban was the only option that was seriously considered.

In the Central Asian states, Lebed's rhetoric about the threat of the Taliban was often discounted. For example, from Almaty the Secretary of Kazakhstan's own Security Council, Baltash Tursumbayev, maintained in an interview with Russia TV that Lebed had grossly exaggerated the Taliban threat:

If one says that tomorrow they will be posing a threat to Uzbekistan and Kazakhstan, this is said in haste and is groundless. Who are the Taliban? The Taliban are bandit formations. If one is saying that bandit formations can do something to regular armies, the people should not believe this.[7]

These and other criticisms emanating from Central Asia of Russia's exaggeration of Taliban power had little impact. The Russian mass media gave generous coverage to bleak and sometimes alarmist assessments. Thus the influential Moscow newspaper *Rossiiskaia gazeta* warned that the long-term impact of the Taliban's rise to power might well mean the forced withdrawal of the Russian army from Central Asia:

[6]   Interfax news agency report, 1 October 1996.
[7]   Quoted in *Inside Central Asia*, no. 141 (30 September-6 October 1996).

The Taliban's successes and their proclamation of an Islamic state are significantly changing the geostrategic situation in the Central Asia region, and this very directly affects Russia's interests. Indeed, it is no accident that the Pakistani authorities are supporting the Taliban as a means of putting pressure upon Iran and India in the struggle for trade routes to the markets of former Soviet Central Asian republics.

Faced with this threat, the presidents of former Soviet Central Asia, observers believe, could unite around Moscow. But it could be that something else will happen: for example, a successful northward advance by the Taliban. Then it would become difficult to hold the Tajik border on the river Pyandzh, and at worst we might have to quit the Central Asian republics, which would mean the exodus of ten million Russian-speaking refugees from the region.[8]

The implications for Central Asia of continuing instability in Afghanistan as well as the prospect from the spring of a renewed and successful Taliban offensive north of the Hindu Kush were the subject of talks held in Tashkent in February 1997 by the defence ministers of four republics (Uzbekistan, Kazakhstan, Tajikistan and Kyrgyzstan) together with Russia's Defence Minister Igor Rodionov. Their discussions preceded but actually obscured the regional summit conference in Almaty convened originally to discuss environmental issues and aspects of the Aral Sea disaster. President Karimov of Uzbekistan warned of an imminent offensive by Taliban forces which might bring them to the very borders of the Central Asian states, and was quoted as stating:

The Taliban, who represent a large aggressive force, are now preparing to take the north in the spring after the snow melts and the roads reopen, in order to be the only representative of all ethnic minorities in Afghanistan. It is difficult to imagine the consequences of the euphoria in which Afghanistan's Taliban forces will be, should they come close to the Amu Darya river.[9]

On behalf of Tajikistan, President Rakhmonov deplored the imminent flood of refugees (claimed as being at least one million) into his republic from the fighting in Afghanistan, going on to criticise the international community's indifference to the grave situation in Afghanistan. 'During the Afghan war in Soviet times, that country was spoken about every minute, while now everyone is silent'.

---

8 *Rossiiskaia gazeta*, 1 October 1996.
9 Interfax and ITAR-Tass news agency reports of late February 1997; and see further *Inside Central Asia*, no. 161 (24 February-2 March 1997).

According to Interfax, three contingency plans were discussed at the closed meeting in Tashkent, one of them being the creation of two motorized army divisions by the CIS states. Rodionov reportedly stated, 'I am approaching our working conference deeply impressed by my conversation with Karimov', as also by Karimov's (unspecified) 'concrete proposals'. Rodionov was quoted as expressing concern over what he described as 'plans by military circles in Afghanistan and Pakistan relating to an escalation of tension on the borders of the Central Asian states, with which Russia is linked by good, close relations'.[10]

The Taliban's northern campaign

When Taliban forces advanced north of the Hindu Kush and claimed in May 1997, after the defection of Abdul Malik, to be on the point of a dramatic breakthrough and virtual takeover of Mazar-e Sharif along with most northern border areas, a further meeting, hastily summoned, of leaders of Central Asian states and Russia warned that a military response was not ruled out. For many observers, this was held to mean possible air strikes against Taliban-held positions from air bases across the border in Central Asia–a pattern which had been very common during the Soviet war in Afghanistan.

It might have been expected that the three Central Asian states with contiguous borders with Afghanistan, totalling 2,000 kilometres in length, would be naturally far more apprehensive about instability and a potential spillover of Islamic activism from Afghanistan than the two more distant republics, Kazakhstan and Kyrgyzstan. However, Turkmenistan–here as in most policy areas–took care to distance itself from the other governments of the region. Of the three states with land borders, it was Uzbekistan, with by far the shortest border, which was most active and vociferous, at once reinforcing anti-tank defences of the bridge over the Amu river border crossing at Termez and soon closing the town to foreign visitors and effectively sealing the border into northern Afghanistan.

More in control of its own remodelled military forces than the other states, as well as being the aspiring regional power, Uzbekistan had its own goals to fulfil. In circles in Tashkent close to the president's office, it was maintained that Uzbekistan was not afraid of the Taliban, nor did it believe the Moscow-promoted idea that the Taliban would go on to cross the borders north of Afghanistan if they secured the entire country. What was feared was the *impact* of any

10 *Inside Central Asia*, no. 173 (19-25 May 1997).

Taliban victory: refugees would flee to the Central Asian states, drugs would flow more easily, and ideological influence would grow in certain groups in Uzbekistan susceptible to Islamic rhetoric.

Uzbekistan had shown itself far more independent of Moscow than either Turkmenistan or Tajikistan could afford to be in foreign policy. Turkmenistan's relationship to Russia has been compared with good reason to that of a colony, where the Niyazov regime relied absolutely upon Russian-controlled military power. Tajikistan's government was too weak and heavily embroiled in its own civil war to have its own independent policy over Afghanistan. With the economy fatally weakened, the Rakhmonov government was bankrupt, and utterly dependent upon Russia and Uzbekistan for its survival. However, confronted with instability and the real possibility of a hostile Islamic regime in control of Afghanistan, the Karimov government aligned itself firmly to Moscow.

After the Taliban started their major northern offensive in May 1997, a nervous reaction set in across the region. With the dramatic realignment of anti-Taliban forces, seen in the open split in General Dostum's party, the Jumbesh, and the declaration of General Abdul Malik in favour of the Taliban, the city of Mazar-e Sharif changed hands on 24 May. Thousands of Taliban were rushed by road to Mazar, to link up with their new allies. Russia announced at once that it would be prepared to take military action to protect the southern borders of the Commonwealth of Independent States. A communiqué declared:

The Russian leadership states that in the event of a violation of CIS borders, the mechanism of the treaty on the collective security of the CIS member states will immediately be brought into effect [...] There is a threat to the security of the CIS countries, above all Uzbekistan and Tajikistan.[11]

From Tehran, where he was attending another round of peace talks intended to end the civil war in Tajikistan, President Rakhmonov expressed 'grave concern' about Afghan developments but went on to assert boldly that border security 'will be ensured in any event; the country has the appropriate forces and means, making it possible to repulse any attempt at armed intervention'. On the issue of refugees fleeing from Afghanistan (both Afghans and Tajik citizens already based there) Rakhmonov admitted the Tajik government was concerned. Although Tajikistan was unable to give refuge to a potentially large number of Afghan refugees who might attempt to cross over, 'the republic will not leave these people in the lurch and will do all it can to help them in every way'. However, he pointed out

11 BBC *Summary of World Broadcasts*, SU/2928/B/8, 26 May 1997.

the obvious fact that in this humanitarian area–as in so many others–
the Tajikistan regime was impotent by itself. 'The main hope in this
respect is pinned on other countries and international organizations'.[12]

In Kyrgyzstan too, separated though it is from Afghan territory by
the buffer of the Gorno-Badakhshan region of Tajikistan, there was
alarm at the apparent collapse of anti-Taliban coalition forces.
President Askar Akayev called an emergency meeting on the Sunday
following the fall of Mazar-e-Sharif, at which it was decided that
military officers and security chiefs should make a tour of inspection
to the Osh region in the south. National Security Minister Felix
Kulov stated that Kyrgyzstan, 'so far sees no direct military threat to
its borders', but did express concern over the prospect of large numbers
of refugees from the fighting in Afghanistan.

As for the Russian border command of 5,000 troops based along
Kyrgyzstan's southern border, a much stronger and sharply contrasting
appreciation of strategic danger was voiced. According to one military
spokesman, Russian border guards had been placed on high alert, and
candidly stated they would not be 'able to protect the southern borders
of the republic on their own against a possible attack by armed
Taliban units'.

Kazakhstan's Foreign Minister Tokayev had warned even before the
flight of Dostum and his loss of Mazar-e Sharif that 'appropriate
political measures' would be taken by the CIS states if the Taliban
forces moved further northwards beyond Afghanistan's border. 'The
Taliban', he stated, 'must fulfil their promises and confirm that they
have no plans to carry out any combat operations against
neighbouring countries'.[13]

Alone among the Central Asian states, Turkmenistan appeared to
take a more sanguine view of Taliban power extending over northern
Afghanistan in areas adjacent to its border. A Turkmen official
spokesman described the situation along the border as stable, going on
to declare that 'Turkmenistan does not expect any complications
caused by the Afghan developments. The country views them
traditionally and hopes for the soonest normalization in the
neighbouring country'. Before the end of the month, President
Niyazov himself offered to help the peacemaking process in
Afghanistan, in conversations held with Pakistan's ambassador in
Ashgabat:

Turkmenistan, in view of its internationally recognized neutral status, is
completely ready to cooperate in the constructive efforts of the Afghan

---

[12] *Inside Central Asia*, no.173 (19-25 May 1997).
[13] Interfax news agency report, 21 May 1997.

people, the international community and the UN in establishing peace and stability in the state as soon as possible.[14]

Turkmenistan had been careful to cultivate good relations with the key regional warlord Ismail Khan as long as he ruled Herat and other northwestern provinces of Afghanistan, helping with supplies of fuel and other items in short supply. There was reportedly no interruption in these smooth relations when Ismail Khan was ousted by Taliban forces in September 1995. For Turkmenistan, the priority in its dealings with Afghan local warlords or any new government of this broken-backed state was clearly construction of the long-awaited gas and oil pipeline routes across Afghanistan to world markets. The growing urgency of the pipeline projects for the Niyazov regime could be measured by the acute financial crisis it faced and the desperate economic straits of the ordinary population, who had been promised wealth beyond their dreams by President Niyazov on independence. Five years on, Turkmens now found that the plentiful gas on which the vaunted 'Kuwait on the Caspian' was to be built could find no foreign-currency clients, and that they lacked even the basic essentials they had been used to in the Soviet era.[15]

A further special meeting on the Afghanistan crisis was held in Moscow on 27 May 1997. Representatives of nine former Soviet republics, all signatories to the CIS Collective Security Treaty of 1992, attended, including Russia, Kazakhstan, Uzbekistan, Tajikistan, and Kyrgyzstan of the Central Asian states, but as usual Turkmenistan stayed away. Statements by Russian officials were often opaque or ambiguous about the military option which might be exercised by Russia. However, the chief of Russia's Federal Border Service, Andrei Nikolayev, declared on 29 May that 'if the situation entails a negative aftermath, more measures will be taken, not military however, but political'.

From the Taliban side, messages from Mullah Mohammad Rabbani were sent to some of the participating governments in an attempt to reassure them that the military offensives in Afghanistan did not constitute any threat to the Central Asian states. Radio Shariat (formerly Radio Kabul) broadcast details of the messages on 29 May:

---

[14] BBC *Summary of World Broadcasts*, SU/2930/G/2, 28 May 1997.

[15] Turkmenistan as a gas exporter still 'remains umbilically connected to Russia', as explained in a cogent analysis of the country's severe economic plight: Helen Boss, *Turkmenistan: Far from Customers who Pay* (London: Paper no.4, Former Soviet South Project, Royal Institute of International Affairs, November 1995), p. 6.

The Islamic Republic of Afghanistan wants the establishment of friendly relations with all countries in the world, especially the neighbourly and regional countries, on the basis of accepted international principles, peaceful coexistence and non-interference in the internal affairs of other countries.[16]

Although regional governments clearly remained anxious over the perceived threat from a Taliban takeover of the whole of Afghanistan, by the end of May Uzbekistan's state media were emphasising that normal conditions, not a dangerous crisis, let alone panic, prevailed along their border with Afghanistan at Termez:

Here, calm prevails. Defenders of our motherland are performing their everyday service as usual. There is calm in the houses, streets and educational establishments near the military units. In short everything is as usual on the territory adjacent to Afghanistan and in Termez.[17]

Arms supplies

Claims and counter-claims of foreign weapons deliveries along with other forms of involvement in the Afghan conflict became more strident in late summer, with renewed heavy fighting for control of northern Afghanistan. While the Taliban claimed that Russia, Uzbekistan and Tajikistan, along with Iran, India and France, were all implicated in arms transfers and help for the northern alliance, spokesmen for the alliance parties maintained that Pakistan had airlifted Taliban reinforcements from Pakistan besides supplying more arms and ammunition. According to the Taliban radio station, Afghan fighter pilots of the northern alliance had flown to Kulyob airbase in southern Tajikistan. 'That airport has been transformed into a base for the Islamic State of Afghanistan's opposition rebel forces. The rebel forces, on instructions of their masters, have ordered those aircraft to take off from that airport and to bombard residential areas in the north of Afghanistan'. The radio went on to 'strongly denounce such intervention by foreign countries and ask the Tajik authorities to return the five aircraft', warning that 'if foreign enemies do not refrain from their open intervention in the internal affairs of our country and continue to intervene, the responsibility for the dangerous consequences stemming from such intervention will rest with the government of Tajikistan and other interventionist countries'.[18]

16 BBC *Summary of World Broadcasts*, FE/2933/A/5, 31 May 1997.
17 Quoted in *Inside Central Asia*, no. 174 (26 May-1 June 1997).
18 BBC *Summary of World Broadcasts*, FE/3023/A/5, 13 September 1997.

Though the government of Tajikistan was directly addressed in this and other complaints, it was common knowledge that Kulyob airbase was actually in the hands of the Russian military responsible for guarding CIS borders. By mid-September, Taliban officials were claiming that this and other foreign interference had reached 'intolerable levels', warning of 'dangerous consequences' in the form of future retaliation. 'We seriously warn the Dushanbe government to stop playing with the fire kindled in Afghanistan by Iranians and Russians'.[19] Russia itself was repeatedly accused of supplying long-range missiles to Ahmad Shah Massoud after eight Frog-7 (Lunar) rockets landed near Kabul airport in mid-September. It was claimed that Yuri Baturin, a senior adviser to Russia's President Boris Yeltsin, had made a recent visit to the Panjsher valley, soon after which missiles were delivered by air.[20] These and other circumstantial reports of 'increasing and flagrant Russian interference' were, however, completely denied by Massoud, who stated that his forces had many Lunar and Scud missiles stockpiled in the Panjsher bases where they had been transported from Kabul the previous year, just before the Taliban capture of the capital.[21] The sudden return in mid-September of the ousted General Dostum from almost four months' exile in Turkey revealed the cracks within Jumbesh ranks, and just how fluid loyalties were. When Taliban forces succeeded on 17 September in taking control of the port town of Hairatan on the Amu Darya border with Uzbekistan, troops from the northern alliance detachment defending Hairatan reportedly fled across the border into Uzbekistan. Although Taliban officials maintained that the Uzbekistan government had a hand in the return of General Dostum, as well as apparently backing northern alliance efforts to regian control of Hairatan, no convincing evidence was offered in support of the allegations. What was certain, though, was that as long as Taliban forces kept control of the port along with its bridge, the simplest supply route for any military supplies being sent from Central Asia or Russia was now effectively blocked.

In analysing and interpreting the diverse statements, speeches and blunt warnings made to the Taliban regime regarding retaliation and an effective military response in the event of cross-border attacks, it should be noted that whether coming from Russia, or the Central Asian capitals–or indeed from Iran–many shrewd observers assess them as being in reality more directed to the two governments of Pakistan and Saudi Arabia than to the Taliban regime as such. It was Pakistan

---

19 Radio Shariat, Kabul, 13 September 1997.
20 BBC *Summary of World Broadcasts*, FE/3026/A/2, 17 September 1997.
21 BBC Radio World Service interview, 15 September 1997.

and Saudi Arabia, together with US oil interests behind the UNOCAL-Delta pipeline project (often held to be backed by the CIA, rightly or wrongly) which were jointly held responsible for coordinating, providing logistics and financing the series of Taliban military successes.[22] It had, indeed, become widely accepted that by these means Iran as well as Russia and its CIS allies were warning Pakistan and Saudi Arabia to rein in their Taliban clients and moderate Taliban attempts to conquer all the northern provinces of Afghanistan adjacent to Central Asian states. Tensions between Afghanistan and its northern neighbours looked likely to continue indefinitely, yet there were also some prospects of improvement by mid-1997. There were obvious potential benefits for all the regional states if peace and stability came to Afghanistan, thus enabling construction of an oil and gas pipeline. In Tajikistan the signing of a peace accord between the rival factions in the civil war (not however the first, nor possibly the last) together with the formation of a Joint Commission to promote harmony in the country and to encourage the return of Tajik refugees and guerrilla fighters from Afghanistan did indeed look more hopeful than many previous failed initiatives. Whether the Central Asian governments or Russia could conquer their own fears and suspicions that Afghanistan under Taliban rule would inspire Islamic activism among their own populations, possibly leading on to political instability or even an Islamic-style revolution, still remained in the nature of things uncertain.

---

[22] See for example, Ahmed Rashid, 'Power Play', *Far Eastern Economic Review*, 10 April 1997, pp. 22-24; and Ahmed Rashid, 'Highly Explosive: renewed fighting alarms Central Asian neighbours', *Far Eastern Economic Review*, 12 June 1997, pp. 24-26.

SAUDI ARABIA, IRAN AND THE CONFLICT IN AFGHANISTAN

Anwar-ul-Haq Ahady

This chapter deals with the interaction of the interests of Saudi Arabia and Iran–two major regional powers–and its impact on the conflict in Afghanistan given their support for opposing factions. Currently, Saudi Arabia is believed to be supporting the Taliban while Iran is backing their opponents. Both countries have strong reasons for their involvement in Afghanistan; but before discussing Iran's and Saudi Arabia's current postures in Afghanistan, it is helpful to review briefly the evolution of their involvement in this conflict.

The development of Iran's and Saudi Arabia's involvement in the Afghan conflict falls into three discernible phases. The first began with the Soviet invasion in December 1979 and ended with the 1988 signing of the Geneva Accords, which provided the framework for the withdrawal of Soviet forces from Afghanistan. The second started with the beginning of the withdrawal of Soviet forces in mid-1988 and ended with the collapse of the Communist regime in April 1992. The third began with the outbreak of the civil war which coincided with the Mujahideen's assumption of power in 1992 and is still in progress as of January 1998. The objectives of both Iran and Saudi Arabia have of course fluctuated; during the last two phases, the conflict between the objectives of these two countries has intensified tremendously, thus hindering the conflict's resolution and increasing its complexity. Although this chapter does not deal with Pakistan's involvement in the Afghan conflict, it is the regional power that is most dominant in Afghanistan. Because Saudi Arabia's involvement in Afghanistan is closely coordinated with Pakistan's policy regarding that country, Saudi Arabia, in its rivalry with Iran, is the beneficiary of Pakistan's dominance in Afghanistan.

Saudi Arabia maintained a very high profile in Afghanistan during 1980-88. Since the Second World War, Saudi Arabia's foreign policy has had three major objectives: the promotion of Islam; guaranteeing

117

the security of the country and the royal family; and general stability.[1] Riyadh felt that its security was threatened by the Soviet invasion of Afghanistan. The Saudis believed that the Soviets had aggressive intentions in the Persian Gulf and that their invasion of Afghanistan was a first step in their desire to control Persian Gulf oil.[2] Even if the Soviets did not intend any direct military action in the Gulf, the Saudis believed that the rise of communism in Afghanistan would promote political instability in the region and hence jeopardise the security of the royal family. Saudi Arabia's distaste for the invasion was fuelled further by the fact that it was against a Muslim country, and that it installed a communist regime in Kabul whose domestic policies were directed against Islam.[3] Thus, for Saudi Arabia, opposition to the Soviet invasion was rational because Soviet behaviour contradicted all the major objectives of Saudi foreign policy.

Saudi Arabia's support for the Afghan resistance was also influenced by the Islamic revolution in Iran. Islam has always had a special importance in Saudi foreign policy. Saudi Arabia has claimed the leadership of the Islamic world since the late 1950s, when Egyptian President Gamal Abdul Nasser's Arab nationalism posed a threat to the legitimacy of the Saudi rulers. To counter Nasser's ideological offensive, Saudi Arabia offered pan-Islamism as an ideological alternative to Arab nationalism. In this connection, Saudi Arabia established the Organization of the Islamic Conference to coordinate the foreign policy of Muslim countries, and the Muslim World League to institutionalise Saudi influence in Muslim cultural and religious activities throughout the world. The defeat of Nasser in the 1967 Arab-Israeli War and the rise of Saudi Arabia as a major financial power in the 1970s established its position as the leader of the Islamic world.[4]

The Islamic Revolution in Iran soon challenged Saudi Arabia's pre-eminence. Indeed, Tehran argued that monarchy was incompatible with Islam and that Saudi Arabia's close relations with the United States

---

[1] For a discussion of Saudi Arabia's foreign policy objectives, see Adeed Dawisha, *Saudi Arabia's Search for Security* (London: Adelphi Paper no. 158, International Institute for Strategic Studies, 1982).

[2] For a discussion of threats from the Soviet invasion of Afghanistan to Persian Gulf security, see Thomas L. McGaugher, *Arms and Oil: U.S. Military Strategy and the Persian Gulf* (Washington DC: The Brookings Institution, 1985), pp. 23-46.

[3] For a discussion of anti-Islamic policies of the communist regime in Afghanistan, see Anwar-ul-Haq Ahady, 'Afghanistan: State Breakdown', in Jack A. Goldstone, Ted Robert Gurr, and Farrokh Moshiri (eds.), *Revolutions of the Late Twentieth Century* (Boulder: Westview Press, 1991) pp. 162-193.

[4] For a discussion of Saudi Arabia's efforts to establish its leadership in the Islamic world, see Dawisha, *Saudi Arabia's Search for Security*, pp. 8-13.

were against the interests of the Muslims. In the 1980s, the Saudi leadership believed that Iran posed a greater threat to its legitimacy than did Nasser's Arab nationalism in the 1950s and 1960s. The Saudi leadership became particularly alarmed when a group of Saudi zealots, asserting the illegitimacy of the royal family, occupied the Grand Mosque in Mecca in 1979.[5]

Period One: 1979-1988

The Afghan conflict allowed the Saudi leadership to strengthen its Islamic credentials at home and to assert Saudi Arabia's leadership in the Islamic world against the challenge from Iran. Saudi Arabia supported the immediate withdrawal of Soviet forces and the right to self-determination of the people of Afghanistan. Saudi Arabia, with the United States, became one of the two major financial backers of the Afghan resistance organisations. For both political and ideological reasons, Saudi Arabia also promoted the Sunni Islamic fundamentalists within the Afghan resistance[6] and deliberately emphasised the Sunni and Shiite division in Islam.[7]

In contrast to Saudi Arabia, even though Iran accepted over two million Afghan refugees and the Soviet invasion threatened its security, during the period 1980-88 Iran played a minor role in the development of the Afghan conflict. This was due to two factors: first, less than a year after the Soviet invasion, the Iran-Iraq War broke out. Iran did not want the Soviets to support Iraq and thus refrained from antagonising the Soviets and maintained a low profile in the Afghan conflict. And second, the struggle for power within Iran between the radical clerics and the democratic nationalists was resolved in the favour of the clerics; this resulted in an Iranian policy that focused on the Shiite cause in Afghanistan instead of the struggle against the Soviet occupation. When democratic nationalists such as Mehdi Bazargan, Abol-Hassan Bani-Sadr, and Sadeq Qutbzadeh were in charge of Iran's foreign policy, Iran did not differentiate between the Shiite and Sunni Afghan resistance organisations. The democratic

---

5 For a discussion of Iran's challenge to Saudi Arabia's leadership of the Islamic world, see Jacob Goldberg, 'Saudi Arabia and the Iranian Revolution', in David Menashri (ed.), *The Iranian Revolution and the Muslim World* (Boulder: Westview Press, 1990), pp. 155-170.

6 See William B. Quandt, *Saudi Arabia in the 1980s: Foreign Policy, Security and Oil* (Washington DC: The Brookings Institution, 1981), pp. 41-46.

7 For a discussion of the intensity of sectarian conflict between the Wahhabis and Shiites, see Martin Kramer, 'Tragedy in Mecca', *Orbis*, vol. 32, no. 2, Spring 1988, pp. 231-247.

nationalists in Iran emphasised the Soviet threat to the security of Iran and the region, and wanted an active role for Iran in the Afghan conflict. In 1981, however, after the triumph of the radical clerics, they focused their efforts on the Afghan Shiites and shied away from confrontation with the Soviet Union. Among the Shiites, Iran decided to weaken the traditionalist resistance organisations and promoted two new pro-Iran Islamic revolutionary groups–Nasr and Sepah–to dominate the Afghan Shiites.[8]

Iran's narrow focus on revolutionary Shiite organisations not only offended the Pakistan-based Sunni resistance, but the more traditional Shiite organisations as well. Indeed, Iran's caution regarding the Soviet Union, and her refusal to commit significant resources to the Afghan hostilities, caused a great deal of dissatisfaction even among the revolutionary Shiite organisations that Iran helped to create–Nasr and Sepah. Although Iran supported the Afghan demands for the withdrawal of Soviet forces, and the right to self-determination for the people of Afghanistan, it did not play any major role in the realisation of these objectives during 1980-88.

Period Two: 1988-1992

The second period in the evolution of the Afghan conflict began with the implementation of the Geneva Accords that stipulated the withdrawal of Soviet forces from Afghanistan. These accords did not address the domestic Afghan conflict, specify the future of the communist regime in Kabul, or determine the form of government that would rule Afghanistan in the future.[9] Thus, the major issue in the period 1989-91 was the role of Najibullah's government and his party, the Hezb-e Watan, in Afghanistan's political future. In this period, the Afghan conflict acquired greater complexity at both the national and regional levels as the objectives of various participants contradicted each other.

At the regional level, period two brought about a visible change in Saudi Arabia's position. After the withdrawal of Soviet forces, Saudi Arabia was no longer concerned about the threat that Afghanistan posed to the security of the Persian Gulf. After the signing of the ceasefire between Iran and Iraq in 1988, nor was the Saudi leadership

---

[8] For a discussion of the evolution of Iran's Afghan policy during period one, see Zalmay Khalilzad, 'Iranian Policy Toward Afghanistan Since the Revolution', in David Menashri (ed.), *The Iranian Revolution and the Muslim World* (Boulder: Westview Press, 1990), pp. 235-241.

[9] For a discussion of the Geneva Accords, see Rosanne Klass, 'Afghanistan: The Accords', *Foreign Affairs*, vol. 66, no. 5, Summer 1988, pp.922-945.

particularly worried about the challenge that Iran's Islamic revolution posed to it. From 1989, Saudi Arabia wanted to consolidate the influence that it had gained during 1980-88 and insisted on the establishment of a pro-Saudi Arabia and pro-Pakistan Islamic government in Kabul.[10] Saudi Arabia was not interested in self-determination for the people of Afghanistan. Riyadh, like Islamabad, believed that a military defeat of the communist regime in Kabul would facilitate the realisation of its objectives in Afghanistan. Thus, from mid-1988 to 1991, Saudi Arabia, like Pakistan, insisted on the military resolution of the conflict.

These changes in Saudi Arabia's (and Pakistan's) position brought about rigorous opposition from Iran. The beginning of period two of the Afghan conflict coincided with the end of the Iran-Iraq war; consequently, Iran could afford to pay greater attention to the war in Afghanistan. Period two also marked the end of direct Soviet military involvement in the conflict and a significant decline in Soviet ambitions in the area. This in turn created a vacuum of power, which Iran believed Pakistan and Saudi Arabia were trying to fill in Afghanistan. Iran thus encouraged the Iran-based Shiite organisations to demand 25 per cent of the representation in the resistance institutions and in any future government in Kabul. The Shiite demand was forcefully rejected by the pro-Saudi and pro-Pakistan Sunni resistance organisations in Peshawar, not least because the Shiites constitute about 12 per cent of Afghanistan's population. Furthermore, the Sunni leadership argued that the Shiites had played an insignificant role in the war against the Soviet occupation forces and so were not entitled to any major role in the future government of Afghanistan. The Saudis (and the Pakistanis) had similar attitudes toward Iran's efforts to gain influence in Afghan affairs. To improve their bargaining position, Iran and the Shiite Afghan organisations cultivated both Najibullah's regime and the Soviets. They also questioned the legitimacy of the Peshawar-based transitional Afghan government and supported the political resolution of the conflict. But in 1989-90, Iran lacked the political influence or military power to frustrate the designs of Saudi Arabia in Afghanistan. The Persian Gulf War of 1990-91, during which the Saudi-backed Afghan resistance groups backed Iraq rather than their patron, led to yet another change in Saudi policy. Saudi Arabia cut off its financial assistance to these organisations and also supported the UN plan for a political resolution of the Afghan conflict.

[10] See Barnett R. Rubin, 'The Fragmentation of Afghanistan', *Foreign Affairs*, vol. 68, no. 5, Winter 1989-90, pp. 150-168; and *Far Eastern Economic Review*, 23 January 1992, p. 22.

Period two of the Afghan conflict coincided with a major change in Iran's foreign policy. During the Khomeini era ideological considerations dominated Iran's foreign policy, but after his death in 1989, Tehran attached greater importance to the interests of the state and Persian nationalism in its foreign policy.[11] This change had a tremendous impact on Iran's involvement in Afghanistan. Thus, in late 1991 Tehran embarked quietly on a new strategy in Afghanistan. It had realised that its emphasis on the rights of the Afghan Shiites was rather narrow and provided Iran with minimal influence in Afghan politics. Furthermore, Iran had observed that with the exception of Burhanuddin Rabbani's Jamiat-e Islami, Pushtuns were dominant in all of the Pakistan-based resistance organisations. This was particularly true of the pro-Saudi organisations. To strengthen its influence among the Persian speaking, but Sunni, Afghans, Iran, in late 1991, signed an agreement with Tajikistan and Afghanistan's Jamiat-e Islami for increasing cultural interaction between the Persian speaking Iranians, Afghans, and Tajiks. It also decided to unite non-Pushtun ethnic minorities into one anti-Pushtun front.

In addition to establishing formal ties with the predominantly Tajik Jamiat-e Islami, Iran also contacted the Ismaili Shiites and the Uzbeks in Afghanistan. Its efforts to form a coalition of anti-Pushtun ethnic minorities proved fruitful when the Tajik commander Ahmad Shah Massoud, Uzbek General Abdul Rashid Dostum, Ismaili Shiite commander Jaffar Naderi, and the Hazara Hezb-e Wahdat, led by Abdul Ali Mazari, formed the Northern Alliance that brought down Najibullah's government days before the scheduled transfer of power to a UN-selected team of neutral Afghans. Most members of this alliance had close relations with Iran, which gave Iran great leverage in Afghan affairs.

Period Three: 1992 to the present

The third period in the evolution of the Afghan conflict began with the downfall of the communist regime in April 1992 and is still in progress. It is characterised by an intense struggle for power among various Afghan groups, the breakdown of the state, and the continuation of the civil war, which has a strong ethnic dimension.

---

[11] For a discussion of realism and idealism in Iran's foreign policy, see R.K. Ramazani, 'Iran's Foreign Policy: Contending Orientations', *The Middle East Journal*, vol. 43, no.2, Spring 1989, pp. 202-217; Hanna Yousif Freij, 'State Interests vs. The Umma: Iranian Policy in Central Asia', *The Middle East Journal*, vol. 50, no. 1, Winter 1996, pp. 71-83; and Henry Precht, 'Ayatollah Realpolitik', *Foreign Policy*, no. 70, Spring 1988, pp.109-128.

Within this period, the first two years were characterised by the decline of American and Russian involvement in the conflict and a corresponding increase in the involvement of regional powers. Although with the disintegration of the Soviet Union, developments in Afghanistan had obvious implications for the newly independent states of Central Asia, during 1992-94, the primary objective of the regional powers' rivalry was to influence events in Afghanistan itself. Since 1994, not only have Russia and America once again become interested in Afghanistan, but Central Asian considerations loom large in the development of the Afghan conflict.

In the immediate aftermath of the collapse of the communist regime, the Northern Alliance of ethnic minorities, led by Commander Ahmad Shah Massoud, emerged dominant. This change in the balance of power within Afghanistan was immediately reflected in the composition of the Mujahideen government that succeeded the communist regime. Massoud and his resistance organisation, Jamiat-e Islami, led by Burhanuddin Rabbani, became the dominant force within the Mujahideen government in Kabul. But they were quickly challenged by the Hezb-e Islami, led by Gulbuddin Hekmatyar, which resulted in the breakdown of the state, outbreak of civil war, and the virtual destruction of Kabul.

In addition to intense rivalry for power among the Afghan groups, conflict among regional powers reached a new height. Soon after the formation of the Mujahideen government, both Saudi Arabia and Pakistan realised that Iran had played a major role in the formation and success of the Northern Alliance whose dominance in the Rabbani administration had tremendously increased Iranian influence in Afghanistan. Saudi Arabia (and Pakistan) did not want direct confrontation with Massoud and Rabbani, but decided to strengthen Hekmatyar and encouraged him violently to contest Massoud's and Rabbani's power in Kabul. Because the Northern Alliance had an anti-Pushtun orientation, during 1992 Saudi Arabia supported the Pushtuns, especially Hekmatyar's Hezb-e Islami. Although the precise extent of Saudi support for Hekmatyar remains unclear, in its June 1993 issue, *The Middle East* reported that in the previous two years Saudi Arabia had spent two billion dollars in Afghanistan, with Hekmatyar as a major beneficiary.[12] In the same period, Iran provided substantial material support for the Northern Alliance.[13]

The period 1992-94 was also characterised by shifting alliances and opportunism on the part of most of the participants. As discussed

[12] See *The Middle East,* June 1993, p. 22.
[13] See *The Middle East International,* 12 June 1992: *FBIS*-NES, 27 January 1993, pp. 72-73.

earlier, the Northern Alliance was made up of the Uzbek force led by General Dostum, the Hazara force led by Mazari, the Ismaili Shiite force led by Naderi, and the Tajik force led by Massoud. Subsequently, the anti-Pushtun members of Najibullah's Watan Party and the armed forces also joined the alliance. Most of Mazari's Hazaras acquired arms with the help of other members of the alliance and of the Iranian embassy in Kabul at the time of the collapse of Najibullah's regime. Because of their new-found military strength and backing from Iran, the Hazaras were able to extract major concessions from Sebghatullah Mojadiddi, the first Mujahideen transitional head of state, who agreed to award three ministerial portfolios, eight seats in the Jihad Council, and one seat in the Leadership Council to the Hazaras. The Hazaras were able to extract similar concessions from Rabbani, the second Mujahideen transitional head of state. However, in late July 1992, relations between the Hazaras and Massoud's forces deteriorated, resulting in heavy fighting between them. The conflict erupted over control of the western part of Kabul. Massoud wanted the government forces (actually his own Shura-i Nazar forces) to control the western part of the city. The Hazaras in Hezb-e Wahdat were loath to relinquish control over the area.[14] The conflict created a difficult situation for Iran, which had good relations with both the Shiite Hazara Hezb-e Wahdat and Massoud-Rabbani. Although Iran condemned the atrocities committed against the Hazaras and provided material aid to the victims of the fighting, it could not take a clear position against the Rabbani-Massoud government.[15]

The Hazara-Massoud conflict, however, facilitated the Hazaras' eventual alliance with Hekmatyar which was conceived despite the fact that during the first few months after the collapse of the communist regime, Pushtuns and Hazaras committed large-scale atrocities against each other. The Sunni Pushtun dominated Hezb-e Islami and the Shiite Hazara Hezb-e Wahdat alliance brought together Afghan groups that were supported by regional rivals, Saudi Arabia (and Pakistan) and Iran. Similarly, the emergence of the Massoud-Hazara conflict facilitated an alliance between Abdul-Rab al-Rasul Sayyaf, the Pushtun leader of the pro-Saudi Ittehad-e Islami, and Massoud, the Tajik leader of Shura-i Nazar, who was initially supported by Iran. In these conflicts, Dostum, the Uzbek leader, changed sides a number of times. Although he supported Rabbani and Massoud in 1992, in early 1993 he tilted toward Hekmatyar and the Hazaras. Dostum's conflict with Massoud and Rabbani was due to his insistence on having a greater share of power in Kabul but not sharing power with Rabbani's

14 See *FBIS*-NES, 21 July 1992, pp. 52-54

15 See *FBIS*-NES, 17 February 1993, p. 52; and 24 February 1993, p. 37.

and Massoud's party–Jamiat-e Islami–in northern Afghanistan. Rabbani and Massoud, on the other hand, desired Jamiat's dominance in the north and a limited role for Dostum in Kabul. In January 1994 Dostum, Hekmatyar, Mazari, and Mojadiddi formed a united front against Rabbani and Massoud. Thus, alliances in this period were extremely fragile and, in their struggle for power, most of the participants preferred opportunism over idealism.

This was also true of Iran's and Saudi Arabia's behaviour. As discussed earlier, Iran was deeply involved in the formation of the Northern Alliance. However, in 1993 and 1994, Massoud, the leader of the Northern Alliance, repeatedly and openly criticised Iran's interference in Afghan affairs. Although in the immediate aftermath of the collapse of the communist regime Iran was the major source of material support for Dostum's forces, after 1992 Dostum distanced himself from Iran. Indeed, for a while, Massoud pursued an anti-Iran and anti-fundamentalist strategy to gain the support of the West. Some observers believe that in addition to conflict over control of the city, Massoud's attack on the Hazaras was motivated by his desire to portray himself as anti-fundamentalist and anti-Iran. This situation, of course, brought Iran and Hekmatyar closer, despite the fact that before the outbreak of hostility between Massoud and the Hazaras, Iran had repeatedly criticised Hekmatyar's stand in the Afghan conflict, and Saudi Arabia's and Pakistan's support for Hekmatyar.[16]

Similarly, to enhance its influence in Afghan affairs, Saudi Arabia tried to establish links with other forces beside Hekmatyar. Thus, Saudi Arabia provided financial support for Dostum, hoping to prevent an alliance between Dostum and Iran.[17] It also cultivated relations with Massoud and Rabbani; Massoud had openly criticised Iranian interference in Afghan affairs. Consequently, during 1993-94 Saudi Arabia provided $150 million in aid to the Rabbani-Massoud government.

The most significant development in the Afghan conflict in 1994 was the rise of the Taliban movement. The overwhelming number of the Taliban are Pushtun Islamic studies students in seminaries in Pakistan and southwest Afghanistan. Most of these seminaries in Pakistan are controlled by the Jamiat-e Ulema-i Islam of Pakistan, led by Maulana Fazlur Rahman. There are two major views about the rise of the Taliban. One theory explains the rapid success of the Taliban in capturing southwest Afghanistan in terms of local conditions such as anarchy, the people's need for security, and the immoral conduct of

---

16 See *FBIS*-NES, 14 July 1992, p. 51; 29 September 1992, p. 40; and 15 September 1992, p. 41.

17 See *FBIS*-NES, 29 January 1993, p. 47; *The Middle East*, June 1993, p. 22.

many warlords. The other theory argues that the Taliban movement was organised by Pakistan to promote her interests in Afghanistan.[18] Probably the combination of the two theories is closer to the truth than either one alone. The rise of the Taliban was certainly a response to the anarchic conditions in the Pushtun-populated areas, but without Pakistan's support, the movement would have not become so powerful as to defeat major warlords.

When the Taliban captured four provinces in the southwest in late 1994, they did not generate much controversy among the regional powers. Even though Pakistan quickly established good relations with the Taliban, Iran did not oppose the movement during the first few months of its rise. The Taliban's conflict with Iran began in March 1995 when the Taliban defeated Hekmatyar's Hezb-e Islami and Mazari's Hezb-e Wahdat forces–both allies of Iran–in the southern and western outskirts of Kabul, murdered Mazari himself, and threatened to capture Kabul from Rabbani and Massoud. It was at this juncture, when the Taliban movement emerged as a serious contender for national power, that Iran began to see the Taliban as an anti-Shia and anti-Iran force.

Consequently, Iran decided to cooperate with Rabbani and Massoud in opposing the Taliban. Rabbani and Massoud welcomed this opportunity to improve relations with Iran because, in spite of their efforts in the previous two years to align themselves with America, the United States was not forthcoming. Meanwhile the Taliban movement had gained control over a very large part of the country and was adamant about capturing Kabul. Iran had taken a public stand against the Taliban and was willing to provide financial and military support to their opponents. Thus, despite the fact that during 1993 and 1994, Massoud had accused Iran of supporting the opponents of the Kabul regime (the 'Council of Solidarity' alliance of Hekmatyar, Mazari, Dostum and Mojadiddi), after March 1995, Iran developed very close relations with Kabul. This change of relations between Iran and Kabul added coherence to Iran's position in western Afghanistan where Iran was supporting Ismail Khan's rule in Herat.

Ismail Khan was a member of the Rabbani-led Jamiat-e Islami organisation and was part of the Kabul administration. Iran's friendship with Rabbani and Massoud also facilitated the rise of an informal alliance between India, Russia, and Iran supporting the

---

18 For views about the identity and the rise of the Taliban, see John F. Burns and Steve LeVine's report in *The New York Times*, 31 December 1996, p.A1, 6; and Hasan Kakar 'Dar barai nawishtahi ghiv masuh shaghali Ghoriani wa digara' [A Response to Ghoriani and others], *Afghan Mellat* (in Persian, published in Peshawar, Pakistan), 13 May 1997, pp. 3-5.

Rabbani-Massoud government in Kabul. Because the major opponents of the Kabul regime–Hekmatyar before 1995 and the Taliban in 1995 and 1996–were supported by Pakistan, India found it very advantageous to strengthen relations with Rabbani and Massoud. Russia had all along had good relations with Massoud. Moscow believed that a radical Islamist government in Kabul would most probably pursue the cause of Islam in Central Asia and undermine Russian interests there. Russia also believed that a Rabbani and Massoud-led government in Kabul was the best insurance against the spread of Islamic fundamentalism in Central Asia. Thus, in early 1995, with the spectacular rise of the Taliban to national prominence, the interests of Iran, India, and Russia converged to support Rabbani and Massoud and to oppose the Taliban.[19]

This rapprochement between Tehran and Kabul, however, led to a deterioration of relations between Riyadh and Kabul. In this new realignment between Afghan contenders for power and foreign powers, Saudi Arabia supported the Taliban. Saudi Arabia's support for the Taliban was consistent with its longstanding policy of opposing Iran and the Shiites, and supporting Pakistan and the Sunni Pushtuns. As in the past, Saudi Arabia's involvement was largely confined to providing financial support.

In September 1995, the Taliban captured Herat. This caused great anger in both Kabul and Tehran as both governments accused Pakistan of military intervention in support of the Taliban. Tehran attached special importance to Herat and considered the presence there of a hostile force such as the Taliban a national security threat. Thus, Tehran reacted strongly to events leading to the capture of Herat by the Taliban and, reportedly, sent a one thousand-strong force to help Ismail Khan's forces against the Taliban.[20]

With the loss of Herat by the pro-Iran Afghan forces, and increasing hostility between Iran and the Taliban, Iran developed an elaborate theory regarding the rise and the objectives of the Taliban. Iran believes that the United States, Saudi Arabia, and Pakistan have cooperated in the creation and the rapid military success of the Taliban. According to Iran, Pakistan has been responsible for the logistics to create the group, Saudi Arabia for financing the movement, and the

---

[19] For a good discussion of convergence of interest between Iran, India, and Russia on the one hand and Pakistan, Saudi Arabia and the United States on the other, see Ahmed Rashid, 'Back with a Vengeance: Proxy War in Afghanistan', *The World Today*, vol. 52, no. 3, March 1996, pp. 60-63.

[20] See *Al-Hayat* (London), 15 May 1995, pp. 1, 6.

United States for the overall strategy.[21] Since 1993 the United States has been pursuing a policy of containment against Iran. It has concluded defence agreements with Gulf Cooperation Council members in the Persian Gulf which are aimed at containing Iran and Iraq there.[22] In 1995 the United States intensified its efforts to isolate Iran further, especially in Central Asia. Iran and Afghanistan are the two gateways to Central Asia.

Shifting interests and strategies

Iran attaches great cultural, political, and economic importance to Central Asia. Iran–Persia–was culturally a significant influence in Central Asia before the Russian conquest of this region. The disintegration of the Soviet Union and the emergence of independent states in Central Asia have revived Iran's ambition for the renewal of its political and cultural influence in these countries. Furthermore, Iran believes that given the development of its transportation facilities, it should serve as the link connecting Central Asia to the outside world. Tehran believes that its relations with Central Asia and the Caucasus states can help defeat the US policy of containing Iran.[23] Thus, Central Asia looms large in Iran's foreign policy. According to Iran, the United States fears its cultural, economic, and political influence in Central Asia and hence would rather support the claims of Pakistan and Afghanistan as the alternative gateway to Central Asia. Pakistan's economic interest in Central Asia depends on its becoming a major route for the transportation of goods to and from Central Asia. Pakistan also sees other great economic opportunities there. Pakistan has already signed agreements with Central Asian countries for

---

[21] See *FBIS*-NES, 7 March 1996, p. 82; and 'Iran Calls for Reconciliation', <http://afg-news.home.ml.org>, 4 October 1996.

[22] For the US policy of containment of Iran, see Martin Indyk, Graham Fuller, Anthony Cordesman, and Phebe Marr, 'Symposium on Dual Containment: U.S. Policy Toward Iran and Iraq', *Middle East Policy*, vol. 3, no. 1, 1994, pp. 1-26. For US efforts to exclude Iran from a Persian Gulf security system, see Anwar-ul-Haq Ahady, 'Gulf Security After Desert Storm', *International Journal,* vol. 49, no. 2, Spring 1994, pp. 219-240.

[23] For Iran's policy in Central Asia, see Freij, 'State Interests vs. The Umma: Iranian Policy in Central Asia'; and John Calabrese, *Revolutionary Horizons: Regional Foreign Policy in Post-Khomeini Iran* (New York: St, Martin's Press, 1994), pp. 75-143.

building highways and railways, but, because of the civil war in Afghanistan, these projects have not been implemented.[24]

Furthermore, since the disintegration of the Soviet Union, large quantities of oil and gas have been discovered in the Caspian Sea area. According to reliable reports, the Caspian Sea area has about 178 billion barrels of oil. Most of this oil belongs, in descending order, to Kazakhstan, Turkmenistan and Azerbaijan. Some of this oil will be exported through the existing pipelines owned by Russia. Iran wants to build pipelines so that a large quantity of Central Asian oil and gas can be exported through Iran.[25] UNOCAL, the California-based oil and gas company, has signed an agreement with Turkmenistan, Afghanistan and Pakistan for the construction of two pipelines which will carry Turkmenistan's gas to Pakistan and her oil to international markets beyond the region.[26] Delta, the Saudi oil and gas company, is UNOCAL's partner in the pipelines project. Iran believes that the United States wants to play an important role in the exploitation of Central Asian oil and gas. The United States also wants large quantities of Central Asian oil and gas to be exported through pipelines that go through Afghanistan and Pakistan. A corollary of this is American objections to pipelines that go through Iran. Thus, the United States' and Pakistan's economic objectives in Central Asia converge. Although Saudi Arabia does not have very strong economic interests in Central Asia, it considers Pakistan and the United States strategic allies and Iran a regional rival. Thus, according to Iran, a counter informal alliance of Saudi Arabia, Pakistan, and the United States has emerged which supports the Taliban in Afghanistan. The Taliban are supposed to defeat pro-Iran Afghan factions, pacify and unify the country, and thus improve the attraction of Afghanistan and Pakistan as an alternative gateway to Central Asia. Iran believes that denying it a significant role in Afghanistan and Central Asia is part of the general US policy of containing Iran.[27]

Consequently, Iran has been very vocal in its opposition to the Taliban and has provided military, financial, and political support for their opponents. Militarily, after the capture of Herat by the Taliban,

---

[24] See Vsevolod Polonsky, 'Taliban Increases Its Presence in Afghanistan', <http://afg-news.home.ml.org>, 12 October 1995; and 'French Expert on Taliban Role', <http://afg-news.home.ml.org>, 3 October 1996.

[25] See Freij, 'State Interests vs. The Umma: Iranian Policy in Central Asia', pp. 81-82.

[26] See Ralph H. Magnus, 'Afghanistan in 1996: Year of the Taliban', *Asian Survey*, vol. 37, no. 2, February 1997, pp. 111-117.

[27] See 'Washington's Benign Views of Taliban', <http://afg-news.home. ml.org>, 11 November 1996.

Iran reportedly created an 8,000-strong force which was supposed to support Ismail Khan against the Taliban. In this connection, in 1996, some reports indicated that Iran might launch a major offensive in western Afghanistan against the Taliban. Furthermore, Iran provided two billion Afghanis–Afghanistan's currency–to Ismail Khan to buy off some of the Taliban commanders. Although Ismail Khan was captured by the Taliban in May 1997, the existence of the 8,000-strong force that Iran has created remains a potent threat to the Taliban.[28]

Similarly, after the capture of Herat by the Taliban, Iran redoubled its efforts to strengthen the Rabbani-Massoud government in Kabul, in particular by establishing an air bridge between Mashad and Bagram to supply the Rabbani-Massoud regime with necessary military and civilian goods. India also flew in its material support to the Rabbani-Massoud regime through Iran. Of course, Russia remained the major supplier of weapons to the Rabbani-Massoud regime.[29]

Politically, Iran intensified its efforts to persuade all pro-Iran Afghan factions to participate in the Rabbani-Massoud government in Kabul. As discussed earlier, between 1992 and 1995, the major contenders for power in Afghanistan were the Jamiat-e Islami, led by Rabbani and Massoud, and the Hezb-e Islami, led by Hekmatyar. In spite of their common ideology–Islamism–relations between these two organisations had usually been hostile. Indeed, after the Mujahideen victory over the communists in 1992, the breakdown of the state, and the outbreak and continuation of the civil war were largely the consequences of the inability of these two organisations and their leaders to cooperate with each other in ruling the country. Iran has had friendly and hostile relations with both organisations at different times. After the capture of Herat by the Taliban, it engaged in tireless diplomacy to reconcile Hekmatyar and Rabbani.

Iranian efforts finally paid off in early 1996 when Hekmatyar agreed to serve as Prime Minister in a government headed by Rabbani. Iran argued with the Afghan Islamists that unless they cooperated with each other, the United States would marginalise all Islamist groups. In this respect, Iran's efforts were helped by the Pakistani Islamists, especially the leader of the Jamaat-e Islami of Pakistan, Qazi Hussain Ahmad, who has been a longtime supporter of Hekmatyar. After the capture of Herat by the Taliban, Hussain Ahmad subscribed to the Iranian view that the United States aimed at marginalising the Islamist groups in the region, and at isolating Iran, and that the Taliban served

---

[28] See *Dawn*, 21 February 1996, p. 1.
[29] See *Al-Hayat* (London), 22 April 1997, pp. 1, 6.

American interest in the region.[30] Hussain Ahmad used his influence with Hekmatyar and helped Iran to reconcile him with Rabbani. Iran was very satisfied with this outcome, and accused the United States of trying to undermine Iran's success by pushing for a political solution of the Afghan conflict outside the framework of the pro-Iran Rabbani-Hekmatyar government.[31] During the summer of 1996, Iran persuaded the Shiite Hezb-e Wahdat to join the new government. There were reports that General Dostum might also join the new government.

Iran seems to have a clear strategy regarding Afghanistan. Ideally, it prefers pro-Iran Afghan factions to dominate the government in Kabul. If such an objective cannot be realised, Iran insists that at least some pro-Iran Afghan groups be included in the government. It does not want a pro-West and anti-Iran government in Kabul and believes that its influence in Kabul will help the realisation of its objectives in Central Asia. Iran accepts Pakistan's role in Afghanistan but opposes American and Saudi Arabian influence in Afghanistan. It believed that the Rabbani-Hekmatyar government was compatible with its interest in Afghanistan.

However, the Rabbani-Hekmatyar government was not even four months old when the Taliban consolidated their hold on all Pushtun-populated provinces and captured Kabul in September 1996. This was probably the most significant political change in Afghanistan since the collapse of the communist regime in 1992. The Taliban gained control over two-thirds of the country, including the capital, and their opponents were pushed so far back that they could not hit Kabul with artillery fire or rockets. Of course, the loss of Kabul by the pro-Iranian forces was a devastating blow to Iran's power in Afghanistan. As expected, Iran once again accused Saudi Arabia, Pakistan, and the United States of helping the Taliban to capture Kabul. Not only did it not recognise the Taliban government, but it insisted that Rabbani was the legitimate head of the Afghan state. To prevent the consolidation of power by the Taliban throughout the country, Iran continued its financial and military support for the Tajik Massoud, the Shiite Hazara Hezb-e Wahdat, and for the Uzbek General Dostum. India and Russia also continued their support for Massoud. Among other weapons, Russia provided twelve airplanes to Massoud and must have advised Tajikistan to allow Massoud to operate an airport in Kolyob, inside Tajikistan.[32]

---

[30] See *FBIS*-NES, 8 August 1996, p. 31.
[31] See *Kayhan International,* 8 July 1996, pp. 7-8; and *FBIS*-NES, 28 June 1996, p. 52, and 1 July 1996, pp. 59-70.
[32] See *Al-Hayat* (London), 22 April 1997, pp. 1, 6.

The influence of the wider world

The counter informal alliance of Pakistan, Saudi Arabia and the United States seems to be supporting the Taliban. In addition to frequent charges from Iran, India and Russia regarding Pakistan's military support for the Taliban, numerous reputable journalists have also reported strong military support from Pakistan for the Taliban.[33] Although there is no hard evidence to substantiate Saudi Arabia's support for the Taliban, the Taliban must be receiving some financial support to sustain their military operations. Pakistan simply does not have the kind of financial resources to support the military activities of an Afghan faction which is opposed by Iran, Russia and India. Therefore, most probably, Saudi Arabia is providing the financial support for military operations.[34] Similarly, although the United States publicly supports the political resolution of the Afghan conflict, and occasionally criticises the insensitivity of the Taliban to women's rights and human rights, the official US position regarding Afghanistan can be interpreted as qualified support for the Taliban.[35] Furthermore, when the Taliban captured Kabul, the California-based oil company UNOCAL immediately issued a statement asserting that this was a positive development for peace and the implementation of the pipeline project in Afghanistan.[36] The strongest support for the validity of the assertion that the Taliban are supported by the United States, Pakistan, and Saudi Arabia came from the former Prime Minister of Pakistan, Benazir Bhutto, who, on 14 October 1996 told the BBC that 'the United States and Britain supplied weapons to the Taliban on money provided by Saudi Arabia'. Bhutto also added that the Taliban movement 'met the interests of Pakistan, too'.

Thus, there seems to be a convergence of interests between the United States, Pakistan, and Saudi Arabia favouring the Taliban in Afghanistan. This informal alliance seems to be based on relatively strong strategic interests which have survived at least one major change in government. Thus, even though during the recent election campaign, candidate Nawaz Sharif announced that, if elected, his

---

[33] On Pakistan's military involvement in Afghanistan, see *The New York Times,* 31 December 1996, pp. A1, 6; and Roger Howard's report, <http://afg-news.home.ml.org>, 31 May 1997.

[34] On Saudi Arabia's financial support for the Taliban, see 'Washington's Benign Views of Taliban'.

[35] For indirect US support for the Taliban, see *FBIS*-NES, 3 November 1995, p. 56; 'Washington's Benign Views of Taliban'; 'French Expert on Taliban Role'; and the statement by Robin Raphel, US Assistant Secretary of State for South Asia, at the UN Meeting on Afghanistan on 18 November 1996.

[36] See Magnus, 'Afghanistan in 1996: Year of the Taliban', pp. 116-117.

government would review Pakistan's policy in Afghanistan, Prime Minister Sharif has not changed former Prime Minister Benazir Bhutto's policy of supporting the Taliban. Indeed, Pakistan's willingness to risk friendly relations with Iran and allow India to develop very close relations with Iran,[37] indicates the strategic strength of this informal alliance between Pakistan, Saudi Arabia, and the United States.

Afghanistan does not have surplus resources to support the continuation of the civil war. Foreign interference, especially foreign financial assistance to various contenders for power, is a major cause of the continuation of the civil war in Afghanistan. Foreign powers also prevent a quick victory by any Afghan faction. Whenever one group comes closer to prevailing over its opponents, foreign support enables the opposition to resist and to establish a new and short-lived equilibrium.

After the capture of Kabul by the Taliban in September 1996, a new military stalemate between the Taliban and their opponents emerged in January 1997. In this stalemate, the Taliban had control over 70 per cent of the country, Massoud over two provinces, Hezb-e Wahdat over one province, and General Dostum over six provinces, all north of the Hindu Kush mountains. Iran and Russia were instrumental in enabling the opponents of the Taliban to resist any further territorial expansion by the organisation.

This stalemate was broken when on 19 May 1997, General Abdul Malik defected from Dostum and formed an alliance with the Taliban. Apparently, Pakistan had a major role in striking a deal between the Taliban and General Abdul Malik.[38] General Abdul Malik's defection quickly led to the capture of Mazar-e Sharif on 25 May 1997 by the joint forces of the Taliban and General Malik. Had the alliance not been broken on 28 May 1997, this would have been the beginning of the end of the civil war and the reunification of the entire country under the Taliban. Such a consolidation of power by the Taliban would have been a major gain for Pakistan, Saudi Arabia, and the United States, and a major setback for Iran, Russia, and India. That is why immediately after the capture of Mazar-e Sharif by the joint forces of Taliban and Malik, Pakistan, Saudi Arabia and the United Arab Emirates quickly recognised the Taliban government. The United

---

[37] For growing differences between Pakistan and Iran over the Taliban, see *The Muslim*, 17 November 1995, pp. 1, 4. For closer relations between India and Iran, see Shireen T. Hunter, *Iran and the World* (Bloomington: Indiana University Press, 1990), pp. 131-139; and Calabrese, *Revolutionary Horizon*, pp. 125-130.

[38] For the text of the Taliban-Malik agreement, see 'Afghan Reconciliation on the Cards', <http://afg-news.home.ml.org>, 7 June 1997.

States also signalled that it would accept any Taliban-appointed diplomat to Afghanistan's mission in Washington DC.[39] In contrast, Iran encouraged the Shiite Hezb-e Wahdat to challenge the Taliban in Mazar-e Sharif and when the Taliban alliance with General Abdul Malik broke down, Iran was instrumental in forging an alliance between the Uzbek forces of General Abdul Malik, the Shiite Hazara forces of Hezb-e Wahdat, the Ismaili Shia forces of Jaffar Naderi, and the Tajik forces of Ahmad Shah Massoud. This new northern alliance of ethnic minorities attacked the predominantly Pushtun Taliban forces in Mazar-e Sharif, Shibar, Pul-e Khomri, and Jabal Saraj, inflicting very high losses on them. According to some reports, the Taliban lost (casualties and prisoners) between one and ten thousand fighters.[40] This is the most serious military reversal for the Taliban. The informal alliance of Iran, Russia, and India is once again trying to provide enough support for the opposition to deny the Taliban control over the entire country. During the first two weeks after the break-up of the Taliban-Malik alliance, Iran and Russia, respectively, provided twenty and forty airplane loads of ammunitions and weapons to opponents of the Taliban.[41]

Thus, the stakes are very high in the struggle for influence in Afghanistan. After the end of the Cold War, Afghanistan had lost its strategic importance. But the breakup of the Soviet Union, the emergence of Central Asian states, the discovery of large quantities of oil and gas in the Caspian area, the US policy of containment against Iran, Iran's determination to be an influential power in Central Asia, and the possibility that Afghanistan can be an alternative gateway to Central Asia, all have revived Afghanistan's strategic importance for Iran, India, and Russia on the one hand, and Saudi Arabia, Pakistan, and the United States on the other. Both of these informal alliances still believe that they can prevail in Afghanistan. Both informal alliances seem to be willing to spend a considerable amount of resources to deny their opponents a conclusive victory. This does not bode well for peace and stability in Afghanistan. Most probably, the conflict will continue for quite a while, not only because of quarrels among Afghans, but also because of intense rivalry between foreign powers, including Saudi Arabia and Iran.

---

[39] See *The Washington Post,* 29 May 1997, p. 29
[40] See *Associated Press* report, 31 May 1997.
[41] See 'Afghan Reconciliation on the Cards'.

DILEMMAS OF HUMANITARIAN ASSISTANCE IN AFGHANISTAN

Michael Keating

There can be little doubt about the profundity of Afghanistan's humanitarian crisis. The country holds Asia's or the world's worst records in a number of fields, including infant and maternal mortality, life expectancy, adult and female literacy, access to safe water, the estimated number of land mines, the proportion of mentally or physically disabled people, the numbers dependent upon food support, and the number of refugees and internally displaced people. It is estimated that well over a million people have been killed, and 700,000 women made widows in the fighting over the last 18 years.

Facts are scarce, but the evidence, as any visitor to the country will confirm, speaks for itself. The difficulties in gathering data are such that Afghanistan was actually dropped from rankings in the 1997 edition of the *UN Development Report*. This relegation is perhaps symbolic–of the lack of international interest in Afghanistan's social problems, and of the ignorance about how Afghan society is coping, or failing to cope, with its continuing nightmare.

The days when Afghanistan was glamorous for the aid community have long gone. In the years immediately after the Soviet invasion, there was a cause–to show solidarity with the underequipped rural Mujahideen's resistance to the blunt might of the Soviet Army–that attracted not only every self-respecting war reporter but thousands of humanitarian aid workers, many of whom had visited and fallen in love with the country and its people as tourists. They were prepared to endure terrible hardship and danger to bring basic services, usually medical, to embattled communities. There was an innocence about assistance that gradually evaporated as the 1980s wore on and as aid became less a gesture of solidarity and more enveloped in politics, particularly once the US stepped up its involvement in the war from the middle of the decade.

Today, there is little innocence left. There is no obvious cause, other than the purely humanitarian. The aid community has become less idealistic, more self-conscious, more wary of its own role and the impact that its activities are having on Afghanistan. In part, this is owing to recognition that, in a country whose industrial productivity has collapsed and employment market evaporated, the aid industry is no longer peripheral; after agriculture, it is the second biggest sector of what is left of the licit economy. Dilemmas for humanitarians abound. Some of these predate the arrival of the Taliban on the scene, but nearly all have been intensified by their arrival.

Key dilemmas

The most fundamental is whether the humanitarian effort is contributing to–or at least facilitating–the conflict. There is something both alarming and perverse about the possibility that the net effect of the assistance effort may be to make it easier for the authorities to sidestep or abdicate their responsibility for the welfare of ordinary people.

It is an open question to what degree authorities in Afghanistan have ever seen provision for the social welfare of the population to be a basis of their legitimacy, notwithstanding Islamic injunctions and tradition in this regard. Certainly, during the days of the Soviet occupation, the Mujahideen were not noted for giving social issues a priority. In the late 1980s, when aid funds seemed abundant, dozens of Afghan NGOs came into being under the aegis of the resistance parties. Although some were staffed by Afghan technocrats with the noblest motives, many seemed to exist to soak up funds rather than to deliver any verifiable service. The availability of funding for NGOs in any case owed much to the West's overall political objective of supporting the resistance to eject the Soviets from Afghanistan.

But even today, when there is no such political motor to drive Western donor generosity, aid workers cannot help but wonder what the political impact of their hard work is. One Western ambassador came back from a trip to Kabul in September 1997 with a story to illustrate the point. He was kept awake much of the night by successive planes landing and taking off from the airport–presumably not delivering cuddly toys. Bleary eyed, in the morning he met medical NGO workers struggling to resist pressure from the Taliban authorities who were demanding that they pay the salaries of government health workers.

Some would argue that the Taliban have repeatedly demonstrated powerful commitment to the welfare of the population–that indeed, this has motivated their cause from the beginning. The Taliban themselves repeatedly point out that security has improved, particularly for women, in areas under their control. But the Taliban's and international community's notions of what comprises social wellbeing are hardly comparable. Attendance at mosques and provision of facilities for female medical patients cannot be measured on the same scale.

But one might argue that the Taliban–and other Afghan leaders–are not alone. Their abdication of what is normally thought of as social responsibility is matched by the failure of the international community to accept responsibility for the overall humanitarian crisis. As is argued elsewhere in this book, the Afghan conflict has been characterised by an extraordinarily high degree of external interference. There would appear to be little domestic or international pressure upon those governments interfering in Afghanistan's internal affairs to desist, even though such governments are often paying a high price as a result of the continuation of the Afghan war, as smuggling, corruption, drug addiction, and terrorism seep back into their own lands.

Exasperated aid workers often ask why greater pressure is not brought to bear on Afghanistan's neighbours to create the external conditions for peace. It is difficult not to assume that Afghanistan simply no longer matters–that it is merely a dim flicker on the global geopolitical radar screen. And that to the degree that it does matter, the suffering borne by hundreds of thousands of Afghans is of little consequence in the larger scheme of things.

This naturally raises another dilemma. Should the international community's political activities be more integrated with its social, economic and development work, or might that risk compromising and politicising humanitarian activities?

In the late 1980s, UN humanitarian and development workers were under instruction to make a clear distinction with Afghan interlocutors between their work and that of the high level political negotiators such as Diego Cordovez. But by late 1997, with the work of the UN Special Mission on Afghanistan apparently going nowhere, and the Taliban showing steely determination to achieve a military solution, the separation is often described as a disconnect. Whether because of the mandate handed to the UN Special Mission on Afghanistan, or the manner in which its Head has chosen to animate it, the perception is that, at least until the involvement of Ambassador Lakhdar Brahimi, UN peacemaking efforts had for too long been confined to a narrow and fruitless world characterised by ceasefires, exchanges of prisoners and talks about talks.

Reservations about the UN's agenda

Reservations about the UN's political role have raised doubts on a number of scores. First were doubts that issues relating to the deteriorating conditions under which humanitarian workers are obliged to operate were not being pursued by the Head of the Special Mission–the assumption being that only he was in a position to do so with sufficient authority. Second were concerns that the whole issue of human rights and gender raised by the Taliban–and for many, long overdue in Afghanistan--were not being factored into political discussions with Afghan leaders. But third, and most substantially, were worries that the UN was failing to address the bigger picture–the geopolitical and economic context within which both the conflict and the assistance effort take place.

The perceived disconnect is therefore between the international community's professed concern for the victims of the conflict and its failure, through its chosen vehicle, the UN Special Mission on Afghanistan, to square up to and open dialogue with the parties, whether in neighbouring states or with their powerful allies, whose actions, or failure to act is, arguably, prolonging the war. But how, in operational terms, might the reconnect be made?

Any suggestion that aid be a bargaining counter in the pocket of the UN political negotiator raises the contentious issue of the validity of making aid subject to conditionality. Few would dispute that it is quite reasonable for the international community to hold out the prospect of major reconstruction funding as a carrot to bring parties to the table. But the apparent disregard of the authorities for aid, and the absence of development funding, means in reality that the only bargaining counter is humanitarian assistance.

The International Committee of the Red Cross has traditionally had a clear and fixed position--that political considerations should in no way compromise the provision of humanitarian assistance or prevent the agency from reaching people in need. This position is being tested to breaking point by the Taliban–for example, in their insistence that female health facilities be segregated, regardless of the resource and practical implications that this has for those trying to meet women's needs. If the ICRC is compelled to suspend some of its activities, it is more likely to be on grounds of breach of contract than human rights, such is the agency's commitment to fulfilling the humanitarian imperative. But the UN has a far less fixed position, and has found itself dancing around this dilemma for years.

The issue of conditionality is the slipway to a further set of dilemmas. The subject of conditionality more usually arises in the context of human rights and the treatment of women. Is it reasonable or realistic to expect the public and politicians in Western countries to provide aid to a country whose authorities have regressive human rights and gender policies? The closer to the field one gets, the less obvious the answer to this question becomes.

The challenge of the Taliban

The Taliban are not the first Afghan authorities to abuse human rights, and it is often remarked that little concern was expressed by

Western politicians in the past, either in the 1980s or more recently since the rise of the Taliban–until they shocked the world by capturing Kabul. Not much notice was paid in early 1996 when in Herat the Taliban refused to meet female staff from aid agencies, banned all women from working except in the health sector and refused to countenance any discussion about reopening girls' schools. Nor, one might argue, do politicians seem to be so vociferous about official gender discrimination in other countries, least of all important oil-rich Muslim ones.

Others point out that while the Taliban have totally unacceptable attitudes towards the place and role of women in society, even by Islamic standards, the impact of these is confined to Kabul and a few areas of the major towns. They argue that the Taliban, like waves of Afghan ideologues before them, including the communists, are few in number and neither have the power, nor can afford, to alienate the vast majority of the population, with whom they have reached a *modus vivendi*. This has meant, for example, that where female education is locally valued, it is permitted. Indeed, a study by the Swedish Committee for Afghanistan in the summer of 1997 showed that the proportion and total number of females in SCA schools in six southern provinces had actually increased over the last 10 years.[1]

But whatever the mitigating circumstances, the brazenness of Taliban gender policies can only be received as an insult to the women–and, one would hope, men–of the world who have struggled for equal opportunity and the full realisation of human rights. On the spot, there is broad consensus on the need to adopt a principled but non-confrontational attitude towards Afghan authorities over the issue of women. But explaining the nuances of this to a distant public which consumes news reports that verge from the horrific to the ridiculous about restrictions upon women will be an almost impossible task. This dilemma is here to stay.

However, aid agencies could make their lives easier. Many demonstrate remarkably little understanding of who the Taliban are, and the Pushtun culture from which they spring. This is a poor basis for any form of dialogue, whatever the intended outcome. The range of responses to Taliban edicts by aid agencies has created confusion and given the impression, which in some cases may be fair, that agencies are not themselves committed to respecting and implementing international human rights norms and standards. The Taliban

---

[1] See A.W. Najimi, *Report on a Survey on SCA Supported Girls' Education and SCA Built School Buildings in Afghanistan in Regions under Southern and Eastern SCA Regional Management* (Peshawar: Educational Technical Support Unit, Swedish Committee for Afghanistan, 29 August 1997).

themselves have grounds for accusing the agencies, some of whom do not exemplify commitment to gender equity in their own staffing and operations, of inconsistency and even hypocrisy.

The issue of conditionality is made no easier by the difficulty of drawing the line between humanitarian and non-humanitarian assistance. Where does rehabilitation fit in? No-one would dispute that providing emergency food to the hungry is an activity protected from any form of conditionality by International Humanitarian Law. But what about giving the hungry the means–an income, perhaps some tools, or help with irrigation, or seed and fertiliser–to reduce their dependency upon handouts? Is it even ethical, whatever the political hue of the authorities, to limit aid to humanitarian assistance when it is clear that rehabilitation work is both possible and arguably essential to preventing hundreds of thousands of Afghans from becoming beggars on their own land?

But perhaps the biggest dilemma of all facing the assistance collectivity is how to deal with a group which claims to be a government and which controls most of the country, but which, in reality, is more usefully described as a movement and which has demonstrated no significant administrative capacity.

The internal dynamic of the Taliban movement remains obscure to outsiders and makes the Chinese politburo look transparent. Aid agencies, not least the UN, naturally seek governmental counterparts but are repeatedly frustrated by what they see as the indifference or ignorance of Taliban authorities towards them and the sectors in which they work–whether in health, education, agriculture or otherwise. Communication between ministries would seem to be rare, and agreements struck with officials in Kabul often seem to hold no sway either in other parts of the country or, in some cases, in the street outside. The Taliban do little to support what remains of the country's demoralised civil service which, amazingly, manages to carry on in some cases.

How should the aid community react to this absence of governmental interlocutor? It has done so in a variety of ways–for example, at one extreme, by bypassing central authorities altogether; or by treating them as a source of, effectively, non-objection certificates but certainly not as an administrative partner; or, at the other extreme, by seeking Taliban endorsement and involvement in programming decisions.

There are other problems which at first glance may seem lesser in scale but which pose enormous practical and political dilemmas. Much of the assistance community, the ICRC being a notable exception, is based in a neighbouring country, Pakistan. There are good practical and political reasons for this. But it makes simply travelling to Afghanistan an almost political act. Moreover, there is nothing like being on the spot, in the Afghan environment, for decision making and inevitably there is something artificial about assistance by remote control. The logistical and communication problems are formidable and compounded by the absence of Afghan infrastructure.

Another formidable problem is finding and supporting female UN or NGO staff, Afghan or international. Working inside Afghanistan is not easy for anyone, and infinitely more difficult for women in the current environment. Security is one issue. In addition, special arrangements are needed tor local transportation, in offices, and at meetings. Agencies have long discussions about how far they should go to respond to local authorities' diktats or sensitivities. At what point do practical arrangements become unprincipled accommodation, or amount to an abandonment of educated Afghan women's own liberal traditions, which have just as much validity as other Afghan traditions?

The eyes of the world

Many of these dilemmas are common to other prolonged crises but in Afghanistan they seem to be in sharper focus than elsewhere. This may in part be due to sustained international media interest in Afghanistan, largely limited to the military situation and to reporting of restrictions upon women by the Taliban. Their introverted ways and zealotry never cease to intrigue and outrage world public opinion. Indeed, the Taliban's beliefs and behaviour, powerfully advertised in a series of incidents such as the stringing up of former President Najibullah from a traffic light in downtown Kabul or, more recently, the detaining of European Commissioner Emma Bonino and CNN star correspondent Christiane Amanpour, seem to have an almost mesmeric fascination in a world preoccupied by altogether more mundane concerns.

There may be greater focus on Afghanistan too, certainly for those in the world of international relations and aid, as the result of a decision by an obscure but powerful UN committee to single out Afghanistan as a test case for improving the world's ability to address and resolve the problems of countries in crisis.

In April 1997, the Administrative Committee on Coordination, which includes the UN Secretary-General and the executive heads of UN programmes, specialised agencies, the World Bank and the IMF, met in Geneva for one of its regular meetings. Its members agreed to strengthen efforts in crisis countries where the UN operates political programmes mandated by the Security Council or the General Assembly. It chose two countries as test cases–Afghanistan and Mozambique (although the latter was subsequently changed). Sadako Ogata, UN High Commissioner for Refugees, was said to have been the most vocal in support of the choice of Afghanistan, not that surprising as Afghans represent one of the largest and oldest refugee caseloads in the world.

The decision by Administrative Committee on Coordination members to choose Afghanistan was a happy one in that, probably unbeknown to them, much had been going on in the region already to bring all the players in the international aid community together to address some of these very dilemmas. In January 1997 an international forum had taken place in Ashgabat, Turkmenistan, to try to get some consensus on the objectives, principles and elements of external assistance to Afghanistan.

But whether the Administrative Committee on Coordination had quite realised what it was taking on by choosing Afghanistan is another question. The Taliban phenomenon has added a further dimension to all the dilemmas that the international community is facing in 'failed states'. Some of these dilemmas will never be resolved but a concerted attempt is now being made in Afghanistan at least to manage them better. The Strategic Framework for Afghanistan, prepared in late 1997, which resulted from the Administrative Committee on Coordination decision, is a major step forward in this regard. It attempts to make explicit the responsibilities for the prolongation of the social, economic and humanitarian crisis in Afghanistan, and to place the assistance community's work in a realistic geopolitical and economic context. It proposes a holistic approach in which political and non-political efforts to achieve peace inform each other and in which the aid community's work is based upon recognition of comparative advantage, common identification of needs, agreement as to priorities and consistent implementation of human rights principles and norms.

More specifically, it makes a number of proposals, including a common vision for the whole assistance community: the creation of productive livelihoods; a single assistance programme for all actors, operating under a single board of stakeholders; a unitary funding mechanism; an independent monitoring and evaluation mechanism; and an enhanced coordination role for the UN, both at the national and regional level inside Afghanistan. This, of course, is heady and radical stuff with implications not just for the way the international community works inside Afghanistan but for its business in all complex emergency countries.

Inevitably there will be resistance to this agenda. Some donors, no matter how much they may bay for reform of the UN, will resist or baulk at the implications of a unitary funding mechanism for assistance to Afghanistan if only because the money comes from so many different bureaucratic sources, each with their own regulations and procedures. An additional complication may also be posed by the enhanced role being offered to donors as stakeholders; being absent from Afghanistan, many simply do not have the local capacity to respond. Many donors are also likely to be sensitive to the concerns of their national NGOs, some of whom, in the absence of a diplomatic community inside Afghanistan, have exceptional influence in shaping donor foreign policies.

The NGOs are often the most critical of the UN's performance in the field. They consider the UN to be expensive, cumbersome and having staff ill-suited to the difficult jobs they have been given. Some NGOs have a better institutional memory than UN agencies and are highly critical of the UN's overall performance in the last decade–beginning with the UN's heralding of a massive, and as it turned out, totally premature reconstruction programme after the Geneva Accords were signed, continuing through to the Action Plan for Immediate Rehabilitation which was overshadowed by a particularly vicious, and perhaps the most destructive, phase of the civil war, through to UNDP's PEACE Initiative, launched in early 1997 in which, as with previous UN plans, they felt they had little input. Their wariness about the Strategic Framework process is therefore hardly surprising.

NGOs, particularly international, have also been critical of the apparent inability of UN agencies to coordinate among themselves, particularly the way in which the UN has handled the Taliban phenomenon, not least of all in the fields of education and health care. They have seen the way different UN agencies have interpreted the various thunderous proclamations from distant headquarters on how to handle the human rights and gender issues and are exasperated by what they consider to be the accommodation that WHO in particular has reached with the Taliban authorities.

It is therefore no surprise that NGOs are unlikely to be thrilled at the prospect of the UN taking on an even greater coordination function–let alone the idea that assistance funding to them should be through a unitary funding mechanism. Nor will they be easily persuaded by the UN's offer to include them in overall management and policymaking–firstly, because they doubt some UN agencies' integrity in this regard, and secondly because they are the first to admit the problems that NGOs themselves face in reaching common positions, or in representing themselves through a single body.

Existing NGO coordination structures, notably the Peshawar-based Agency Coordinating Body for Afghan Relief, or ACBAR, despite funding problems, have proved to be invaluable networking, information exchange and policy fora, but none can claim to be representative of the geographically and culturally diverse range of NGO bodies. Indeed, most would argue that it is the variety of NGOs–Western, Islamic, Afghan, rights-centred, delivery-focused, emergency-oriented, developmental, and so on–that constitutes the sector's strength, and that to attempt to homogenise this group for whatever purpose is both impractical and counterproductive.

But ironically, the greatest resistance to the proposals being made in the Strategic Framework will probably be from within the UN. Despite the operational flexibility that many UN agencies have shown inside Afghanistan, most are notoriously protective of their mandates, resistant to fundamental change, and suspicious of predatory behaviour by their sister agencies. Within Afghanistan, effective coordination will be possible if the individuals involved have a positive attitude towards coordination, and if a relatively new discipline–professional coordination–is given a chance to work.

The higher up the UN system one goes, the more resistance there will be, as institutional agendas and executive egos clash. Ultimately, the authority of the Secretary-General, backed up by Member States, will be needed to push through the agenda being proposed in the Strategic Framework. But even then, cynics–or sages–will warn against any underestimation of the independence of individual agencies, many having their own executive boards consisting of governmental representatives who may or may not have any truck with their compatriots or peers on other executive boards.

Afghanistan is thus currently the crucible for many dilemmas facing the global assistance community, including how to operationalise UN human rights and gender equity principles, how to reconcile these principles with the dictates of International Humanitarian Law, how to reorder the way in which the assistance actors work with each other in complex emergency situations, and how to re-energise and reform the UN, not least with a view to more muscular approaches to saving future generations from the scourge of war. The way they are handled, if not resolved, in Afghanistan could have ramifications well beyond the local scene.

AFGHAN WOMEN UNDER THE TALIBAN

Nancy Hatch Dupree

After so many years on the periphery, Afghan women stand centre stage in the full glare of world opinion. Since the takeover of Kabul by the Taliban Islamic Movement, the women's issue has been raised to a pinnacle with equal fervour by both the Taliban and the international community. Each stands steadfast on foundations of fundamental principles guaranteeing women a dignified place in society. Yet they stand poles apart.

The divide lies in the complex realms of defining roles and determining appropriate means by which these roles may be realised. This discussion seeks to describe what the Taliban have done to so enflame the outside world, and the major international and Afghan responses, with an interweaving of brief comments on the cultural matrix in which the arguments rage.

The avowed purpose of the Taliban Islamic Movement is to complete the unfinished agenda of the jihad: to install a pure Islamic state, cleansed of evils perpetrated by their predecessors. Great stress is placed on the creation of secure environments where the chasteness and dignity of women may once again be sacrosanct. When they first appeared, the Taliban acted against a Mujahideen commander in Kandahar who had reportedly abducted, raped and killed three women in mid-1994.[1] The first decrees announced after each major takeover require women to curtail their movements in public, and then only when decently covered and in the company of close family relations (*mahrammat*). As an extension of these restrictions, female work outside the home is proscribed and girls' schools are closed. Not so well publicised, but upsetting to women, was the closing of women's bath houses (*hammam*) in Herat and in Kabul where, on 19 October 1996, the municipality closed 32 public baths reserved for women.[2]

---

[1] See Kristian Berg Harpviken, 'Transcending Traditionalism', *Journal of Peace Research*, vol. 34, no. 3, August 1997, pp. 271-287.

[2] 'Taliban close women's bath', *The News*, 20 October 1996. In addition to being an inconvenience in a city facing a harsh winter without running water and electricity, with fuel scarce and so expensive as to be beyond the means of many families, this act also presented a potential health hazard for women: Tanya Power Stevens, 'Women, children out in the cold', *Aina*, vol. 1, no. 3, Winter 1996-97, p. 19.

Initially, these instructions on work and education were enforced in a haphazard manner, varying from region to region. Through patient dialogue, aid providers operating in provincial Taliban-held Pushtun communities, where secluded female behaviour was already the norm, were frequently able to continue their programmes after an initial hiatus. In many provincial areas, central administrative control was and is still indifferently imposed; policies are unclear; and individual attitudes among local authorities reflect a wide spectrum of personal opinion, from ultra-conservative to moderate. In the cities, hard-line conservatives dominate and strict adherence is demanded, although the influence of moderates at lower levels can be detected and even called upon. This has led to frustrating contradictions and inconsistencies.

Actions and Reactions

The aid providers within the international community have doggedly sought clarifications since 1994, particularly regarding education and employment for women. With equal consistency, the Taliban, on all levels, have insisted that the movement considers it an Islamic duty to provide education for all, including women, as long as Islamic rules and regulations are properly followed. This requires separate facilities, which are currently unavailable, and security in the streets, also unavailable. They vow the suspension is only temporary, pending review and the establishment of law and order. They ask for time and criticise the aid community for their insistence on linking assistance to women.[3]

When after a year no policy changes were forthcoming, the international community took action. On 10 November 1995 UNICEF issued an official communiqué announcing that it was suspending assistance to education programmes in those parts of Afghanistan where girls were excluded from education. In taking this position UNICEF cited its commitment to the principles of the UN Convention on the Rights of the Child, to which Afghanistan is a party.[4]

---

[3]   A familiar refrain repeatedly employed since the very beginning. See, for instance, in 1995 the Governor of Khost speaking to *The Frontier Post* ('No substitute to Shariat punishments, vow Taliban', *The Frontier Post*, 24 September 1995); and in 1997, the First Secretary of the Afghan Consulate in Peshawar speaking to the General Assembly of the Afghan NGO Coordination Bureau in Peshawar, ('NGOs asked to coordinate with Taliban to improve efficiency', *The News*, 5 June 1997.)

[4]   *Girls Education is a Human Rights Issue* (Geneva & Peshawar: UNICEF, PR/GVA/95/45, 10 November 1995); Jaya Dayal, 'UNICEF cuts aid as Afghan girls barred from schools', *Dawn*, 19 November 1995.

This argument made no impression, for the Taliban recognise only the validity of the Sharia; they do not feel bound by UN human rights instruments, which they regard in good part as vehicles of Western cultural imperialism. Not surprisingly, the written response to UNICEF called the UNICEF action 'unfortunate and unjustifiable', adding, rather unkindly, that as their assistance was 'a lot of paperwork and a few vehicles', UNICEF should reconsider its position, do something practical and stop indulging in politics.[5]

By the beginning of 1996 with the 'temporary' bans yet to be lifted and as restrictions on the employment of women as well as their access to basic services worsened, the Save the Children Alliance in Afghanistan announced the suspension of its operations in Herat on 4 March 1996.[6] On 8 March, Save the Children called for all humanitarian aid organisations to follow UNICEF and consider the suspension of every non-emergency programme in sectors where women's employment was prohibited.[7]

This call went largely unheeded. Most assistance providers felt that to use threats or suspend assistance during a rapidly evolving situation would be inappropriate and lead to a hardening of attitudes and a breakdown in communications which would ultimately jeopardise large populations in need of assistance. Nevertheless, the women's issue was tabled at every meeting, much to the increasing irritation of the Taliban. Why, they asked, had there been no condemnation of the excessive violations against women by the Mujahideen? Abductions, forced marriages, rape and trafficking in little boys and girls were universally acknowledged, but the international community chose not to make an issue of these violations.[8]

Furthermore, the former regime, while by no means as stringent in their restraints, also hampered women's activities in the name of Islam. Female education was encouraged and thousands of women worked in government offices, but occasional constraints were imposed for reasons of female propriety. In July 1995, the Women's High Association in Kabul hosted 300 women at a 3-day workshop to

---

5   'Taliban flay Unicef for stopping education aid', *The News*, 28 November 1995.

6   *Suspension of Operations in Western Afghanistan* (London: Save the Children, 4 March 1996). The Alliance consisted of the Swedish Radda Barnen, Save the Children (UK) and Save the Children (USA).

7   *Action on Gender and Development in Afghanistan: A call to Humanitarian Aid Organizations* (Islamabad: Save the Children (UK), 8 March 1996). The call was repeated in *Gender Equity Essential to Development: Save the Children Calls for Action in Afghanistan* (Islamabad: Save the Children (UK), 20 October 1996).

8   For an extensive account see Iram Noor, 'Abuse of women in Afghanistan persists', *The News*, 27 June 1995. Also Amnesty International reports, although much of their material is repetitive, anecdotal reporting of fears and rumours, lacking adequate verification.

prepare guidelines for the Afghan delegation to the Fourth World Conference on Women in Beijing on 4 September. As they were about to depart on 31 August, the Deputy Foreign Minister, Abdul Rahim Ghafoorzai, announced that the government had cancelled the delegation because 'there are a lot of issues to be discussed that the High Council considers are against the basic Islamic principles governing life in the Islamic society in Afghanistan. We are concerned about a number of issues that we consider unIslamic. They include the question of parental control over their children, the right of a husband to control the women of the family, matters of family planning, including abortion, and the concept of pre-marital relations for boys and girls.'[9]

As Taliban challenges increased, harsher restraints were implemented. In November 1995 the Eastern Shura in Jalalabad banned women from working. The NGOs negotiated and continued their programmes; the UN suspended all Afghan female employees, earning a flurry of well-publicised reproof from female activists in the United States.[10] On the whole, however, the Western media reported on women only peripherally from the end of 1994 until the Taliban swept into Kabul on 27 September 1996. Then, suddenly, Afghanistan, Kabul and women were at the top of every agenda and the real clamour began.

Predictably, within hours after they took Kabul, orders from the High Council were announced over Radio Kabul[11] instructing women to cease attending workplaces, to move outside the home only when necessary, and then only with faces covered and accompanied by a male family member (*mahram*). Schools were closed.

World leaders launched a barrage of statements throughout October. The Director-General of UNESCO, Federico Mayor, called for a spirit of tolerance.[12] The European Commissioner for Humanitarian Aid, Emma Bonino, feared that Afghanistan's new rulers were set to take the country 'back to the Dark Ages'.[13] The Secretary-General of the

---

9   'Afghanistan pulls out of women's moot', *Dawn*, 1 September 1995. The delegation included officials from the Ministries of Health, Education, Foreign Affairs, Civil Aviation, and Rural Development, the Department of Family Guidance, and the Dean of the Faculty of Law, Kabul University. UNHCR and various UN agencies funded the workshop and were prepared to underwrite the expenses of the official delegation. UNICEF, WHO and various NGOs sponsored a number of Afghan women from Peshawar and Islamabad, who attended the parallel NGO Forum which met in Beijing at the same time.

10 'UN Cutting women from staff in Kabul', *The Frontier Post*, 11 November 1995.

11 Renamed Radio Shariat in October 1996.

12 'Director-General Calls for Tolerance in Afghanistan', Paris, 30 September 1996.

13 'Taking Afghan women back to the Dark Ages', *The News*, 7 October 1996.

United Nations, Dr Boutros Boutros-Ghali, pointed out that the United Nations system is obliged to be guided by the norms stated in its Charter and that the restrictions imposed by the Taliban could have serious repercussions on the ability of the United Nations to deliver programmes.[14] The UN High Commissioner for Human Rights, Jose Ayala Lasso, only mildly noted that Afghanistan was party to various conventions protecting women's rights.[15] Dr Norbert Holl, the UN special peace mediator, warned that it was not up to Taliban leaders to rule on human rights, since 'Whoever is controlling Afghanistan is bound by the Charter of the UN'.[16]

While the US Permanent Representative to the UN (now Secretary of State), Madeleine Albright, dubbed the Taliban decrees 'medieval and impossible to justify or defend',[17] a State Department spokesman warned that the Taliban should not expect recognition unless they showed respect for women's rights, observing that Taliban 'directives threaten to generate international isolation, which would deny Afghanistan international assistance'.[18] Even Maulana Fazlur Rahman, Chief of Jamiat-e Ulema-i Islam, the alleged patron of the Taliban, criticised the regime 'for their unrealistic attitude towards women.'[19]

Taliban officials were stung by the outcry. Their only purpose, they said, was 'to protect their sisters from corrupt people'.[20] Some bristled at the arrogance of outsiders in assuming that Western

---

[14] United Nations, New York, 7 October 1996; 'Taliban crackdown on women can affect aid: Gali', *The Frontier Post*, 8 October 1996.

[15] 'Diplomats see oil reserves as the booty in Afghan fighting', *Dawn*, 10 October 1996; US Department of State, *Country Reports on Human Rights Practices for 1996* (Washington, DC: U.S. Government Printing Office, 1997), pp. 1407-1417 at p. 1414. Afghanistan is party to the Convention on the Political Rights of Women (1953), the International Convention on the Elimination of All Forms of Racial Discrimination (1965), and the International Covenant on Economic, Social, and Cultural Rights (1966). It signed, but did not ratify, the 1979 Convention on the Elimination of All Forms of Discrimination against Women.

[16] 'Holl asks Taliban to ensure human rights', *The Nation*, 22 October 1996.

[17] 'US condemns human rights abuses in Afghanistan', *The Nation*, 26 October 1996.

[18] 'US warns Taliban over women's rights', *Dawn*, 8 October 1996.

[19] 'JUI to create Afghanistan like situation, warns Fazal', *The Nation*, 19 October 1996. Qazi Hussain Ahmad, chief of Pakistan's other ultra-conservative political party, the Jamaat-e Islami, also spoke out against Taliban bans on female education and employment, and the compulsory wearing of the burqa: 'JI doesn't back Taliban: Qazi', *The Frontier Post*, 30 May 1997.

[20] Acting Minister of Information and Culture, Amir Khan Muttaqi: 'Aid agencies for Taliban compromise on women rights', *The Frontier Post*, 9 October 1996.

standards must be imposed.[21] It soon became clear that threatening international disapprobation and cuts in assistance would not move the authorities toward moderation. In Kabul, at a meeting on 8 October 1996 with the Acting[22] Foreign Minister, Mullah Mohammad Ghaus, the aid community observed that humanitarian projects dependent on female staff would be suspended unless UN and NGO female employees were allowed to work, and that this would badly affect some 30,000 widows who were the sole earners in their families. The Minister expressed his 'astonishment' at the level of international concern for 'such a small percentage of the working population' and stressed the fact that the movement was still coming to grips with establishing a government.[23]

This is still a valid but little heeded point. The central government is far from functioning effectively. Its base of power lies primarily in a very young militia nurtured in the isolation of ultra-conservative madrassas (Islamic seminaries) where they imbibed ideas by rote without encouragement to reason or dispute. Schooled in the belief that unveiled women in public must by nature be morally suspect, they arrive in Kabul fervently imbued with the conviction that as instruments and arbiters of Islamic rectitude their task is to rid the city of its sinful ways, personified by cosmopolitan Kabuli women.

Privately, not a few in positions of authority sincerely fear that individuals within the young Taliban militia who have never been exposed to urban living may easily be led astray. They point to the equally inexperienced young Mujahideen who came to Kabul in 1992 with similar ideas about upright female behaviour: 'good' women stay home, 'bad' women expose their faces and mingle with men in public places. Young immature Mujahideen who had grown up on the battlefield under the influence of conservative leaders marvelled at the unveiled Afghan female newsreaders on TV, concluded they must be promiscuous, and–Kalashnikovs at the ready–waylaid the ladies at the studio gate saying, 'Tonight you are mine'. Several former TV celebrities have told me how relieved they were when the Rabbani government finally put a ban on female TV appearances, an act denounced by Westerners as being discriminatory to women. Initially women in Kabul were terrified of these zealous Mujahideen but in time, because the former regime was lax in its vigilance, women lost their fear and began to act more assertively, moving about the city as

---

21 'Taliban say no to Western values for women', *The Frontier Post,* 9 October 1996.

22 Taliban officials use the designation 'Acting', since they have insisted from the beginning that their goal is to install an Islamic government, not to rule it.

23 'Aid agencies for Taliban compromise on women rights', *The Frontier Post,* 9 October 1996.

they had in the past. The change was rapid and extraordinary. At first so terrified they dared not leave their homes, a scant four months later women walked the streets with confidence, returning measure for measure when young men deigned to question the appropriateness of their apparel. At the same time, the Mujahideen lost their fervour, became weak, gave in to the lures of women and succumbed to corrupt city ways.

The authorities are dependent on their young militia as a base of power, but they are less than sanguine about their real ability to control them.[24] Nor do they dare risk losing the loyalty of these fighting forces by modifying their stand on women, an important symbol of the movement's Islamic legitimacy.[25] Then, of course, there are those who simply have no doubt that women appearing in public in any capacity are instruments of moral corruption and agents of sexual anarchy.

Whatever the reasoning, many in the leadership worry that women could be sexually dishonoured. The movement would then be sullied. To avoid this, women must be kept covered, out of sight and off the streets. By imposing strict restraints directly on women, the society's sensitive component symbolising male honour, the regime sends a message of its intent to subordinate the personal autonomy of every individual, thereby strengthening the impression that it is capable of exercising control over all aspects of social behaviour, male and female. In short, although official pronouncements regarding women may be couched in Islamic rhetoric, the web of hidden attitudes governing official actions and colouring public statements is woven of many complexities.

The Taliban vigorously enforce the requirement that women wear the *chadari*, a voluminous head-to-toe pleated covering, also referred to by the Arabic term *burqa*. This garment totally encompasses the body, leaving only a mesh square over the eyes to permit minimal vision. The *hejab*, adopted by many refugee women on orders from the Mujahideen is not acceptable 'because it is not from our culture and because it does not conform to Islamic Sharia since it is very smart and draws attention', according to Haji Mawlawi Qamaluddin, Deputy Director, *Amr bil-Maroof wa Nahi An il-Munkir*, the department responsible for the Promotion of Virtue and Suppression of Vice, a

---

[24] A rare public acknowledgement of this was made in Kandahar in May 1997 by the Governor of Kandahar. One reason for postponing the opening of girls' schools was, he said, the fear that girls might be 'raped or abducted' on their way to school: 'Kandahar Visit 12-14 May 1997', ACBAR, Peshawar, n.d., p. 3 (mimeo).

[25] Barnett R. Rubin, 'Women and pipelines: Afghanistan's proxy wars', *International Affairs*, vol. 73, no. 2, 1997, pp. 283-296 at p. 291.

religious police force which is one of the most powerful arms of the Taliban Movement.[26] *Hejab* is a general Arabic term for body covering. Various forms are worn in the Middle East. The style of *hejab* that evolved in Pakistan among Afghan refugees consisted of an ankle-length, long-sleeved coat worn with a waist-length headcovering which is drawn across the face just below the eyes when moving in the streets or in mixed gatherings. These *hejab* were typically black or navy blue. Even little girls in primary schools run by the political parties wore uniforms in this *hejab* style. Many women, a majority, who objected to the *hejab* because it was a foreign import, wore instead the traditional Afghan *chader*, a large shawl-like headscarf draped over the hair and falling to cover about three-quarters of the body. The *chader* leaves the face open, although it also can be drawn across the face when needed.[27] In July 1996, after Gulbuddin Hekmatyar became Prime Minister in June, he warned women that they would be required to wear black *hejab* if they wished to continue working.[28] Many women in Kabul at that time were already wearing the long coat over Western-style suits and dresses, under which they had added the *shalwar* (full trousers). Headcoverings were sometimes so small, however, they covered the hair inadequately.

The new Taliban dress codes and restrictions on movement were alien to women in Kabul; many were slow to comply. Daily confrontations between women and young Taliban militia resulted in insults and beatings. These incidents, captured on TV and graphically described by Western journalists, hardened Western attitudes toward the Taliban. Women adapted quickly out of fear of the consequences, but the beatings continue, often for such inconsequential reasons as the length of the *chadari* or the colour of the shoes.[29] Seldom do women suffer extensive physical injuries from these beatings. The intent is to humiliate. This, of course, causes considerable psychological damage.

Thus cosmopolitan Kabul has reverted to the days before 1959 when the government of Prime Minister Daoud Khan announced the

[26] 'Taliban toughen beard code', *The Nation*, 23 February, 1997.

[27] See Nancy Hatch Dupree, *The Present role of Afghan Refugee Women and Children* (The Hague, The Netherlands: Bernard van Leer Foundation, 1992), pp. 3-5.

[28] 'Hekmatyar lays down strict Islamic policy', *The Nation*, 11 July 1996.

[29] To give only one example of the ubiquitous, arbitrary and petty nature of the harassment, when six women were beaten for the inadequacy of their veils on 9 April 1997, the 'appalled' policeman from the department of religious police is quoted as saying: 'The ankles of the women could be seen and even their faces were not covered. They were half naked!': 'Taliban beat 3 male shavers, 6 women', *The Frontier Post*, 11 April 1997.

voluntary end of seclusion and removal of the veil.[30] The key word then was voluntary; whether to shed the veil and move in public was strictly up to individual families to decide. Those who did come out, however, were immediately and fully prepared to make significant contributions since governments from 1929 onward had strongly supported women's education and employment in separate institutions, even while keeping women in *purdah*. *Purdah*, literally meaning curtain, refers to the practice of secluding women inside their homes, and includes veiling in public places. King Amanullah (1919-29) urged women to come out from *purdah*, and many élites did so. The conservative tribesmen who overthrew Amanullah in 1929 put women back into *purdah* and the *chadari*. Nadir Shah (1929-33) and his successors until 1959, realising that their base of power was too weak to confront conservatives on this sensitive issue, kept women behind the veil, in seclusion away from the public domain. After 1959, women in ever-increasing numbers took education and professional careers for granted, a trend that escalated after 1978.[31] Now that momentum has been abruptly halted.

Of the many rules and regulations governing women, the international community has reacted with the greatest concern to restrictions on education and employment. The dilemma is to find ways in which congenial environments can be created where assistance may be delivered according to internationally recognised human rights standards without compromising national cultural perspectives.[32] To these ends, the issue of female education is hit hard by both sides. According to a UN survey conducted in May 1996, Kabul had 158

---

[30] Louis Dupree, 'The Burqa Comes Off', *American Universities Field Staff Reports*, vol. 3, no. 1, August 1959, pp. 1-4; Louis Dupree, *Afghanistan* (Princeton: Princeton University Press, 1973), pp. 530-533.

[31] For a comprehensive account, including statistics, see Wali M. Rahimi, *Status of Women: Afghanistan* (Bangkok: UNESCO, 1991). For a history of the women's movement through the communist period, see Nancy Hatch Dupree, 'Revolutionary Rhetoric and Afghan Women', in M. Nazif Shahrani and Richard Canfield (eds.), *Revolutions and Rebellions in Afghanistan: Anthropological Perspectives* (Berkeley: University of California Press, 1984), pp. 306-340. Increasingly after the 1978 leftist coup d'etat, women expressed new-found freedoms by flaunting their sexuality. This embarrassed even liberal males; conservatives were convinced sexual anarchy was imminent: see ibid, at p. 322. This attitude still affects many within the Taliban movement.

[32] During October 1996 aid providers were as prolific as the world leaders in issuing statements. The most thoughtful was 'A Position Statement of International Agencies Working in Kabul', The Kabul Information Forum, Kabul, 5 October 1996. 'Policy Guidelines for Fieldwork of UN Agencies in Afghanistan', issued by UNOCHA on behalf of all heads of UN agencies in Afghanistan, Islamabad, 31 October 1996, is a detailed statement of the official UN stand.

public schools, accommodating 148,223 boys and 103,256 girls, taught by 11,208 teachers of whom 7,793 were women. Because of the high percentage of female teachers, the restrictions effectively deprived boys as well.[33] Efforts to reactivate the shattered education sector remain deadlocked. The voices of moderates are muted; the hard liners dominate. Contradictions and inconsistencies abound; hopes rise only to evaporate. In December 1996, there was a flurry of optimism that the ban on girls' schools would be lifted after the winter recess. In meetings with the Ministry of Education, UN agencies declared themselves ready to commit an estimated $300,000 toward the rehabilitation of schools, provided half of the facilities would be utilised for girls.[34] The final government document, beginning with an introduction flaying former regimes for damaging the entire education system by utilising a foreign curriculum, simply requested repairs for buildings, furniture and funds to print textbooks. The expected commitment for girls was nowhere mentioned.[35] On 9 March 1997 when the schools opened, headmasters were directed not to register girls; Kabul University opened with no female teachers or students.[36]

The most recent round on education took place in Kandahar on 12-13 May 1997 at which the Governor of Kandahar, Mullah Mohammad Hassan, candidly observed that in the overall scheme of things, the conclusion of the war and the establishment of law and order are uppermost priorities, against which the question of girls' education is

---

[33] United States Department of State, *Country Reports on Human Rights Practices for 1996*, at pp. 1415-1416.

[34] Much attention has been given to physical facilities, but little has been paid to the more crucial question of curriculum, even though numbers of Taliban officials have stressed that girls should be taught only 'Islamic' subjects. Personal communication.

[35] 'Immediate Rehabilitation of Schools of Ministry of Education of Islamic Republic of Afghanistan', document signed by Mawlawi Abdul Salam Hanafi, Minister of Education, Kabul, 19 January 1997. It should be noted that many Taliban officials, probably a majority, keep their families in Pakistan, one reason being the availability of education for their daughters. Personal communication.

[36] According to the then Rector of Kabul University, Amir Shah Hassanyar, of the 10,000 students at the university when it closed in September 1996, 4,000 were women; of 360 professors, 60 were women. At the opening ceremony, The Minister of Higher Education, Mawlawi Hamidullah Noumani, emphasized the ban on women was temporary because of a lack of resources. However, he also said that when women are reinstated they may not be allowed to study engineering, but would be confined to such subjects as medicine, home economics and teaching: 'Kabul university reopens without women, funds', *Dawn*, 10 March 1997.

a 'minor matter.'[37] Because so little action has been taken, the early optimism generated by conciliatory remarks apparently designed to mollify Western critics and the aid community is rapidly turning into cynicism.

Slightly better progress can be noted regarding women's employment, although initially many distressing incidents occurred. Various reports estimated that anywhere from 40,000-150,000 women, including teachers plus doctors, nurses, administrators and other civil servants, were affected by the prohibition on women's employment. Three days after taking Kabul, Mawlawi Wakil Ahmad, member of the Central Shura and Senior Adviser to the founder of the movement, Mullah Mohammad Omar, announced that the government would continue to pay female government employees, but that 'we stand by our decision that women cannot work in government offices in the future.'[38]

Harsh realities have forced some modifications. Kabul is overcrowded with Internally Displaced Persons and homeless returning refugees reeling under the affects of escalating inflation in an environment with limited earning opportunities. Government services have mostly collapsed,[39] and the safety net of traditional closely-knit extended family support networks has been severely damaged. For the first time in its history, beggars roam the streets of Kabul or huddle outside relief agencies. A high proportion are children and women, many of whom are widows or those responsible for disabled men unable to work. A January 1997 survey by ICRC recorded the presence of 50,000 widows, each with an average of 7-9 children.[40]

---

[37] 'Kandahar Visit 12-14 May 1997', ACBAR, Peshawar, n.d., p. 3. The workshop was part of an ongoing series of meetings initiated by the UN Coordinator, Alfredo Witschi-Cestari, on 19 March 1997 to establish closer relationships and better understanding between responsible Taliban officials. UN agencies and members of the NGO community.

[38] Rahimullah Yusufzai, 'Afghan women to get salaries without working', *The News*, 30 September 1996. The women were paid the first month, then less frequently until it was announced that no further payments would be made as of 1 May 1997.

[39] Ministry of Public Health hospitals are still functioning, assisted by various agencies, as are clinics run by the Afghan Red Crescent assisted by the International Federation of Red Cross and Red Crescent Societies. The Municipality provides potable water systems, garbage, human waste disposal and other services, with assistance from UN agencies and NGOs.

[40] *Report of the Senior Coordinator for Refugee Women on Mission to Afghanistan and Pakistan 30th April to 9th May 1997* (Peshawar: UNHCR, May 1997), p. 3. One wonders how the authorities can countenance the sight of so many destitute female beggars while still maintaining that a pillar of their existence is to guarantee the dignity of women.

Restrictions on female employees drastically interfered with the ability of many organisations to continue delivering emergency assistance to this vulnerable population, as well as services for others in need of assistance in the deteriorating economic environment. Without female staff it was impossible to access families or monitor programmes. Programmes were scaled down; some suspended operations altogether. Conditions in hospitals where women were forbidden to be seen by male doctors became desperate without female medical professionals.

Continually pressured on these matters, a set of eleven rules for female medical personnel, signed by *Amir al-Momineen* Mullah Mohammad Omar as well as the Minister of Public Health, was issued in November 1996; a comprehensive set of regulations for both men and women was announced on 17 December by the *Amr bil-Maroof wa Nahi An il-Munkir*.[41] These cleared the way for women to work in the medical sector, as long as they dressed appropriately, 'in simple clothes ... with no cosmetics and makeup', worked in segregated spaces and travelled with escorts. Allowances were made for male physicians to examine female patients as long as the female was accompanied by a *mahram*, both doctor and patient were dressed in Islamic dress and the male doctor did 'not touch or see other than the affected part' of the female patient.

Of the general regulations, only three pertained to women. Number 1 stated that in order to prevent 'sedition and uncovered females', no drivers were allowed to pick up females wearing the Iranian *burqa* which did not cover the face, or seductive clothing, or those unaccompanied by a *mahram*. In case of violation the driver would be imprisoned and the husbands would be punished. Number 12 required that it should be announced in all mosques that women found washing clothes in the river would be picked up in a 'respectful Islamic manner' and taken to their homes where their husbands would be severely punished. Number 15 announced that tailors found taking female body measurements and displaying fashion magazines would be imprisoned. The emphasis on punishing males for infractions committed by females reflects the universal acceptance of male

---

[41] Both sets of regulations are included in the *Final report on the situation of human rights in Afghanistan submitted by Mr. Choong-Hyun Paik, Special Rapporteur, in accordance with Commission on Human Rights resolution 1996/75* (United Nations: E/CN.4/1997/59, 20 February 1997): Appendix II Rules of work for the State hospitals and private clinics based on Sharia principles; Appendix III Rules and regulations of the Administration Department, the General Presidency of *Amr bil-Maroof wa Nahi An il-Munkir*. Such written statements are primarily for the benefit of the UN and NGOs. The general populace is informed of regulations over Radio Shariat.

responsibility for females, which is a natural consequence of the belief that males have a duty to exert control over female members of their families. Even under normal circumstances evidence of a loss of male control affects family as well as individual standing within the community. Female behaviour therefore becomes the ultimate determining factor of family status.

Although the modification of constraints on working women in the health sector paved the way for thousands of women to work with various humanitarian projects, especially those serving vulnerable women,[42] the absence of recognised channels of authority allows serious incidents to erupt. On 24 May 1997 five CARE International female employees, duly armed with written authorisation from the Ministry of Interior to conduct monitoring and survey work for emergency feeding programmes for widow-headed households, were forcibly ordered from their car by members of the *Amr bil-Maroof wa Nahi An il-Munkir*. Summarily dismissing the letters of authorisation, the guards publicly insulted the women over a loudspeaker, calling them prostitutes because they worked for foreigners, and proceeded to strike them several times with a metre-and-a-half-long whip made of metal and leather.[43] The ladies escaped unhurt but badly humiliated, the driver was arrested, and apologies were eventually extended by the Deputy Director of the religious police, with the explanation that the action had not been authorised. Work resumed. The ladies now carry yet another letter of authorisation, from the *Amr bil-Maroof wa Nahi An il-Munkir*.

This incident vividly illustrates several important realities. First, unacceptable acts are being carried out by individuals without the sanction of the authorities, either because of a misguided sense of righteousness or, very often, simply because of personal whims and grudges. It is against official policy to punish women in the streets,[44] but incidents continue to be reported. Rank-and-file members of the

---

[42] For example: emergency food distribution, income generation such as quilt making, gem cutting, textiles, nylon shopping bags, poultry. Hundreds of women are employed by women's bakeries producing bread at subsidised prices for needy families, a WFP supported activity. In the Ministry of Repatriation five Afghan women, two of whom are reinstated civil servants, administer two revolving fund projects for returning refugees, many of whom are widows, a project supported by UNHCR: United Nations, *Humanitarian Assistance for Afghanistan: Weekly Update*, No. 214, 5 May 1997, p. 2.

[43] 'Beating of CARE Female Staff in Kabul', Press Release, CARE International in Afghanistan, Peshawar, 26 May 1997.

[44] According to the head of the religious police: 'Since we cannot directly punish women, we try to use taxi drivers and shopkeepers as a means to pressurize them into wearing the chadari': 'Taliban toughen beard code', *The Nation*, 23 February 1997.

religious police are especially notorious for being undisciplined and often act counter to official policies as they cruise about in jeeps patrolling the streets. Regulations are often misunderstood or misinterpreted by this poorly-educated mass of militia. But the Taliban are not a homogeneous monolith. There are moderate Taliban in the government who seek equitable alternatives, as well as men who are not taliban, numbers of whom are distinguished professionals, who do not approve of the excesses.[45] But with ultraconservatives entrenched at the higher echelons of power, their efforts must for a time be kept at a low level if they are eventually to persuade.

Second, women work at risk. They have no security for they may be beaten without provocation even when wearing the *chadari* and carrying credentials. Thus there is danger that women may be sacrificed to worthy principles during this period of violent transition. It is important for all aid providers to be aware of, and remain sensitive to, all the nuances of the volatile environment in which the women they wish to help must move.

Third, the incident is a sterling example of increasing antipathy toward foreigners, especially regarding their influence on women. Distrust of foreign cultural encroachments thought to be inimical to Islam has festered ever since Afghanistan's ruling élites turned toward the West at the beginning of the century and largely isolated themselves from values cherished outside Kabul. Westernised parliaments, constitutions, architecture, city plans, dress, education, literature, food, music, entertainment were all part of the government's modernising zeal, with highly visible women at the centre of the whirl. For women of this era, Western dress, with skirts to the knee and heads uncovered, was a symbol of emancipation, as potent as Islamic dress is for the Taliban.[46]

But the Taliban regard Western lifestyles with anathema, equate Western dress with moral laxity, and denounce freedom for women as antithetical to Islamic morality. Thus when women were warned over Radio Shariat on 8 December 1996 that they were forbidden to enter the offices of foreign agencies, fervid members of the militia

---

[45] The Deputy Minister of Public Health, Abdul Sattar Paktis, for instance, is an orthopaedic surgeon with a world renowned reputation. Unless the movement can attract more such specialists in all fields the chances of establishing a viable government are bleak because institutional capacities are so weak. The absence of girls' education is a deterrent.

[46] Nancy Hatch Dupree, 'Victoriana Comes to the Haremserai in Afghanistan', in Paul Bucherer-Dietschi (ed.), *Bauen und wohnen am Hindukush* (Liestal, Switzerland: Stiftung Bibliotheca Afghanica, 1988), pp. 111-149.

responded to the announcements by attacking women seen leaving UN and NGO offices.[47]

Current pressures by Westerners are also viewed as aggressions against Islam, deepening Taliban convictions that the society is in danger from outsiders.[48] Referring to their Western critics, Mullah Mohammad Hassan Akhund, number three in the ruling hierarchy, told a group of Pakistani academics in Kabul: 'They won't be satisfied unless we obey them and turn our face from Allah, but we do not care about anybody, as long as the religion of Allah is maintained.'[49] The Acting Deputy Foreign Minister, Sher Mohammad Stanekzai, put it more bluntly: 'This is our country and we know better what to do with our women, do not interfere in our internal affairs.'[50]

But even for sympathetic observers, some acts are excessively repugnant to Western sensibilities. In July 1996, a woman and her lover were stoned to death in Kandahar.[51] On 29 March 1997 Radio Shariat announced that a woman from Laghman was stoned to death on charges of adultery.[52] Protests objecting to such summary justice are answered by the argument that harsh times demand harsh punishments if the populace is to be made to comply with the new laws of the land: 'If we do not implement this, many other problems may arise.'[53]

Afghan Responses

If indeed the vigorous enforcement of regulations is intended to ensure that women conform, the policy has succeeded in some ways. City women moving in public spaces are inevitably shrouded in the *chadari*. A few Afghan and expatriate women grumbling about gender apartheid find dress codes and separate institutions 'unacceptable', but most professional Afghan women, while they may not like the

---

47 'Afghan women warned not to enter foreign offices', *The Frontier Post*, 9 December 1996. Restricting contacts with foreigners is not a Taliban innovation. The secret police in governments before 1978 kept an eye on Afghans visiting the homes of foreigners, often interrogating them as they left; Afghan women were not permitted to work as domestic servants for foreigners before 1978, but many worked as maids, cooks and laundresses for NGO personnel during the tenure of President Rabbani. Personal experience.
48 'Taliban defend Sharia enforcement', *The Frontier Post*, 4 October 1996.
49 'Taliban dismiss Western Critics', *The Nation*, 27 April 1997.
50 Mohammad Khurshid, 'Taliban and the Western media', *The Frontier Post*, 8 October 1996.
51 Kathy Evans, 'Afghan Premier Bans Music', *Dawn*, 17 July 1996.
52 'Afghan woman stoned to death for adultery', *The News*, 30 March 1997.
53 Mawlawi Nik Mohammad, representing the Governor of Laghman. 'Eastern Zone meeting', ACBAR, Peshawar, 7 April 1997, p. 4.

inconvenience and the retrogressive image of the *chadari*, are willing
to don it if that is what is now necessary to deliver humanitarian
assistance.[54]

Rural and nomadic women do not typically wear the *chadari*,
unless they have travelled to the city or their husbands have acquired
education or secured government employment, in which case they
wear it proudly as a symbol of status and sophistication. Instead,
women in each tribal or rural ethnic group wear distinctively designed
veils. All are draped over the head and can be demurely pulled over the
face for modesty as occasion demands; many are of bright colours,
some are heavily embroidered with silk and set with small mirrors.
The cut, the colour, and the decoration are expressions of group
identity and individual creativity. The purpose is modesty, not
effacement.

But in Kabul the Taliban have attempted to impose a measure of
standardisation by insisting on the *chadari*. They equate it, perhaps,
with greater anonymity and thus more effective protection and
'dignity.'[55] But women are already making their own fashion
statements, despite the fact that the prices of *chadari* can amount to
more than an average month's salary which is next to intolerable for
many families.[56] Burnt orange and forest green are fashionable in
Jalalabad; various clear shades of blue accented by an occasional canary
yellow flit about Kabul; black was never usual, except among some
groups in Herat. Made mostly of soft artificial silk, the veils shimmer
and billow with a certain mysterious seductiveness. This, of course, is
far from the intent of the authorities.

Beneath the veil, undercurrents of frustration roil. At home, family
harmony is being severely jeopardised by the mental stress that afflicts
working women unaccustomed to forced confinement. The curtailment
of normal social interactions creates a sense of isolation and

---

[54] A young, sophisticated monitor of aid projects who travels inside Afghanistan
with her brother by public transport, avoiding all contact with UN or foreign
agencies, observed: 'When the Taliban tell me I cannot enter certain areas, I am
incensed. After all this is my home. I go, wearing my chadari, but they make me
feel like a spy in my own country'. For a general discussion of various attitudes
regarding the *hejab*, see Nancy Hatch Dupree, 'Kvinnor som symboler:
utvecklingstendenser och reaktion', in *Islams Mangfald* (Stockholm: Svenska
Afghanistankommitten, 1990), pp. 267-279; reprinted in English as 'Women as
Symbols: Trends and Reactions', *WUFA*, vol. 5, no. 2, 1990, pp. 30-41.

[55] Announced on Radio Shariat: 'Islamic hijab cannot be completed by wearing a
scarf alone. All honourable sisters are informed that the observance of Islamic
hijab is for the sake of their own dignity': 'Taliban define stricter standard of
Islamic veil for Afghan women', *The Frontier Post,* 6 December 1996.

[56] 'Islamic fashion boom after Taliban takeover', *The Frontier Post,* 30 October
1996.

frustration causing depression. There has been an increase in the flow of refugees because parents feel obligated to provide their daughters with education; those with gifted sons fret over the deplorable quality of the little education that exists. Being herded into the back seats of rickety buses, instead of enjoying relative privacy at the front as was customary before, is not only humiliating but formidably uncomfortable on the badly damaged roads. Restrictions on movement inhibit women from seeking necessary medical treatment, for themselves and for their children; attendance at pre-natal and post-natal facilities is down; family nutrition worsens because inflation keeps prices high and women are restricted in shopping for their families. While improvements in physical security are appreciated, the absence of economic security is universally deplored. To watch their children suffer because of deteriorating family income is heartbreaking. Women are angry beneath their veils.

Tensions are being held under great pressure which could erupt at any time, but so far few have been emboldened to stage overt group expressions of discontent inside Afghanistan. Those that have erupted have been quickly quelled, because there is no effective leadership to sustain them. As usual in Afghanistan there is always an exception. Early in 1996, 150 women demonstrated in front of the Governor's office in Kandahar. These were poor beggar women objecting to shopkeepers who refused to accept bank notes of small denominations. That night the Governor announced over the radio that shopkeepers would accept the notes, or be closed down.[57]

The Taliban staged a women's demonstration on their own behalf, in Kabul, on 17 October 1996, to protest against foreign interference. It was a half-hearted affair with both men and women, and lots of energetic little boys, attending.[58] Following this, on 23 October, women rallied for five hours in Mazar-e Sharif raising slogans such as 'Taliban law is not Islamic law' under the inspiration of a lady judge in General Dostum's administration.[59] In Herat a demonstration on 21 December 1996 by 50 women protesting the closing of women's bath houses turned ugly. Twenty were arrested and several others were hospitalised after being beaten.[60]

---

[57] Personal communication in Kandahar.

[58] The women wore *chaders* or *hejabs*, not yet the full *chadari*: *The Nation*, 18 October 1996.

[59] 'Afghan women lambast Taleban rule', *The News*, 24 October 1996. Balkh University was completely co-educational at this time. See Nancy Hatch Dupree, 'Les universités d'Afghanistan en 1995', *Les Nouvelles d'Afghanistan*, no.71, 1996, pp. 17-20 at p. 18.

[60] *Final report on the situation of human rights in Afghanistan submitted by Mr. Choong-Hyun Paik, Special Rapporteur, in accordance with Commission on*

So much for inside Afghanistan. In Pakistan, the highly politicised Revolutionary Association of the Women of Afghanistan (RAWA) continues to hold demonstrations in Islamabad, Peshawar and Quetta, from which they inevitably emerge bloodied by Pakistani police lathi charges. They have now transferred their vitriolic rhetoric from their erstwhile enemy, Gulbuddin Hekmatyar, to the Taliban.[61] Other Afghan women's groups engage mainly in forming networks which periodically hold seminars and issue statements.[62]

Afghan women are fortunate in enjoying the staunch support of one male-directed agency, the Cooperation Center for Afghanistan based in Peshawar, which publishes and holds seminars on human rights in addition to implementing women's projects inside Afghanistan.[63] Aside from CCA and a handful of others quietly working on in-country programmes benefiting women, most Afghan males are conspicuously silent. Some frankly observe that since men enjoy so few rights, they see no reason why such a fuss should be made over women. Truly, it must not be forgotten that Afghan men are being disadvantaged as well. Nevertheless, most Afghans, I believe, agree that women are being disadvantaged to a greater extent.

The community seems to be rather evenly split between those who believe the Taliban should be given the benefit of the doubt and time in which to resolve their problems by themselves, and those who view all Taliban promises with cynical scepticism. 'Give them time? We have. All we get with time is worse than before. When changes are always negative, hope must die.'

Even men who may be sympathetic hesitate to speak publicly, partly because they fear to do so may jeopardise their projects in

---

Human Rights resolution 1996/75 (United Nations: E/CN.4/1997/59, 20 February 1997), p. 16.

[61] Among their many publications, *The Burst of the 'Islamic Government' Bubble in Afghanistan*, January 1997, gives an exhaustive overview of their activities.

[62] For example: the Afghan Women's Council, based in Peshawar, issues periodic news releases and holds seminars on various pertinent subjects, such as 'Women and the Hejab: Yesterday, Today, Tomorrow', held on 23 June 1997; the ACBAR Women's Affairs Sub-committee, in Peshawar in April 1997, called on aid donors to give priority to projects benefiting women; the Advisory Group on Gender Issues in Afghanistan, in Islamabad, on 2 October 1996 and again on 30 May 1997 issued a 'Statement' calling upon the United Nations and national governments to confirm their commitment to women's rights by closely examining Taliban policies before considering Taliban requests for membership and assistance. Afghan women delegates at the International Forum on Assistance to Afghanistan (IFAA) held in Ashgabad, Turkmenistan, 21-22 January 1977, provocatively tabled a 'Statement from Afghan women (independent of men)'.

[63] *Proceedings of the Seminar: Women's Human Rights in Afghanistan, 15-19 October 1994, Mazar-i-Sharif* (Peshawar: Cooperation Center for Afghanistan, 1994).

Taliban-held areas. Looking deeper, one sees more significant reasons for their reticence. Many sophisticated professionals, technicians, administrators and managers, within the UN and NGO systems, prefer to keep their wives and daughters safely secluded within prescribed social networks which do not include mixed study or working environments, particularly where there are foreigners. This mirrors pre-war attitudes. Even during the freedom of the 1960s, working women were expected to socialise within the family, rather than with their colleagues. Women then, as now, chafed under traditional attitudes which bound them too tightly to family choices, a state they described as 'family sickness'.[64]

This discussion has so far focussed largely on women in cities. That is where the tensions lie. Nomadic and rural women have been little affected by the controversies. Rural women mostly live in secure kin-related settings where they move about with considerable freedom. When they venture beyond these protected areas, they travel swathed in *chaders* escorted by male relatives. Handicrafts are made at home; when they work outside, women work in family groups. Above all, their primary ambition in life is to become a mother, preferably of many sons. Through motherhood, the creativity of handiwork and efficient household management, rural women achieve status and a sense of personal fulfilment.

For all Afghans, rural and urban, the family functions as the paramount social institution to which individuals look for rights and owe recognised obligations. For women, a primary obligation is to uphold family honour by conforming to accepted behavioural norms. Although rules governing female behaviour vary from group to group, Afghan society is consistent in its innate belief in male superiority, giving to men the prerogative to determine the dos and don'ts for women. Few challenge this.

Thus the Taliban are reinforcing patriarchal norms wrapped in the mantle of Islam. The basics underlying their intent are understood by most Afghans and do not jar. But Taliban interpretations of Islamic injunctions are viewed as extreme, their conceptions of social values exaggerated, their measures harsh, their manner aggressive, and their stance apparently so rigid that many, even in rural and small town societies, find their austerity unacceptable. The coercive aspects of their administration that impinge on personal choices are undermining tolerance, a highly valued attribute in Afghan society, and this is universally deplored.

---

[64] Erika Knabe, 'Women in the Social Stratification of Afghanistan', in C.A.O van Nieuwenhuijze (ed.), *Commoners, Climbers and Notables* (Leiden: E.J. Brill, 1977), pp. 329-343 at p. 330, fn. 1.

The Taliban resent these disparaging characterisations and expound, repeatedly, on their commitment to female education and promises to provide some female employment–whenever the situation is secure.[65] They ask for time. Some would give them that time. Others are sceptical, convinced that Taliban procrastination and inconsistency belie their sincerity. At least some tendencies toward positive action are needed before the negative images can be redrawn; visible action, not rhetoric is required. The Taliban must come to realise that one can be a good Muslim without a beard or a *chadari*.[66]

The Taliban also seem not to appreciate that war and exile have fostered expanded expectations. Before the war neither the education nor the health system stretched very far into the rural areas. Only about three per cent of school age females went to school; preponderantly in urban areas, mostly in Kabul; in some provinces virtually no girls were enrolled.[67] Infant and maternal mortality rates were, and still are, the second highest in the world; the highest next to Africa.[68] But now women have learned that health services can ease their suffering, that they need not grieve over so many infants. They have seen the benefits of education. They have experienced the satisfaction of raising livestock and poultry, of growing kitchen gardens and learning skills for better child care and extra income.

While the public skirmishes take place at the upper levels, the aid programmes that quietly function in districts held by the Taliban build on these heightened expectations. Steady progress at community levels occurs when aid providers are willing to be flexible in seeking imaginative alternatives[69] and, equally important, when communities learn to persuade authorities to modify the harshness of their restraints. While some programmes function semi-clandestinely, ultimate success is possible only when communities commit

---

65 For example, the Consul General in Karachi at a press conference: Guinevere David, 'Taliban will protect women, human rights', *The Nation*, 28 May 1997.

66 In June 1997, Afghans in Peshawar were startled by the rumour that the *Amir al-Momineen*, Mohammad Omar, had announced that beards were recommended, but not compulsory. Therefore the authorities should ease up on their harassment of men over this issue. Athough unconfirmed, beardless friends recently visited Jalalabad with no adverse effects. Can a similar softening toward the *chadari* possibly be in the offing?

67 *The Status of Education in Afghanistan* (Peshawar: University of Nebraska/Omaha Education Support Section Project, 1994) vol.I, p. 17.

68 *United Nations Human Development Report 1996* (New York: United Nations Development Programme, 1996), p. 159.

69 For descriptions, see *Aina*, the UN Afghanistan Magazine, published in Islamabad by UNOCHA. In addition, the BBC soap opera 'New Home, New Life' includes episodes on everything from conflict resolution and psychological trauma, to health and archaeology. It is a demonstrable success.

themselves to action by presenting their desires to local authorities. Evidence suggests that numbers of communities are doing so.[70]

There are those who belittle these programmes, referring to them as bandaids, useful, perhaps, in periods of transition, but far from satisfactory in the long term. 'Our objective must be to break the walls. Home schools are not enough. You cannot train doctors and engineers in a home school', says an Afghan lady poet and NGO director.[71] The critics deplore compromises made in the name of pragmatism, warning that the larger central issue of basic rights for women will be ignored, if not forgotten. Many donors such as the Nordic countries have clearly stated that they will not support programmes if women's rights are not respected. Yet they recognise that under current circumstances flexibility is required and thus agree to endorse programmes as long as it can be demonstrated that they form part of 'broader strategies benefiting females'. Such ambiguity clouds assistance delivery. Lack of consensus is a continuing problem, lofty statements calling for 'one voice' notwithstanding. Both sides have dug in their heels. In the standoff, one can imagine each side asking of the other, 'Will they never learn?'[72]

Since access to women under the Taliban is so perplexing, it is useful perhaps to view the totality of Afghan women as a pyramid. The sound base is broad and consists of a majority who live in rural areas cherishing aspirations that are almost exclusively oriented toward children and family. Their needs lie in all aspects of basic and non-formal education, in health and in skills training for better family welfare. Here some progress, albeit slow, is taking place in a non-confrontational manner.

At the tip are the small number of Western-oriented, assertive working women who have taken a leading part in the emancipation process begun in 1959.[73] They have become accustomed to formal employment in mixed environments, often in association with foreigners who are now joined in battle on their behalf. These women call for the right to participate fully at all levels of decision-making. They bear the full brunt of Taliban ire.

---

[70] Two examples are given in 'Statement by the Afghan Community', presented to the International Forum on Assistance to Afghanistan (IFAA) in Ashgabad, Turkmenistan, 21-22 January 1997, p. 3.

[71] Home schools which began tentatively as an experiment have expanded to include many thousands of students, boys and girls, in many diverse areas.

[72] It is a pleasure to acknowledge my debt to Mr Zivan Damato for this observation.

[73] Fahima Rahimi, *Women in Afghanistan/Frauen in Afghanistan* (Liestal: Stiftung Bibliotheca Afghanica, 1986).

In the centre is the solid core of professional teachers, medical practitioners, engineers, judges, administrators, businesswomen, social workers and civil servants of every sort which has grown in magnitude and strength since the beginning of the century. Largely from middle class, conservative but progressive families, these women neither wish to deny their society's values nor compromise Islam. Over the years, they have shown by their comportment that Afghan women can function in the public sphere with no loss of dignity to themselves, their families or the nation. Tragically, many have been lost to Afghanistan through resettlement. Many thousands remain, nevertheless, and thousands of others are being trained even though opportunities for utilising their training looks bleak. It is this strong central core that most urgently needs to be uncaged if Afghanistan is to recover and move forward.

IS AFGHANISTAN ON THE BRINK OF
ETHNIC AND TRIBAL DISINTEGRATION?

Bernt Glatzer

Introduction: The ethnic system

Afghan society is usually labelled as 'tribal', a notion which is not the same as 'simple' or 'primitive'. Afghan society is complex, the product of thousands of years of imperial policies, of conquests, of state building and political decay, of far-reaching spiritual, artistic and social achievements as well as of destruction and chaos. Studying complex societies involves identifying lines of structure and order, finding models or threads in order not to get lost in a sea of confusing phenomena and events. Not only do outsiders wanting to understand a society use simplified models; local people too use mental social maps to find their way through their own society.

Gender and age are primary dimensions of such social maps; locality and sources of livelihood are other ordering criteria. In ecologically well-defined mountain areas, the valleys and river banks may be used to categorise a population further. In open areas with little economic variation–note in this respect that 70-80 per cent of pre-war Afghans were peasants–other social categories gain importance, for example kinship group and tribe or ethnic grouping. This does not mean that tribal and ethnic structures are the necessary outcome of a given demographic, economic and geographic setting, but once tribal and ethnic structures are culturally available and acceptable and part of the historically-given arsenal of social institutions, they are quite practical to structure an economically rather homogeneous population in a vast area with little infrastructure.

Anthropologists and demographers have tried hard to count the ethnic groups and tribes of Afghanistan, with widely differing results. The most serious attempt to list the ethnic groups in Afghanistan to my knowledge is that of Erwin Orywal and collaborators.[1] They list 55 ethnic names in Afghanistan. Orywal also cautions that ethnic

---

[1] Erwin Orywal (ed.), *Die ethnischen Gruppen Afghanistans: Fallstudien zu Gruppenidentität und Intergruppenbeziehungen* (Wiesbaden: Dr. Ludwig Reichert Verlag, 1986).

groups and identities are local categories (*emic*). They are relative, variable and dynamic.[2] Orywal has listed the following ethnic groups in Afghanistan: Arab (Arabic speakers), Arab (Persian speakers), Aimaq, Baluch, Baluch (Jat-Baluch), Brahui, Eshkashimi, Farsiwan, Firuzkuhi, Gavarbati, Ghorbat, Gujar, Hazara, Hazara-Sunni, Hindu, Jalali, Jamshidi, Jat, Jogi, Kirghiz, Kutana, Maliki, Mawri, Mishmast, Moghol, Mountain-Tajik, Munjani, Nuristani, Ormuri, Parachi, Pashai, Pushtun, Pikraj, Qarliq, Qazaq, Qipchak, Qizilbash, Rushani, Sanglichi, Shadibaz, Sheghnani, Sheykh Muhammadi, Sikh, Taheri, Tajik, Tatar, Taymani, Taymuri, Tirahi, Turkmen, Uzbek, Wakhi, Wangawala, Yahudi, and Zuri.[3]

A closer look at this list reveals the problematic side of ethnic categories: Aimaq, Firuzkuhi, Jamshidi, and Taymani are listed together, but according to most locals and to most authors Firuzkuhi and Jamshidi are sub-categories of Aimaq. Taymani usually deny that they are Aimaq and many of them feel affinity with the Pushtuns, whereas their Pushtun neighbours deny them Pushtun status. The Pushtuns of Badghis call all Sunni Persian speakers 'Aimaq' which is annoying to local Tajiks who are Sunni Persian speakers but fiercely object to being categorised as 'Aimaq'. Self-categorisation and ascription by neighbours differ and often cause dissension. 'Jat', for example, is a derogatory term for non-pastoral migrant groups with a similar connotation to 'Gypsy' in Europe. These people instead use distinct ethnic names such as Ghorbat, Shaykh Mohammadi, Musalli or the terms of their occupation.

To facilitate discussion of the ethnic complexity of Afghanistan I propose the following definition of 'ethnic' deduced from modern anthropological usage: by 'ethnic' I understand a principle of social order and of social boundary based on the identification of oneself and of others with social units or categories which combine the following properties: (a) they comprise both genders, all age groups and transcend generations; (b) they are believed to have distinctive cultural qualities by which the members of that unit would differ from comparable neighbouring units; (c) members identify themselves and their families with the past and future of that unit; (d) members and neighbours give them a name (*ethnonym*); and they are not sub-units of other ethnic groups.

It is important here to note that ethnic categories and systems are part of the regional culture; they can be observed but not defined by outside analysts. Ethnicity is a phenomenon of social boundaries. An ethnic group cannot be identified or characterised only from within.

---

[2]   Ibid, pp. 9, 18f, 73ff.
[3]   Ibid. pp. 18-19. This transcription has been simplified and alphabetically ordered by the author.

Ethnic groups identify themselves in contrast to other groups. Analytically speaking, ethnicity is not a quality *of a* social group, but a relation *between* social groups.[4] Ethnic identities keep changing over time. The pioneer of the *ethnos* theory, S. M. Shirokogoroff, stated as early as 1935 that ethnic units are *processes*, not static phenomena.[5] The speed of such processes varies geographically and leads to unequal developments even within an ethnic group. It seems that those processes tend to accelerate in times of turmoil and violent conflict.

The present civil war in Afghanistan has frequently been analysed as an *ethnic* war: the Pushtuns against the Tajiks, Hazara and Uzbek or others, each of the groups fighting separately under its own commanders and military structure. The predominantly Pushtun Taliban are believed to aim at printing their ethnic stamp on all other ethnic groups of the country, and non-Pushtuns are supposed to fight against Pushtun dominance and against their ethnic marginalisation. Although there is a grain of truth in this view, such a simplification is of little help in evaluating the present situation in Afghanistan and the chances for a peaceful future.

The main ethnic groups in the Afghan conflict

The Pushtuns. There is no doubt that the Taliban polarised the country between a predominantly Pushtun south and east, on the one side, and on the other the centre and north where Pushtuns are only a minority. Pushtuns are estimated to account for between 40 per cent and 60 per cent of Afghan nationals. There are no reliable figures for the total population, and estimates range between 15 and 20 million. Thus the minimum number of Pushtuns in Afghanistan (40 per cent of 15 million) is 6 million, while the maximum (60 per cent of 20 million) is 12 million. In Pakistan the figures are equally unreliable; the last Census (1981) counted 11 million Pushto-speaking Pakistanis.[6] The Pushtuns subdivide themselves into thousands of tribes along a genealogical charter which they use as a basis of unity and solidarity as well as of fission and conflict. Due to their explicit and elaborate tribal system and possession of their own language and code of ethnic values and norms (*Pushtunwali*), ethnic identity for Pushtuns is

---

[4] This point was introduced to international discussion by Fredrik Barth, 'Introduction', in Fredrik Barth (ed.), *Ethnic Groups and Boundaries: The Social Organization of Cultural Difference* (Boston: Little, Brown & Co, 1969), pp. 9-38.

[5] S. M. Shirokogoroff, *Psychomental Complex of the the Tungus* (London: Kegan Paul, Trench, Trubner, 1935), pp. 12-23.

[6] *Statistical Pocket Book of Pakistan 1991* (Karachi: Federal Bureau of Statistics, 1991), pp. 76, 84. The Census of 1981 contains statistics of languages, not of ethnic groups.

straightforward and rarely questioned by themselves or others, although interethnic fluctuation takes place.

The Tajiks. The Tajiks are the second largest group in Afghanistan. Calling them an 'ethnic' group involves stretching the usual ethnic definitions. There is no recognisable cultural, social or political boundary between them and the others. Groups of people called 'Tajik' live all over the country: in the larger cities they form majorities or important minorities. Most of the people in the provinces north of Kabul up to Badakhshan are called Tajik and in almost all Pushtun provinces there are important pockets of Tajiks. Their social groups are organised along local lineages, village clusters, valleys and occupational groups. When asked what people they are, most Tajiks answer by naming their valley, area, or town. 'Tajik' is mainly an analytical term, used by others to designate those who do not belong to a tribal society, who speak Persian and who are mostly Sunni.[7] There seems to be an increasing tendency of non-tribal Persian speaking Afghans to identify themselves as 'Tajik' when speaking to outsiders.[8]

The Hazara. The Hazara are another ethnic group whose members play a major role in the civil war. They are now estimated to number 1.5 million. A majority adhere to the Imami Shiite confession ('Twelver Shia'); minorities among them are Ismaili and Sunni.[9] The Hazara speak their own Persian dialect, Hazaragi, and are geographically concentrated in the Central Afghanistan highlands, in an area called the Hazarajat.[10] Sizeable groups live also in various parts of northern

[7]　In northeast Afghanistan there are also Ismaili Tajik (Islamuddin Sawez, 'Anpassung und Abgrenzung–Die Tagik', in Orywal (ed.), *Die ethnischen Gruppen Afghanistans*, pp. 284-289).

[8]　The western Afghan Shia Persian speakers are referred to in the literature as 'Farsiwan': see, for example, Louis Dupree, *Afghanistan* (Princeton: Princeton University Press, 1980), p. 59. There is obviously no clear ethnic boundary between Tajik and Farsiwan. At least nowadays, there are educated Herati Shia Persian speakers who call themselves 'Persians' (not Iranians) and 'Tajik' (Rameen Moshref, personal communication); compare also Robert L. Canfield, 'Ethnic, Regional, and Sectarian Alignments in Afghanistan', in Ali Banuazizi and Myron Weiner (eds.) *The State, Religion and Ethnic Politics: Pakistan, Iran and Afghanistan* (Syracuse: Syracuse University Press, 1986), pp. 75-103 at p. 78.

[9]　The latter are not to be confused with the Sunni Hazara of Badghis, also called Qala-i Nau Hazara, who are usually counted among the Aimaq or as a separate ethnic group closer to the Tajik than to the Central Afghan Hazara.

[10]　In official publications of the Hezb-e Wahdat, the most powerful political party among the Hazara, their country is called Hazaristan (*Wahdat Newsletter*, vol.6, no. 63, August 1997).

Afghanistan, and in the major cities, particularly in Kabul, in the poorest sector of the society; as well as in Quetta (Pakistan) and Mashhad (Iran). The Hazara are identified by the other Afghans as one ethnic group recognisable by their prevailing Central Asian phenotype. Before the war I found the Hazara reluctant to name themselves 'Hazara', maybe because in Kabul Hazara has the connotation of 'very poor' or 'coolie'. The war has changed this attitude; decades of independence from Kabul have led to a remarkable ethnic self-confidence.

European anthropologists who visited the Hazara before the war even questioned their ethnic unity.[11] A large block among the Hazara are the Sayids, who form their spiritual and political élite. The Sayids believe themselves to be descendants of the Prophet Mohammad and thus separate themselves from the commoners. The latter subdivide themselves into many tribes and clans but without an overarching genealogy. Modern Hazara nationalists claim descent from Chinggis Khan, thus hoping to raise the social status of the Hazara within the Afghan value system of social groups.

A unifying factor is their popular dislike of Pushtuns. The Afghan Government in the 1880s and 1890s subdued the Hazara with a Pushtun army and allotted the best agricultural and pastoral land to Pushtun clans and chiefs. From that time until 1978, Pushtuns intruded into the Hazarajat as administrators, merchants, money lenders, landlords and nomads–in short, as persons who came to extract resources from the Hazarajat but who gave little in return. The Hazarajat liberated itself from the communist regime in 1979; one of the free Hazaras' first actions after that was to deny all Pushtuns access to Central Afghanistan. As a consequence Pushtun nomadism suffered a dramatic decline because it depended to a large part on summer pastures in that part of the country.

The former mosaic of political parties among the Hazara reflects their initial lack of unity, their parties ranging from ultraconservative mullah-networks (Shura-i Ettefaq) to moderate conservatives and to modern Islamist radicals (Nasr), and even to Maoist parties. Pressure from Iran, which supported most of the Hazara parties, and pressure from their adversaries in the post-1992 civil war drove them together politically. Today we hear only of the pro-Iranian Hezb-e Wahdat ('Party of Unity'). The recent successes in Wahdat's battles against the Taliban in Ghorband, Wardak and Mazar indicate a Hazara unity which never had existed before. If this tendency continues the Hazara may

---

[11] Lucas-Michael Kopecky, 'Die Saiyid und die imamitischen Hazara Afghanistans: Religiöse Vergemeinschaftung und Ethnogenese', in Orywal (ed.), *Die ethnischen Gruppen Afghanistans*, pp. 165-203.

become the first major ethnic group in Afghanistan which is able to act as a coherent unit.

The Uzbek. The fourth important ethnic group are the Uzbek (Uzbeg, Özbeg, Uzbak) of North Afghanistan. They speak their own Turkish language, adhere to Sunni Islam, and are ordered in tribes and clans. Most pursue agriculture and sedentary animal husbandry. Their numbers equal roughly those of the Hazara. One part of the Afghan Uzbek are an autochthonous population, living in North Afghanistan for centuries, who were ruled by their own begs and amirs before the Afghan state extended its control to the river Oxus. The other part of the Uzbek population migrated into Afghanistan after the expansion of the Tsarist Empire and again during the Sovietisation of Central Asia. These Uzbek immigrants did not fuse with the autochthonous Uzbek, but formed a sort of distinct ethnic group under the name of *muhajerin* ('refugees').[12] Before 1978 the Afghan Uzbek were known as relatively docile citizens, although anti-Pushtun agitation which had an ethnic target but hardly an ethnic base did exist. During the Soviet-Afghan war, some of the Uzbeks sided with the pro-Soviet government or rather with the pro-minority policy of the new government and were militarily organised under Rashid Dostum's Jawzjani militias; others sided with the Mujahideen, mainly under the Harakat-e Enqelab of Mawlawi Mohammad Nabi Mohammadi, whose leaders, but not commanders, were almost exclusively Pushtun.[13]

The examples of the four largest ethnolinguistic units in Afghanistan may demonstrate that ethnic 'groups' are not organised into opposing political or military blocks. With the exception of the Hazara, who recently succeeded in joining their forces under Khalili's Hezb-e Wahdat, none of these groupings had ever developed a decision-making institution which could express the will of the whole ethnic 'group', or at least of the larger part of it, and which could lead such people to any concerted political or military action. The Pushtuns are said to have ruled the country for 250 years. In fact it was not *the* Pushtuns, but Pushtun rulers. The latter governed a wide range of different people, but never all the Pushtuns, not even a majority of them, and the actual day-to-day administration was left mainly to non-Pushtuns, to a Persian-speaking urban élite.

---

[12] Audrey Shalinsky, 'Uzbak Ethnicity in Northern Afghanistan', in Orywal (ed.), *Die ethnischen Gruppen Afghanistans,* pp. 290-303.

[13] Olivier Roy, *L'Afghanistan: Islam et modernité politique* (Paris: Éditions du Seuil, 1985), p. 175.

The tribal system

The term 'tribe' needs further clarification because it is often confused with 'ethnic group'. In this context tribes are sub-units of ethnic groups. In Afghanistan tribes are based on the notion that their members share a common ancestor through agnatic descent. An individual may be a member of many tribes, each of which is a sub-unit of a larger one. Tribes have 'brother' or 'cousin' tribes, which are situated on the same structural level and define lines of conflict or of solidarity, depending on whether they feel threatened by a common enemy or whether they compete for material or symbolic resources. Tribes are not cultural units; the markers of tribal boundaries are genealogical and sometimes also geographical. This does not exclude notions of qualitative difference ('my tribe is better than your tribe'); such comparisons rest on identical scales of value, not on feelings of cultural difference or strangeness, as in ethnic relations. In the following description and analysis of the tribal system I use the Pushtun model which is more elaborate than that of other ethnic groups.

Local folklore has it that all Pushtuns are descendants of one ancestor, even if there is no agreement about the common grandfather's name. Some call him Qais Abdurrashid; others say he was Daru Nika or Khaled bin Walid–the legendary general of the army of the Prophet Muhammad. The name of the common ancestor is less important than the Pushtuns' sense of belonging to *one* huge kinship group or super-family. Their common ancestor had many sons, grandsons, great-grandsons and so forth, each being the ancestor of one of the innumerable branches and sub-branches or tribes and sub-tribes, clans and sub-clans down to the local lineages and families. The ordering principle of each tribal subgroup is identical to that of the larger group. There have been attempts to codify the Pushtun tribal system, the most famous being the *Makhzan-e Afghani* of Nimatullah, written in the early seventeenth century. Such genealogies list thousands of tribes together with legends and anecdotes about their origins and how they joined or split.[14] The tribal charter is based on patrilineality, but in some conspicuous cases this principle is set aside for notable exceptions. Some of the more famous and powerful tribes such as the Afridi or Ghilzai are connected to the rest of the Pushtuns by adoption or by female links. Adventurous or romantic stories

---

14 Khwaja Nimatullah b. Khwaja Habibullah al-Harawi, *Tarikh-e Khan Jahani wa makhzan-e Afghani* (Dacca: Asiatic Society of Pakistan, 1960-1992) vols. I-II. Dorn issued a translated version in 1829 under the title *History of the Afghans* (London: Susil Gupta, 1965). Another, more handy, genealogy is Hayat Khan, *Hayat-e Afghan* (Lahore: Sang-e-Meel Publications, 1981), originally translated into English by Priestley in 1874.

usually adorn these deviations from the patrilineal rule in the genealogical books. Adaptations to social and political realities were always possible as the tribal system was managed in a flexible manner.

In principle, one has to be born into a tribe, but Afghan pragmatism allows exceptions. Through consensus of the tribe, outsiders may be allowed to reside in their area. If that person and his family honour the tribal code of behaviour the newcomers may be accepted as members after a generation or two.

A few words about terminology. People, ethnic groups and tribes are called *qawm* in Pushto and in most other languages in Afghanistan. This reflects the traditional notion that ethnic groups and tribes are structured equally, that is, by genealogical links. Sub-tribe or clan is *khel* in Pushto, but it may also be called *qawm* as any tribal unit may be a tribe or sub-tribe at the same time; it depends on whether it is seen to be from the root of the tree or from above. A sub-tribe or sub-clan of a *khel* is also a *khel* down to the village level. A common suffix of names of larger tribal units is *-zai* (for example, Mandozai, meaning 'Son of Mando'; the plural form is Mandozi, 'Sons of Mando'), and *-khel* for the sub-units. Some *khel*s have grown to such an extent that they became recognised as tribes of their own, such as the Sulaimankhel, a branch of the Ghilzai. The suffix *-zai* indicates in most cases a southern or western origin (for example, the Yusufzai of Swat originate from Kandahar), whereas most of the eastern tribes lack the typical tribal suffix, such as the Afridi, Mohmand, Zadran, Jaji, Mangal, Shinwari, as well as many smaller tribes of Khost such as the Tanai, Saberi, Lakan, and Ghorboz.

Most of the tribes in Afghanistan are neither corporate nor political entities, yet the tribal system has always served as a blueprint for political alliances. Political entrepreneurs found kinship and tribal links most convenient as a basis for alliances or confederations in order to challenge even imperial powers and to secure areas of freedom and independence for their people. The Confederation of the Ghilzai Pushtuns in the early eighteenth century succeeded in conquering Isphahan and dethroning the Shah of Persia, but their ephemeral tribal cohesion did not allow them to run the empire for more than two years. A few decades later their Pushtun opponents, the Abdali Confederation later renamed as Durrani, established the first Kingdom of Afghanistan, and conquered the lands between Herat and Delhi. After two generations their political power was exhausted, the fissive forces inherent in every segmentary tribal system became stronger than the cohesive forces, and the kingdom and the confederation disintegrated, a striking example of the working of Ibn Khaldun's law of the rise and fall of empires.[15]

There is a dilemma in tribal societies: the very tool which enables tribal leaders to establish powerful political entities, the charter of segmentary solidarity, is also instrumental for segmentary division. Once a charismatic leader who masters the instrument of segmentary alliances loses influence or dies, the divisive character of the segmentary tribal system will gain the upper hand. Tribal systems usually do not develop institutionalised political power which could tolerate fluctuations in the abilities of individual rulers.

The Pushtun ideal of equality is based on the tribal system. The idea is that all Pushtuns are born equal as children of one common ancestor; social and economic inequality, which of course exists, is not given by nature or birth but is supposed to be individually achieved, and is open to be questioned any time. The tribal order discourages social hierarchy, but it defines social nearness and distance. Pushtuns use their tribal order to mark lines of conflict and solidarity. If I see two men fighting I must side with the one who is 'closer' to me, that is, the one with whom I share the nearest common patrilineal ancestor. In the Pushtun tribal areas in eastern Afghanistan and northwest Pakistan we find a sociopolitical division into two opposite factions: the Tor Gund and the Spin Gund. Here is an example from Khost in eastern Afghanistan: the Saberi, Jadran, Chamkani, Tanai, and Mandozai are named Spin Gund in opposition to the Tor Gund, comprising the Mangal, Ismailkhel and others. Today this dichotomy has become practically obsolete, but people clearly remember which tribe belongs to which *gund*. The recent violent land dispute between Chamkani and Mangal, however, is between two opposing *gund* and the sympathies of the Saberi who are not part of the conflict lie with their *gund* fellows, the Chamkani.

Tribes are localised to various degrees. The Ghilzai, for example, are scattered all over Afghanistan; thus there is no proper Ghilzai land. Yet there are areas where Ghilzai and certain of their sub-tribes predominate. Other tribes, such as the Afridi, have a clearly-defined homeland. The latter is true for most of the eastern tribes along the Afghan-Pakistani border. Tribal land is subdivided along tribal subdivisions. Therefore belonging to a tribe means having access to the land of that tribe. There are also landless tribals, for example those who have sold their inherited land to another member of their tribe. If a member of a tribe loses ownership of his land, he retains at least his right to reacquire land if he regains the necessary means. Localised

---

[15] Ibn Khaldun, *Muqaddimah*. The standard translation is by Franz Rosenthal, *Ibn Khaldun. An Introduction to History: the Muqaddimah* (New York: Bollingen Foundation, 1958) vols. I-III.

tribes also own common and undivided property, for example pastures and forests which every member has an equal right to use. A member of a tribe knows that he defends his own security and future of his family when he defends his tribe's land.[16]

Those tribes who inhabit a coherent area are also able to define and enact a common policy. Even where influential persons (*khan*) or commanders have emerged, decisions of importance for the whole community are reached at community councils (*jirga*). According to tribal equality, every free and experienced male person of the tribe has the right to attend, to speak and to decide. Only jirgas on very high levels (provincial or all-tribe) need a system of representation. For example, when the tribes of Mandozai and Ismailkhel sent a joint jirga to Peshawar in order to attract international aid, they nominated two representatives from each sub-tribe to participate.[17] Jirgas traditionally have neither leaders nor chairmen. The participants prefer to sit in circles in order to avoid any dominant position. Decisions are only reached through consensus. Therefore discussions last until everyone is convinced or until it becomes clear that there will be no consensus. Once a decision is reached at a jirga, it is binding on every participant.

During the anti-Soviet war a new political term came into use in Afghanistan: 'shura'. This is the Arabic term referring to the first meetings of the Muslim community (*ummah*). The word 'jirga', on the other hand, is derived from Mongolian and lacks religious connotations. Other differences between jirga and shura are the more representative character of a shura, a relatively permanent membership, and more regular intervals of the meetings. Jirgas in contrast meet *ad hoc* when a problem arises.[18] Tribes traditionally have their own militia, called 'arbaki' or 'lashkar', consisting of young unmarried men who are not experienced enough to participate in jirgas or shuras, but who are strong and loyal enough to sanction the decisions. The classical sanction for not adhering to a decision of a jirga or shura is for the arbaki to burn down the house of the offender, and the worst sanction is expulsion from the tribe and tribal land.

I have mentioned leaders. A closer look at them reveals that their power is rather limited. Whereas tribes and their divisions are relatively stable and dependable, tribal leadership is not. Political

---

16 For a comprehensive account of the legal aspects of the tribal system in Khost see Willi Steul, *Paschtunwali: Ein Ehrenkodex und seine rechtliche Relevanz* (Wiesbaden: Steiner Verlag, 1981).

17 At that time (1991) I worked with the Danish Committee for Aid to Afghan Refugees, an NGO which was approached successfully by that jirga.

18 For a good analysis of the Afghan shuras see Lynn Carter and Kerry Connor, *A Preliminary Investigation of Contemporary Afghan Councils* (Peshawar: ACBAR, 1989).

leaders can hardly build their power on the tribal structure alone because it is egalitarian. They have continually to convince their followers and adversaries of their superior personal qualities and have to procure and redistribute resources from outside their tribal realm; the followers expect from them material or symbolic advantages. In times of political chaos people demand from their leaders security. Followers may be quickly disappointed by a khan or commander and may switch overnight to another big man; there is no institutional safety net for tribal leaders.

In a tribal setting one can gain power by (a) controlling tenants; (b) attracting many regular guests through lavish hospitality; (c) channelling resources from the outside world to one's followers; (d) demonstrating superior rhetorical gifts and regular sound judgements in the shuras and jirgas; and (e) gallantry in war and conflict. All these qualities are transitory and have constantly to be reactivated against ever-present competitors.

In spite of the proverbial unpredictability of tribal leadership, the tribal system is an element of stability and resilience in times of turmoil and when state authority has disappeared. It provides safety, legal security and social orientation in an otherwise chaotic and anarchic world. Where the tribal system is functioning smoothly, the Taliban have not dared to touch it: they continue instead the pre-war practice of Afghan governments of letting peripheral areas (that is, the largest part of the country) be ruled by local authorities and institutions. In the post-communist period, my experience was that in areas where the tribal system was dominant (for example in Khost) the return of refugees and the rehabilitation of the local economy proceeded smoothly.[19]

Although tribal structures are present all over Afghanistan, they do not function everywhere as well as in some areas in the east, because the tribal system and the ethnic factor are only two of many ordering principles in Afghan society. In the predominantly Pushtun south and southwest of Afghanistan, tribalism plays an important role, but the tribes are less localised; most communities and political units are multi-tribal. There a tribesman with political ambitions recruits followers from among his own family, lineage, clan and tribe, but there are limits to this strategy because southern Pushtun tribes live dispersed over very wide areas, with little infrastructural means of being brought together. Hence a man seeking political leadership beyond his village will try to make use of additional or even

---

[19] Bernt Glatzer, 'From Refugee to Resident: Effects of Aid on Repatriation', in E. Eide and T. Skaufjord (eds.), *From Aid During Times of War to Aid for Reconstruction and Development: Seminar Report* (Peshawar: Norwegian Afghanistan Committee, 1992), pp. 161-168.

alternative social structural elements and try to combine as many as possible, for example networks based on locality, economy, sectarianism, Sufi orders, religious schools, political and religious parties and so on.

Tribalism and ethnicity are often lumped together and blamed as the main factors leading to turmoil, war and the breakdown of state order, or to the failure to re-create such an order. I have tried to explain that the tribal structure of Afghanistan is rather a factor for stability, even if it does not provide the basis for durable political leadership. The ethnic principle, on the other hand, is neither a factor for stability nor necessarily for instability. Ethnicity is a phenomenon of social boundary-making, an awareness of sharing a set of cultural values within one group versus another. Members of an ethnic group share a feeling of 'we' versus 'they'.

Ethnicity and tribalism: dangers and opportunities

After this outline of Afghan ethnic and tribal principles, I shall now assess their inherent dangers and implications. As mentioned already, a high degree of ethnic dynamism is observable in Afghanistan; that is, ethnic and tribal boundaries and identities are not fixed since time immemorial, but are often a matter for negotiation. Whether social action is based on ethnic criteria depends on opportunities and tactics and may change quickly. In his public speeches the Pushtun Gulbuddin Hekmatyar initially stressed his attachment to pan-Islamism and the Muslim ummah. Boundaries between Muslim states should be made obsolete, he argued. Later, during his recruitment campaigns in Pushtun areas, he appealed to the ethnic solidarity of the Pushtuns.

During the anti-Soviet war in Afghanistan and later the guerrilla war against the pro-communist regime in Kabul, the frontline divided almost all ethnic groups and the larger tribes. In all those groups there were (a) sympathisers and collaborators of the socialist regimes; (b) fierce enemies of these regimes; and (c) people who decided to wait and see who would prevail. Many families strategically placed one family member among the communists, placed another one or two among the Mujahideen of various parties, and sent yet another as a refugee to Europe or USA while the rest of the family set up their household in a Pakistani refugee camp. Of course the family members all kept in touch with each other.

During the early years of the war foreign observers and Afghan intellectuals on both sides of the front expected a prompt end to tribalism and ethnicity. Some hoped for the 'achievements of socialism' and for the 'brotherly help of the USSR' to transform Afghanistan into a supra-ethnic class society and eventually into a harmonious socialist union; the others expected the grand jihad against the formidable common enemy to do the job of creating one Afghan nation. As the war dragged on, it became obvious that the Kabul regimes and the Mujahideen were divided into numerous hostile factions. It also became obvious that ethnicity and tribalism were contributory factors to this process, but not the most important ones. In early 1980 the Sunni Mujahideen had formed about 100 different parties who ran sixty offices in Peshawar. During the following year the Pakistan Government forced the Mujahideen to unite and acknowledged only seven parties, who were given some administrative tasks with respect to the millions of Afghan refugees in Pakistan. The rest of the parties had to close their offices in Pakistan. The seven parties issued identity and ration cards, thus forcing the refugees to make a choice between one or another of the parties. Even more relevant was the Pakistani policy of distributing military equipment and money for the Mujahideen exclusively through the seven parties. The Shiite Mujahideen formed another eight parties, who found support in Iran. Over the years Iran succeeded in unifying most of them; today the only two significant Shia parties are the Hezb-e Wahdat, which unites the great majority of the Hazara, and the Harakat-e Islami of Asif Mohseni, which appeals more to the urban Shia and is independent of Iran.[20] The Soviet-installed governments, and the army and civil service of Kabul between 1978 and 1992, were divided into hostile factions as well. Two presidents, innumerable ministers, generals and other dignitaries were killed in factional fights.

Ethnicity and tribalism are often held responsible for Afghan disunity. Indeed practically all of the conflicting parties and groups, including the Taliban, show a certain emphasis towards one or another ethnic group. This, however, is no proof that ethnic divisions are the cause of political cleavages and violent conflicts. Every Afghan belongs to an ethnic group; thus a quarrel between two Afghans who by chance do not belong to the same ethnic group may easily be misinterpreted as ethnically motivated.

A closer look at the history of the present conflict reveals that ethnicity was an epiphenomenon in the Afghan war.[21] Or as Canfield puts it, 'Contrary to what might be supposed, the actual operating units of socio-political coalition [...] are rarely genuinely "ethnic" in composition'.[22] The undeniable fact that the parties do have a recognisable ethnic stamp has mainly to do with the local background of their founders and their leaders rather than with their ethnic identity.

---

[20] Jonathan Lee, personal communication.
[21] See Roy, *L'Afghanistan: Islam et modernité politique*; Canfield, 'Ethnic, Regional, and Sectarian Alignments in Afghanistan'.
[22] Canfield, 'Ethnic, Regional, and Sectarian Alignments in Afghanistan', p. 76.

If that local background has a demographic majority of one ethnic group, it is most likely that the closest companions of the founders and leaders will belong to the same ethnic group. They will prefer to recruit from the same area and use the local language, creating a barrier to those unfamiliar with that tongue. Olivier Roy gives the example of the Persian-speaking Nurzai Pushtuns of southwest Afghanistan who initially joined the Jamiat-e Islami (which is mainly Tajik because Persian is the language spoken in that party), whereas the Pushto-speaking Nurzai opted for the Harakat-e Enqelab.[23]

Due to its primordial connotations, ethnic identity, more than other social orientations, has a strong emotional content, leading to particular aggressiveness when conflicts arise. Organisers and leaders of conflicts use ethnic and tribal emotions and the feelings of honour and shame connected with them as a tool or weapon as efficiently as a Stinger or Kalashnikov. Although the national unity of Afghanistan is on the agenda of all these groups, ethnic arguments are increasingly deployed in political agitation and there is a visible tendency towards ethnicisation of the conflict. Anti-Pushtun sentiments among Persian and Turkic-speaking minorities in north and west Afghanistan were fomented and turned against the Taliban as a last resort to activate morale and unity among the northern opposition forces, a tactic which backfires because it alienates Pushtun groups who hitherto participated in the Northern Alliance and encourages them to switch sides. The Taliban too did not do enough to avoid anti-Hazara agitations and killings in Kabul in May 1997 after some Taliban fighters were killed in Mazar-e Sharif, thus boosting the anti-Taliban feelings among the Hazara and other minorities who fear a similar fate.

Another important factor which has a strong impact on the events in Afghanistan is the perception of the Afghan conflict by foreign powers and media who understand this war as an ethnic one. As a consequence warlords of specific ethnic backgrounds are preferred and pampered, thus reinforcing the ethnic factor.

In October and November 1996 I carried out a survey about popular concepts of locality, ethnicity and tribe of about 100 peasants, artisans, traders, and students who recently came from different parts of Afghanistan to Peshawar and intended to return soon. To my surprise all of them without exception stressed the importance of Afghan national unity incorporating all ethnic minorities. A partition of Afghanistan, be it on ethnic or other lines, was seen as a terrifying prospect to be avoided by all means.

To sum up I do not see Afghanistan as being on the brink of ethnic or tribal disintegration, but agree with my interviewees that the breakup

---

[23] Roy, *L'Afghanistan: Islam et modernité politique*, p. 178.

of the country along ethnic lines holds real dangers. Ethnically-motivated aggression is on the rise in Afghanistan as elsewhere in the world, but there are also strong countervailing forces. The awareness of national unity has increased considerably during the last twenty years; this fact easily gets blurred in the daily news from the battlefront. Ethnic groups, including the Pushtuns, are not organised political entities who would be able to pursue a strategy of separation, and tribes have proved in recent years to be a stabilising factor rather than a disruptive one. Even the Hazara, who at present show the highest degree of internal political integration, feel strongly that they are Afghan nationals. What they fight for is the preservation of their local, cultural, and religious autonomy, not disintegration.

The future of Afghanistan will rather depend on whether the protagonists continue using ethnicity as a psychological weapon which invariably backfires against those who use it. It will also depend on Afghanistan's neighbours and on the regional powers who not only continue to fuel the Afghan civil war but also make things worse by applying ethnic criteria when choosing their 'friends'.

THE U.N. AND AFGHANISTAN: 'DOING ITS BEST' OR 'FAILURE OF A MISSION'?

William Maley

In 1940, Sir Nevile Henderson published a memoir entitled *Failure of a Mission*.[1] Henderson had been His Majesty's Ambassador to Germany during the high tide of British appeasement, and his recollections gave evidence of the scale of his own folly, although he certainly did not intend them to do so. Yet Henderson, while by the testimony of his contemporaries a man both dull-minded and hysterical,[2] lived in abnormal times, which ordinary career diplomats are doubtless thankful they need not confront. For most diplomats at most times, diplomacy is a matter of doing one's best in circumstances where the rewards of success are not high, but the costs of failure are not great. It is enough if they manage to do their 'best', even if their best may not be especially 'good'.

In Afghanistan in recent years, times have generally been abnormal, and missions have failed somewhat spectacularly. In April 1992, a United Nations plan for political transition disintegrated along with the regime of communist President Najibullah, who sought and obtained asylum in the UN's Kabul offices, from which he was dragged and murdered on the night of 26-27 September 1996 when the Taliban occupied the Afghan capital. Four months before the Taliban seizure of power, the Head of the UN Special Mission to Afghanistan, Mahmoud Mestiri, had also announced his resignation. While Mestiri's departure from office was not quite as dramatic as that of his predecessor Benon Sevan who had masterminded the failed 1992 plan, it represented every bit as potently the failure of a mission. His successor, the German diplomat Dr Norbert Holl, was left with the unenviable task of negotiating with a resurgent Taliban movement, a

---

[1] Sir Nevile Henderson, *Failure of a Mission: Berlin, 1937-1939* (London: Hodder & Stoughton, 1940).

[2] On Henderson's career in general, see Felix Gilbert, 'Two British Ambassadors: Perth and Henderson', in Gordon A. Craig and Felix Gilbert (eds.), *The Diplomats 1919-1939* (Princeton: Princeton University Press, 1953), pp. 537-554. On Henderson's disposition to hysteria, see Duff Cooper, *Old Men Forget: The Autobiography of Duff Cooper (Viscount Norwich)* (London: Hart-Davies, 1955), p. 217.

task which one experienced analyst has compared to 'grasping smoke'.[3] In October 1997, Holl's own resignation was announced. Why, one might properly wonder, has Afghanistan proved such a graveyard for UN mediation? What are the ingredients of the failure of a mission? To attempt an answer to this question is the objective of this chapter. It is divided into five sections. The first discusses the nature of peacemaking diplomacy, with particular emphasis on the distinctions between interstate and intrastate conflicts. The second traces the history of UN involvement in mediation in Afghanistan, and makes the point that the residues from one episode of mediation can affect the viability of mediation efforts which follow. The third looks at the specific reasons why the Mestiri mission failed, and examines the consequences of that failure. The fourth points to an enduring error of focus in UN mediation efforts. Finally, the fifth addresses the heretical question of whether some forms of mediation can do more harm than good, and offers some suggestions about how peacemaking diplomacy might be structured to generate better outcomes.

Peacemaking diplomacy

From the earliest days of its existence, the United Nations has been heavily involved in attempting to procure peaceful outcomes to political disputes. This is a function of the organisation which is specifically recognised in Chapter VI of its Charter,[4] and which successive Secretaries-General have seen fit to support through the exercise of their 'Good Offices'. The assassination of Count Folke Bernadotte in 1948 in the Middle East pointed to the perils which could attend an active approach to the task of mediation, although the subsequent award of the Nobel Peace Prize to his successor Dr Ralph Bunche showed that a degree of success could in some circumstances be achieved.[5] There is an important sense, however, in which 'failure' is easier to pinpoint than 'success': the successes of peacemaking diplomacy may prove limited, if not downright ephemeral. Even if the disputes which divide the parties are effectively resolved, there is no guarantee that other issues will not emerge to divide them just as deeply. Peacemaking diplomacy does not put an end to politics. Furthermore, a process of mediation is almost certain to fail in the

---

3   Michael Keating, 'Women's Rights and Wrongs', *The World Today*, vol. 53, no. 1, January 1997, pp. 11-12 at p. 12.

4   See Bruno Simma (ed.), *The Charter of the United Nations: A Commentary* (Oxford: Oxford University Press, 1995), pp. 505-565.

5   On the assassination of Bernadotte and the award of the Nobel Prize to Bunche, see Brian Urquhart, *Ralph Bunche: An American Life* (New York: W.W. Norton & Co., 1993), pp. 153-232.

long run if it neglects to address some key issue separating the parties.[6] In crises, where even short-run failure can often lead to catastrophe, this may seem a less-than-compelling argument for seeking comprehensive settlements, particularly in the nuclear age. However, short-run success can arguably lead to even more dire catastrophe, which was why Winston Churchill labelled the September 1938 Munich Agreement 'a total and unmitigated defeat'.[7]

A process of peacemaking diplomacy nonetheless has potentially a great deal to offer, and can embrace such diverse forms as shuttle diplomacy, face-to-face negotiation between parties with a mediator or mediators assisting, and mixtures of the two. Where deep psychological barriers exist between parties, an effective mediator can move to break those barriers down. A mediator can inject a degree of flexibility in negotiations, by giving voice to ideas which the parties may fear to articulate directly. Furthermore, if a mediator is in a position to mobilise resources, he or she may be able to affect the prudential calculations of the various parties, dislodging them from positions of intransigence. A mediator may also be able to weave a veil behind which parties can execute manoeuvres which they might be reluctant to undertake unilaterally. A well-furnished mediator should be in a position to perform all these tasks. However, there are some tasks which lie beyond the ability of even the most deft of mediators. A mediator is not in a position to create a statesmanlike or consensually unified élite. Nor can a mediator bring about fundamental change in the political culture of a particular country or region. Nor can a mediator be expected to play the role of a latter-day Solon, comprehensively restructuring the institutions of a polity to make them function more effectively.[8] To blame a mediator for persistent weaknesses in these spheres is quite unreasonable.

The art of diplomacy, at least since the Peace of Westphalia of 1648, has been viewed predominantly as that of conducting a conversation between states. Such exercises as the Congress of Vienna, the Congress of Berlin, and the Versailles Conference,

---

6   See Robert F. Randle, *The Origins of Peace: A Study of Peacemaking and the Structure of Peace Settlements* (New York: The Free Press, 1973), p. 487.

7   *Parliamentary Debates (House of Commons)* vol. 339, col. 360, 5 October 1938.

8   See William Maley, 'Peacekeeping and Peacemaking', in Ramesh Thakur and Carlyle A. Thayer (eds.) *A Crisis of Expectations: UN Peacekeeping in the 1990s* (Boulder: Westview Press, 1995), pp. 237-250. For a good account of the complex contingencies of mediation in the international sphere, see Jacob Bercovitch and Allison Houston, 'The Study of International Mediation: Theoretical Issues and Empirical Evidence', in Jacob Bercovitch (ed.), *Resolving International Conflicts: The Theory and Practice of Mediation* (Boulder: Lynne Rienner, 1996), pp. 11-35. Many of the points which Bercovitch and Houston make are equally pertinent when one is discussing mediation in internal conflicts.

involved a dialogue between representatives of states, conducted within a framework of rules and norms which dominant élites understood, even if on occasion their commitment to those norms was nominal rather than substantive. The League of Nations provided a venue for such conversations in the period between the two world wars, and the United Nations has provided a similar venue in the period since it was established at the San Francisco Conference of 1945. However, extending the conversation of states to include other parties is a much more recent development in world politics. Even as late as 1988, the UN Secretary-General, Javier Pérez de Cuéllar, was to remark that since the United Nations was an organisation of governments, it would be 'against our philosophy to be in touch with the enemies of governments'.[9] In recent times this has changed, especially when the phenomenon of the 'failed' or 'collapsed' state has imperilled international peace and security by threatening to set the population of some particular disaster area on the march as refugees. In such circumstances, there has been considerable pressure on the United Nations, and specifically upon the Secretary-General through his 'Good Offices',[10] to initiate discussions with all relevant parties, whether representatives of states or not, with a view to averting a descent into chaos and anarchy.

Yet once one extends the scope of diplomatic conversations to include non-state actors, a range of problems can arise. Since the UN General Assembly has very often accepted the credentials of the delegation of some particular group within a country as entitling it to occupy the country's General Assembly seat, it is prima facie committed to accepting the legitimacy of that party as a government. There may be good reasons on occasion for putting this prima facie assumption to one side–for example, where the 'government' in question is clearly a 'puppet government'[11]–but failing this or some other compelling reason, such as an abominable human rights record, it is arguably not the role of the UN to take steps which compromise the legitimacy of member governments, although Pérez de Cuéllar's blanket formulation almost certainly went too far. Choosing which

9   Quoted in Thomas M. Franck and Georg Nolte, 'The Good Offices Function of the UN Secretary-General', in Adam Roberts and Benedict Kingsbury (eds.), *United Nations, Divided World: The UN's Roles in International Relations* (Oxford: Oxford University Press, 1993), pp. 143-182 at p. 150.

10   See Kjell Skjelsæk, 'The UN Secretary-General and the Mediation of International Disputes', *Journal of Peace Research*, vol. 28, no. 1, February 1991, pp. 99-115; Cameron R. Hume, 'The Secretary-General's Representatives', *SAIS Review*, vol. 15, no. 2, Summer-Fall 1995, pp. 75-90.

11   See William Maley, 'The Geneva Accords of April 1988', in Amin Saikal and William Maley (eds.), *The Soviet Withdrawal from Afghanistan* (Cambridge: Cambridge University Press, 1989), pp. 12-28 at pp. 13-14.

actors to engage in discussion may be a politically explosive issue, especially if some actors are the clients of external patrons. The very act of adopting them as parties to negotiation may compromise the mediator in the eyes of other parties. Directly admitting external patrons to discussion may prove equally controversial, as this may appear to legitimate their claims to a role in determining the political future of the country in question. Yet excluding them may doom any negotiating process to failure, as may the exclusion of important domestic actors. More seriously, non-state actors may lack hierarchical authority structures, and be incapable of reaching–or reaching with expedition–the decisions upon which further progress in negotiations may depend. Most seriously of all, non-state actors may deny the authority of the very framework of rules and norms within which conversations between states occur. The normative foundations for binding agreements between parties may in these circumstances prove extremely difficult to establish to the satisfaction of the relevant actors.

UN mediation in Afghanistan

United Nations mediation in Afghanistan has a venerable, and by now rather well-chronicled history.[12] It falls into four phases. The first, which culminated in the signing of the Geneva Accords of April 1988, was quintessentially an example of diplomacy between states, although with some peculiarities not found in routine state-to-state conversations. The mediation team was led by Diego Cordovez. The parties to the Accords were Afghanistan and Pakistan, and the United States of America and the Soviet Union signed as witnesses and guarantors. The parties of the Afghan resistance were neither direct participants in the negotiations, nor signatories to the agreements. The second phase followed the completion of the Soviet withdrawal from Afghanistan in February 1989, the resignation of Cordovez to become Foreign Minister of Ecuador, and the expiry of the mandate of the United Nations Good Offices Mission in Afghanistan and Pakistan (UNGOMAP) on 15 March 1990. In this phase, Benon Sevan, as

---

12 See Riaz M. Khan, *Untying the Afghan Knot: Negotiating Soviet Withdrawal* (Durham: Duke University Press, 1991); Diego Cordovez and Selig S. Harrison, *Out of Afghanistan: The Inside Story of the Soviet Withdrawal* (New York: Oxford University Press, 1995); Barnett R. Rubin, *The Search for Peace in Afghanistan: From Buffer State to Failed State* (New Haven: Yale University Press, 1995); Amin Saikal, 'The UN and Afghanistan: A Case of Failed Peacemaking Intervention', *International Peacekeeping*, vol. 3, no. 1, 1996, pp. 19-34; Frédéric Grare, *Le Pakistan face au conflit afghan (1979-1985): au tournant de la guerre froide* (Paris: L'Harmattan, 1997).

Head of the Office of the Secretary-General in Afghanistan and Pakistan (OSGAP), sought to bring about the creation of an interim government in Afghanistan in accordance with the terms of a statement issued by the Secretary-General on 21 May 1991 calling for 'an intra Afghan dialogue', a 'credible and impartial transition mechanism' and 'free and fair elections, taking into account Afghan traditions, for the establishment of a broad-based government'.[13] Here, the negotiations extended to include various Afghan resistance groups, although not all, and arguably not the most important, notably some of the key commanders operating within Afghanistan itself. This phase came to an end with the collapse of the communist regime in mid-April 1992. The third phase dated from December 1993, when the General Assembly voted for the establishment of a Special Mission to Afghanistan, and continued until the resignation of Mahmoud Mestiri in May 1996. This phase was notable for Mestiri's disposition to treat some factions as if they were the government, and the government occupying the UN seat if it were just another faction. The fourth phase, inaugurated by the appointment of Dr Norbert Holl to replace Mestiri, has been marked by extreme difficulty in finding anyone relevant with whom to negotiate, not least because the Taliban seem largely uninterested in negotiating seriously with anyone else.

The first phase of the negotiations has on occasion been held up as an example of a UN success, not simply by Cordovez, but also by some academic commentators.[14] However, there are two significant grounds upon which this can be questioned. The first is that the Soviet withdrawal from Afghanistan was prompted by fundamental calculations of Soviet interest: at the November 1986 meeting of the Soviet Politburo which took the decision to withdraw from Afghanistan, the Geneva negotiations under UN auspices scarcely rated a mention.[15] It is important to note that this decision came well before Gorbachev's December 1988 speech to the UN General Assembly which signalled a renewed interest on the part of the USSR in reviving the UN as an agency through which international peace and security could be promoted. Thus one can doubt whether the Soviet withdrawal can reasonably be seen as a UN success. Second, given that the exclusion of the Afghan resistance from the negotiations created a high level of suspicion towards the UN as a whole, one can also doubt whether this phase should be judged a success at all, since this

---

[13] Quoted in William Maley and Fazel Haq Saikal, *Political Order in Post-Communist Afghanistan* (Boulder: Lynne Rienner, 1992), pp. 23-24.

[14] See, for example, Thomas M. Franck, *Fairness in International Law and Institutions* (Oxford: Oxford University Press, 1995), pp. 181-183.

[15] See 'Sekretnye dokumenty iz osobykh papok: Afganistan', *Voprosy istorii*, no. 3, 1993, pp. 3-32.

suspicion significantly limited the ability of the UN to play a useful role in bringing the Afghan parties together in the period following the Soviet withdrawal, which of course was the core requirement for conflict resolution in Afghanistan.

The second phase arguably failed for the same basic reason, namely a failure to engage the relevant parties in negotiation, but this failure should not be attributed simply to the legacies of the first phase. The Sevan mission was hampered by a misunderstanding of the fundamental correlation of forces in Afghanistan. On the one hand, Sevan was unduly impressed by the survival of Najibullah's regime in the period after the Soviet troop withdrawal, which resulted not from generalised normative support for the regime, but from its ability to use massive Soviet aid to buy support from particular militias,[16] commitments which manifestly would not survive the cutoff of Soviet aid to which the Soviet and US administrations agreed following the failure of the coup attempt in Moscow in August 1991. On the other hand, Sevan gave far too much credence to the notion that it was possible to bypass existing parties to the conflict and replace them with new forces brought to the fore under UN auspices. Afghanistan's politicians had no interest in cooperating in their own liquidation: few politicians ever do. While there was indeed much to be said for the view that a number of prominent resistance groups–most notably the Hezb-e Islami of Hekmatyar and the Ittehad-e Islami of Sayyaf–were creatures of outside patrons, this charge could not be credibly directed at some of the more prominent commanders who had long struggled against Soviet forces in Afghanistan itself. To attempt to bypass these personalities was inviting trouble. Furthermore, a number of those whom Sevan appeared to view as providing an 'impartial' core of a transitional arrangement in Kabul, in keeping with the Secretary-General's 1991 proposals, were in the eyes of other (powerful) Afghans not 'impartial' at all, but supporters of the former monarchy who had exploited the ignorance of UN officials to paint themselves as Afghanistan's saviours. Where trust has broken down on the scale that occurred in Afghanistan in the 1980s, the very notion of 'interim', 'transitional', or 'impartial' forces lacks credibility, for no-one believes that interim authorities will relinquish power when the time comes for them to do so. It is thus not correct to suggest, as some writers have done,[17] that a workable UN plan for political transition in

---

[16] See Barnett R. Rubin, *The Fragmentation of Afghanistan: State Formation and Collapse in the International System* (New Haven: Yale University Press, 1995), p. 109.

[17] See, for example, M. Hassan Kakar, *Afghanistan: The Soviet Invasion and the Afghan Response, 1979-1982* (Berkeley & Los Angeles: University of California Press, 1995), p. 274.

Afghanistan was thwarted at the very last minute by the ambitions of certain resistance leaders. On the contrary, the belief that it would be possible after many years of arduous struggle to bypass significant elements of the Afghan resistance and instead accord power to a 'credible, impartial transition mechanism' was wishful thinking of the dreamiest possible variety.

But the greatest failure of Sevan's mission was that it concluded with his encumbering the UN with Najibullah as a guest in UN headquarters in Kabul. For the very large number of Afghans whose families had been cruelly persecuted in the years 1980-85 when Najibullah headed the secret police (KhAD),[18] it was simply incomprehensible that an organisation committed to the upholding of human rights should provide protection to such a figure. To them, Najibullah was a fugitive not from persecution but from justice, and the UN was his accomplice. Sevan could perhaps have argued that having offered Najibullah safe passage from the country, he was obliged to do all he could to secure his person, but the question then arises whether Sevan had exceeded his proper mandate by holding out the prospect of escape for Najibullah in the first place. Mediators are not responsible for securing the futures of the often-unappetising individuals with whom they deal, and it is dangerous (and in some circumstances, presumptuous) for them to attempt to do so: Count Folke Bernadotte rightly was prepared to meet with Heinrich Himmler in the dying days of the Second World War, but just as rightly, he did not offer him asylum in the Swedish Consulate in Lübeck from which he operated. The spectacle of the UN regularly raising with the Afghan authorities the question of safe passage for Najibullah from its Kabul premises simply rubbed salt into what was a raw wound, as did the UN's paying for telephone calls made by Najibullah to his family in India, at a time when many Afghans suffered enormously from their inability to communicate with their relatives. During his stay in the UN compound Najibullah privately compared himself to Nelson Mandela, but not many other Afghans shared this grotesque perception, and his slaying by brutal killers accorded at least some Afghans a certain grim satisfaction, since without the brutalising effects of KhAD there would have been fewer brutal killers on the loose in Afghanistan. Again, the UN Security Council's protest at the murder of Najibullah, while understandably focussed on the violation of the integrity of UN premises in Kabul, highlighted the gulf which seemed to divide the UN from many ordinary Afghans, who even if disturbed at the manner of his death had good reason not to mourn his passing.

---

[18] See Jeri Laber and Barnett R. Rubin, *'A Nation is Dying': Afghanistan under the Soviets, 1979-87* (Evanston: Northwestern University Press, 1988).

The failure of the Mestiri Mission

Mestiri's mission was not doomed to fail from the outset. Its mandate, as set out by the UN General Assembly, was appropriately modest, and so were Mestiri's initial contributions to consideration of the Afghanistan issue.[19] However, the mid-1994 first report of the Special Mission, while for the most part low key and sensible, did contain one contradiction which suggested that trouble might lie ahead. On the one hand the Special Mission noted that most Afghans 'opposed a non-Afghan armed military presence, including United Nations peacekeeping troops'.[20] On the other hand, it suggested that free and fair elections 'would be the best way to ensure that all segments of Afghan society participate in determining the future of the country'.[21] What was worrying in all this was that the Special Mission showed no sign of having assimilated one of the central lessons of the UN's experience in Cambodia in 1992-93, namely that in war-torn societies, an effective peacekeeping force is essential if the logistical complexities of holding a free and fair election are to be overcome.

Within a short space of time, the Special Mission unfortunately succumbed to the hubris which had also contributed to the failure of Sevan's mission. Here, it is necessary to talk briefly of the political context within which the Special Mission was operating. The collapse of the communist regime had led to the negotiation of the Peshawar Accord,[22] under which Sebghatullah Mojadiddi held office as President for two months, and was then succeeded by Burhanuddin Rabbani. Gulbuddin Hekmatyar, whose forces had been driven from Kabul by those of Ahmad Shah Massoud in April 1992 in order to avert an imminent Hezb-e Islami coup, began rocket attacks on Kabul in August 1992, at which point Rabbani labelled him 'a dangerous terrorist who should be expelled from Afghanistan'.[23] However, in April 1993, an agreement signed under Pakistani pressure between Hekmatyar and Rabbani and known as the Islamabad Accord provided for Hekmatyar to become Prime Minister, although Hekmatyar's fears for his safety led him not only to remain outside Kabul, but to continue rocket attacks.[24] Nonetheless, by December 1993, when the

---

[19] *Progress Report of the Special Mission to Afghanistan* (New York: United Nations A/49/208, s/1994/766, 1 July 1994).

[20] Ibid., para. 23 (h).

[21] Ibid., para. 40 (d).

[22] For the text of the Peshawar Accord, see *Situation of human rights in Afghanistan* (New York: United Nations A/47/656, 17 November 1992), Appendix I.

[23] BBC *Summary of World Broadcasts*, FE/1461/B/1, 17 August 1992.

[24] For the text of the Islamabad Accord, see *Afghan Peace Accord* (New York: United Nations S/25435, 19 March 1993). For a detailed critique of its provisions,

Special Mission was established, the situation in Kabul was more stable than it had been at any time since the communist regime collapsed.

This changed dramatically on 1 January 1994, when Hekmatyar allied his forces with those of Abdul Rashid Dostum (whom Hekmatyar had long denounced as a 'communist') in order to mount a coup attempt against Rabbani. It might have seemed logical to believe that the opponents of the Rabbani Government, having thereby torn up the Peshawar and Islamabad Accords, were in no position credibly to demand that Rabbani should subsequently step down in accordance with their provisions. Yet this was the very position which Mestiri was to adopt, and it doomed his mission to failure. From this point onwards, he seems to have embarked almost on a crusade to undermine the government whose credentials the General Assembly had accepted. He went so far as to express to journalists the view that he confronted 'a very difficult task–to wrest power from Mr Rabbani'.[25] This suggested objectives different from those which the higher organs of the United Nations had mandated the Special Mission to pursue. In November 1994, the President of the Security Council had issued a statement welcoming

the acceptance by the warring parties and other Afghan representatives of a step-by-step process of national reconciliation through the establishment of a fully representative and broad-based Authoritative Council which would: (i) negotiate and oversee a cease-fire, (ii) establish a national security force to collect and safeguard heavy weapons and provide for security throughout the country, and (iii) form a transitional government to lay the groundwork for a democratically chosen government, possibly utilizing traditional decision-making structures such as a "Grand Assembly".[26]

Not one of these three objectives specifically required that Mestiri approach his task in the way in which he did.

The most serious errors of the Special Mission came, however, in 1995, and here one can argue that they caused more actual harm than did any of the mistakes of Cordovez or Sevan. In early 1995, Mestiri claimed to have received a commitment from Rabbani to step down by late March. That Rabbani had agreed to any such thing was hotly contested by Rabbani's associates, and by late March there was no prospect whatever that it would happen, not least because Mestiri had

---

see William Maley, 'The Future of Islamic Afghanistan', *Security Dialogue*, vol. 24, no. 4, December 1993, pp. 383-396.

25 *Reuters*, 18 March 1995.

26 *Statement by the President of the Security Council* (United Nations: S/PRST/1994/77, 30 November 1994).

failed to secure any credible commitment from the Taliban to accept the UN's plans. In February and March 1995, dramatic military developments had taken place in the vicinity of Kabul. The forces of the Taliban, pushing northeast from Kandahar, in turn prompted the flight of Hekmatyar's Hezb-e Islami forces from their positions near Charasyab, and were then themselves driven from those positions by Massoud's forces. This created a small but significant window for meaningful negotiations between the Taliban and the Rabbani Government, for three reasons. First, the Taliban had suddenly met with battlefield failure; their thitherto largely-uninterrupted run of successes had come to a halt once they were confronted with more conventionally-organised military forces, and this may have given them pause to ponder their future strategy. Second, the Rabbani Government, while at last in a position to exercise full control over Kabul, was still susceptible to incentives to broaden its base, in the form of offers of reconstruction aid conditional upon its being willing to do so. Third, Dostum, whose forces had been ejected from their Kabul positions in June 1994, was under intense pressure from some circles in Russia to reach a compromise with Rabbani, whom the Russians hoped would in exchange move to curtail the operations of elements of the Tajikistan resistance based in the northern provinces of Afghanistan.[27] A realignment of Dostum with Rabbani at this point might well have inclined the Taliban–or their Pakistani backers–to an agreement formalising the de facto control which different power centres enjoyed in different parts of the country. The Special Mission proved incapable of exploiting this opportunity.

Instead, at a UNDP Donors' Conference held in Stockholm in June 1995 to build upon the new atmosphere of stability in Afghanistan, Mestiri with one speech managed to destroy his own credibility. In a background paper circulated for participants, the UN had made the important point that 'Ninety per cent of Afghanistan is now peaceful'[28]–something worth recalling in the light of subsequent claims by the Taliban that only their triumph could bring peace. The Special Mission gave no sign of having absorbed the message of this paper.[29] Furthermore, Mestiri seems not to have had properly-prepared

---

[27] Observations based on detailed discussions with Afghan and Tajik diplomats in Kabul in May 1995.

[28] United Nations, *Briefing of Donors on Afghanistan* (Stockholm: Donors' Meeting on Assistance for Afghanistan's Long-Term Rehabilitation and its Relationship with Humanitarian Programmes, 1-2 June 1995), p. 1.

[29] This remained the case even after Dr Holl took over as Head of the Special Mission. In January 1997, he claimed that the power struggle after the Soviet withdrawal from Afghanistan had 'brought more havoc and death than perhaps during the entire ten years of foreign occupation': see 'Statement by Dr. Norbert Holl' (Ashgabat: International Forum on Aid to Afghanistan, 21-22 January

speech notes–in the text which was supplied to foreign missions, some of the passages most hostile to Rabbani and Massoud were crossed out, but remained clearly legible[30]–and his contribution could only have been taken as an invitation to governments participating in the Donors' Conference to do what they could to challenge the legitimacy of the Kabul government, which he claimed had 'no legal basis'–an astonishing assertion given that it had been granted Afghanistan's UN seat. Of Dostum and the Taliban he voiced no criticisms, and he even expressed his disapproval of the idea of a settlement between Massoud and Dostum, on the grounds that it could provoke 'further ethnic tensions'. The spectacle of a UN mediator actually discouraging parties in conflict from reaching a compromise was truly remarkable in the annals of diplomacy, and doubtless explains why most participants in the meeting were simply aghast at his intervention.

It would of course be wrong to blame Mestiri for everything that has happened in Afghanistan since his disastrous speech of June 1995. That he acted in good faith was never in doubt. He played poorly what cards he had, but he opened with a weak hand. As Rubin has argued, 'the regional powers which voted for the mission in the General Assembly continued to undermine it through their policies of covert aid to the warring factions'.[31] Mestiri had been sent into the field with an extremely limited capacity to offer either inducements or threats to the parties. Indeed, by 1996 there were indications, not least in a speech which he gave in Karachi on the eve of his resignation, that he had come to a much more realistic understanding of the nature of the problems of political order which Afghanistan faced. However, by then it was too late, and it can be plausibly argued that his mis-diagnosis of Afghanistan's problems actually heightened the danger of mass ethnic conflict, which he rightly identified as an evil to be avoided if at all possible. Dostum may well have been inclined to resist Russian pressure anyway, but Mestiri's intervention gave him an additional excuse for doing so. Rabbani and Massoud may equally have been disinclined to compromise with the Taliban, but Mestiri's intervention undermined what moral authority he may have had to encourage such

---

1997), p. 1. In making this claim, Dr Holl exaggerated the level of war-related mortality in post-communist Afghanistan, which according to the highest figures cited in the popular press remains but a small fraction of that experienced according to the most conservative data cited in scholarly discussions of the communist period.

[30] The text faxed to this writer by a Western Embassy in Stockholm was accompanied by a covering note explicitly stating that the amendments to the text were those of the author, and not the Embassy.

[31] Barnett R. Rubin, 'Women and pipelines: Afghanistan's proxy wars', *International Affairs*, vol. 73, no. 2, April 1997, pp. 283-296 at p. 286.

compromise. Ironically, he was also unable to prevent the ultimate crystallisation of two ethnic blocs–Pushtun and non-Pushtun–in the wake of the fall of Kabul. While the formation of such blocs in early 1995 might well have created incentives for effective bargaining, by late 1996 such blocs came into being in a very different political context as a result of the perceived *impossibility* of effective bargaining.

Finally, Mestiri shared one weakness as a mediator with others who had preceded him, namely an almost obsessive reluctance to address the problem of misbehaviour by UN member states. Silber and Little, writing about UN actions in Bosnia, have referred scathingly to the UN's practice 'never to blame any side until you can blame all sides equally'.[32] Such an approach embodies a serious misapplication of the idea of 'neutrality', which is an appropriate position for the UN to adopt when it is conducting a classical 'peacekeeping' operation,[33] but quite inappropriate in situations such as the Bosnian.[34] The same criticism could be applied to the Special Mission's approach to Afghanistan. In 1995 and early 1996, there was an increasing volume of evidence to suggest that the Taliban were receiving significant assistance from Pakistan. The flow of outside assistance to the Taliban put them in a very different position from that of Massoud, who among resistance commanders 'alone lacked a powerful foreign patron'[35] when the communist regime collapsed, and whom UN observers in Kabul were aware had major supply problems, not least because arms sellers in the former Soviet Union demanded payment in hard currency. Mestiri may have hoped to address the matter of Pakistani interference in Afghanistan through 'quiet diplomacy', but for all the value his efforts actually had, he might just as well have been an ostrich seeking to initiate an underground conversation. This reticence actually worked to the disadvantage of moderates in the Pakistani Foreign Ministry, who were unable to draw on international condemnation as a basis for challenging the strategies of military hardliners. Yet pride of place for maintaining an overly-discreet silence rightly belongs not so much to Mestiri as to the senior UN official

---

32 Laura Silber and Allan Little, *The Death of Yugoslavia* (Harmondsworth: Penguin, 1995), p. 299.

33 See Paul F. Diehl, *International Peacekeeping* (Baltimore: The Johns Hopkins University Press, 1994), pp. 7-8.

34 See Michael N. Barnett, 'The Politics of Indifference at the United Nations and Genocide in Rwanda and Bosnia', in Thomas Cushman and Stjepan G. Mestrovic (eds.), *This Time We Knew: Western Responses to Genocide in Bosnia* (New York: New York University Press, 1996), pp. 128-162; William Maley, 'The United Nations and Ethnic Conflict Management: Lessons from the Disintegration of Yugoslavia', *Nationalities Papers*, vol. 25, no. 3, September 1997, pp. 559-573.

35 Rubin, *The Fragmentation of Afghanistan*, p. 273.

who in mid-September 1996, following the fall of Jalalabad, told amazed journalists that there was 'no evidence of Pakistani involvement'.[36] This statement could only have been read in Islamabad as a green light to push ahead with military operations, when what was needed was a firm warning that Pakistan was playing with fire. At this desperate moment, Afghan moderates confronted with an imminent Taliban assault could only have felt that the UN had betrayed not only them, but the humane principles for which the UN purported to stand. The effect of such episodes of studied blindness on the part of the UN may well be ultimately to legitimate a model of 'creeping invasion' by one state of another, in a way which will be profoundly destructive of any hope of consolidating a stable international order in the post-Cold War world.

Dr Holl was left with less room to manoeuvre than any of his predecessors, reflected in the contemptuous way in which the Taliban launched a major offensive in the Shomali Valley to the north of Kabul on 16 January 1997, just one day after the conclusion of UN-initiated ceasefire talks in Islamabad between officials of the Rabbani Government, the Taliban, and Dostum.[37] As long as the Taliban and their backers feel that they are achieving their objectives by military means, the UN Special Mission will be irrelevant to the practice of power politics in Afghanistan. This doubtless was one factor behind Holl's resignation, although the appointment of Ambassador Lakhdar Brahimi in 1997 as the Secretary-General's Special Envoy to report on the Afghanistan issue may also have left him with the sense that he had little worthwhile to do. However, should the Taliban begin to falter or to fragment, or their backers to have second thoughts about the wisdom of their actions, the UN may be able to play a useful role in facilitating a dignified retreat.

Missing the heart of the Afghan problem

If it is to do any more, it will need to improve its diagnosis of the Afghan problem. It is not sufficient (although it may be understandable) to complain, as Dr Holl did in October 1997, that Afghanistan's 'military and political élite' want 'to fight to the last bullet'.[38] Such dismissive remarks, by blaming all parties alike, do little to foster careful analysis of the exact roots of 'spoiler

---

36 *United Press International,* 14 September 1996.

37 *Report of the Secretary-General on the Situation in Afghanistan and its Implications for International Peace and Security* (New York: United Nations, A/51/838, S/1997/240, 16 March 1997), para. 3.

38 *Reuters,* 15 October 1997.

problems'.[39] They also mask the important differences of *vision about Afghanistan's future* which the various combatant parties represent. These different visions need to be recognised and accommodated, even if not ultimately reconciled, if peace proposals are to be of any use. The crisis confronting Afghanistan runs deeper than the mere composition of the *government*. It turns more significantly on the nature, structure and functions of the *state*. This issue has never been properly confronted by the UN, perhaps because its officials, mindful of the terms of Article 2.7 of the United Nations Charter, see it as 'within the domestic jurisdiction' of the state; and the effect of this omission has been to adulterate the credibility of the UN effort as a whole.

To show in detail how this omission might be rectified lies beyond the scope of this chapter.[40] There are no 'magic solutions' to Afghanistan's problems, but merely a range of risky options which may have unanticipated and nasty consequences. Nonetheless, a few brief observations about suggestions which the UN might consider putting to the Afghan parties, should a window of opportunity for a settlement reopen, are in order. In Afghanistan, the state has virtually collapsed, and will not be resuscitated rapidly. Yet if the central state is weak to the point of invisibility, the incentive for any group to seek exclusive control of it will be consequently reduced.[41] A loose federal or zonal system, with national sovereignty perhaps vested in a council of mayors of the capitals of different 'regions', would allow more than one winner, always a desirable potential outcome in a divided society, and minimise the amount of outside force required to secure the durability of a settlement.[42] Very strong UN guarantees would be needed to affirm that federalisation would not lead to the disintegration of Afghanistan, and assistance from the international community in protecting Afghanistan from the predations of its neighbours and from vested commercial interests would certainly be required.

The battle for Kabul arises from the *symbolic* rather than *functional* significance of controlling the capital, and a viable settlement would need to detach Kabul from this symbolic role. The

[39] See Stephen John Stedman, 'Spoiler Problems in Peace Processes', *International Security*, vol. 22, no. 2, Fall 1997, pp. 5-53.

[40] For an elaboration of some of the points which follow, see William Maley, 'Quel Afghanistan?', *Les Nouvelles d'Afghanistan*, no. 79, 1997, pp. 24-26.

[41] See Russell Hardin, *One for All: The Logic of Group Conflict* (Princeton: Princeton University Press, 1995).

[42] See Barbara F. Walter, 'The Critical Barrier to Civil War Settlement', *International Organization*, vol. 51, no. 3, Summer 1997, pp. 335-364 at p. 362; Charles King, *Ending Civil Wars* (Oxford: Oxford University Press, Adelphi Paper no. 308, International Institute for Strategic Studies, 1997).

'corpus separatum' proposal for Jerusalem that was contained in the November 1947 UN General Assembly Resolution proposing the partition of Palestine provides one possible model to follow. However, were Kabul to be put under international administration in perpetuity or for a long period, it would be necessary to prevent it from becoming a 'honey-pot', with millions of internally displaced persons heading for it: one way of doing so might be disperse the head offices of UN humanitarian offices around the country. This could complement the UN's wider humanitarian efforts in Afghanistan, not addressed in this chapter, which have recently focussed on grassroots empowerment of Afghan communities.[43] The UN must also recognise that if it is to contribute to the reconstitution of Afghanistan, it must be prepared to engage in a *long-term* commitment, of a kind which standard UN funding processes have rarely accommodated: it will be difficult if not impossible for the UN to induce Afghans to think of the long-term when its own procedures militate against their doing so.

In the light of this somewhat unhappy history, we are in a position to offer at least preliminary responses to the two questions posed at the beginning of this chapter, namely why has Afghanistan proved such a graveyard for UN mediation, and what are the ingredients of the failure of a mission? Missions can fail in at least six different ways. First, relevant internal issues can be overlooked. Second, relevant internal parties can be overlooked. Third, the contribution to destabilisation of external parties or issues can be overlooked. Fourth, parties can lose confidence in the good faith of the mediator. Fifth, negotiations can be conducted too publicly, in such a way that the glare of publicity limits the flexibility of parties, and encourages them instead to posture for the benefit of their supporters. Sixth, the parties may simply not be interested in reaching an agreement at a given moment: the conflict may not be ripe for settlement. All these reasons for failure have played their role at one time or another in the Afghan case.

Negotiations may fail without doing harm. However, a further lesson from the Afghan case is that the mere existence of a negotiating process may actually be damaging to some parties. From December 1993, the work of the Special Mission directly undermined attempts by the Rabbani government to establish its own legitimacy, for the implication of the Mission was that Afghanistan lacked legitimate national authorities, and that it was the role of the Mission somehow to bring them into being. Furthermore, the presence of the Mission in the field provided a tailor-made excuse for governments which wished to distance themselves from Afghanistan and the Afghans. The US

---

[43] See *Poverty Eradication and Community Empowerment: Afghanistan PEACE Initiative 1997-1999* (Islamabad: United Nations Development Program, 1997).

State Department, for example, routinely covered its lack of any serious policy to help Afghanistan–a country struggling with the bitter legacy of indirect US funding of groups such as Hekmatyar's Hezb-e Islami–by reiterating its support for the UN Mission, even when it was transparently obvious that nothing of value was likely to come from the Mission's activities. Indeed, by November 1997, the UN Secretary-General in a strikingly candid report went so far as to suggest that 'it could be argued that ... the role of the United Nations in Afghanistan is little more than that of an alibi to provide cover for the inaction–or worse–of the international community at large'.[44] Finally, the Mission's existence also had the potential to deter groups from entering compromises on which they might otherwise have embarked had it not been for the hope that if they remained intransigent, the UN might be able to deliver them a larger share of power.

Thus, governments which are offered the assistance of a UN Special Mission would be well advised to tread with caution. Such missions may do good, but they may also complicate still further what is already a fraught and fractious situation, and the losers will inevitably include large numbers of people beyond the ranks of the UN's negotiating partners. Many Afghans–perhaps naively–have put their trust in the dexterity and flexibility of the UN system. The kindest conclusion one can offer is that for too many Afghans, the UN's 'best'–despite all the difficulties it has had to confront–has simply not been good enough.

---

[44] *The Situation in Afghanistan and its Implications for International Peace and Security: Report of the Secretary-General* (New York: United Nations, A/52/682, S/1997/894, 14 November 1997), para. 55.

HAS ISLAMISM A FUTURE IN AFGHANISTAN?

Olivier Roy

From traditional fundamentalism to Islamism ... and back

Traditional fundamentalism–that is, the will to have the Sharia and only the Sharia as the sole law–has been pervasive right through modern Afghan history. Most of the tribal and popular uprisings, whether against an imperial power (Great Britain and the Soviet Union) or a reformist government (King Amanullah in 1928, President Daoud in 1975 or Nur Mohammad Taraki in 1978) were waged in the name of Islam. Rural mullahs were usually at the core of such reactionary movements. Islamism is something different: it is the perception of Islam more as a political ideology than as a mere religion. For Islamists, the Sharia is just a part of the agenda. They address society in its entirety, in politics, economics, culture and law; they claim to reshape society along purely Islamic lines. In this sense Islamism is a modern movement, the last wave of an anti-imperialist mobilisation which dates back to the last century. The Islamists recruit among the intelligentsia and the modern strata of society, including students from 'secular' faculties, mostly in sciences. They have also been able to attract many educated women, who, if wearing the Islamist veil, were accepted into the political and economic arena, which is almost anathema for traditionalists. The Islamists think that a truly Islamic society could be established only through an 'Islamic State', which presupposes a revolution, or at least a struggle for gaining political power–while fundamentalist mullahs rely on any de facto power to implement Sharia. The founding fathers of Islamism were Hassan al-Banna, who founded the Egyptian Muslim Brotherhood, and Abul Ala Maududi, who created the Jamaat-e Islami in the Indian subcontinent.

Afghanistan has been part of this wide movement of Islamic revivalism which had engulfed the Middle East during the 1970s and 1980s. From the political mobilisation of the Kabul students (1965-71) to the war against the communist regimes and the Soviet invasion (1978-92), the Islamists have been in the limelight of the Afghan

199

political scene.[1] They won the student elections at Kabul University in 1971, launched a failed insurrection against President Daoud's regime in 1975, and then, during the exile in Pakistan (1973-78) split between two main parties: the Jamiat-e Islami led by Burhanuddin Rabbani, and the Hezb-e Islami led by Gulbuddin Hekmatyar. Sociologically and ideologically, they were very close to their Middle Eastern counterparts: they recruited among the intelligentsia, and particularly in the scientific high schools or faculties: both Ahmad Shah Massoud and Gulbuddin Hekmatyar were students in engineering. They were joined by many of the educated people who fought inside Afghanistan, and waged the bulk of the fighting against the Soviet troops.

The 1980s saw the peak of the Islamists' influence: they secured the bulk of foreign help for the resistance, and attracted many foreign Islamist militants from the Middle East, who joined their training camps from 1985 until the early 1990s. But after the Soviet withdrawal in 1989, the Afghan Islamist movements also experienced the general decrease of influence and militancy which has pervaded most of the other Middle Eastern radical groups.[2] Even before the fall of Kabul to the Mujahideen in April 1992, ideology played little role in political alignments, which had more to do with the growing ethnic polarisation of the country. Most of the bitter internecine fighting was between the Jamiat and the Hezb, the two Islamist movements in Afghanistan–the former being mainly 'Tajik', a term which is usually applied to the Sunni Persian speakers, and the other Pushtun. But the rise of the Taliban from 1994 onwards suggests that the appeal of Islam for building a new political order has not faded away. Although all parties are nowadays based on an ethnic constituency, none of them promises to create an ethnic state, or even to promote the interests of a specific ethnic group. The Jamiat is Tajik; the Taliban are Pushtuns (from the southern tribal belt, while Hekmatyar recruited mainly among detribalised eastern Pushtuns); the Shiite Hezb-e Wahdat is exclusively Hazara, the Jumbesh of Dostum (and later of Abdul Malik) is mainly Uzbek. But all of them pretend to play for the centre–from the Taliban, who demand nothing less than the recognition of their hegemonic power over the state, to the Hazaras, who simply ask for a fair share of central power and recognition of the Shiite system of law (the 'Jaffari' code). Although there is a huge discrepancy between the mild views of the Jumbesh (and to a lesser extent of the Jamiat) about what Islam means in everyday life, and the strict enforcement of their

1   For a history of Afghan Islamist movements, see Olivier Roy, *Islam and resistance in Afghanistan* (Cambridge: Cambridge University Press, 1990).

2   See Olivier Roy, *The Failure of Political Islam* (Cambridge: Harvard University Press, 1995).

version of the Sharia by the Taliban, all parties advocate an 'Islamic Afghanistan'. So the failure of the Islamist ideology to establish a 'true' Islamic State does not mean that political Islam has no meaning in Afghanistan: it is still a tool of legitimisation for any power. But is this just a cloak for a power whose basis is purely ethnic, or does Islamism still have a future in Afghanistan?

Afghan Islamism and the rest of the Muslim world

Although it had its own momentum, Afghan Islamism has always been closely dependent on other Islamist movements. The ideology of the Afghan Islamists has been entirely borrowed from the two biggest mainstream Islamist organisations, namely the Muslim Brotherhood and the Pakistani Jamaat-e Islami. Moreover, the Afghan movement has sometimes been seen as just an offspring of these organisations. Both were instrumental in the formation of the Afghan Islamist cadres: Burhanuddin Rabbani and Ghulam Mohammad Niazi (founder of the Jamiat-e Islami), as well as Sebghatullah Mojadiddi, spent years at Al Ahzar University in Cairo, where they were involved in Muslim Brotherhood activities. The younger members, like Hekmatyar, were close to the Pakistani Jamaat-e Islami, which regards itself as the 'Godfather' of its Afghan brothers: the fact that Qazi Hussain Ahmad, who was to become the Amir of the Jamaat in the late 1980s, was himself a Pushtun and had been in charge of Afghan affairs during the 1970s, is evidence of this connection. There has been no great Afghan Islamist thinker: the political literature as well as the statutes of both the Jamiat and the Hezb were borrowed from the Muslim Brotherhood, and the radical Egyptian Islamist ideologist Sayed Qutb influenced the Hezb profoundly.

This close connection with Middle Eastern movements was reinforced during the war against the Soviets. With the blessing of the CIA and of the Saudi Intelligence (headed by Prince Turki), and with the active hand of the Pakistani Inter Services Intelligence Directorate (ISI), an international support network was established, channelled mainly through the Muslim Brotherhood. Many Arab militants came to fight in Afghanistan, bringing their own view of radical Islam, but also carrying back home their combat experience in the name of jihad. The hub of these informal networks was established in Peshawar through the 'Office of Services' (*Mektab al-khadamat*), headed by a Jordanian Muslim Brother of Palestinian origin, Abdullah Azzam, in close conjunction with the Saudi activist and tycoon Osama Bin Laden, who founded the 'House of Auxiliaries' (*Bayt al-ansar*), a foundation in charge of recruiting and financing the volunteers. By deciding where to send the volunteers, and who would be the beneficiary of their help (usually Hekmatyar), the foreign Islamists

played a major role in introducing into the Afghan resistance the more
recent features of Middle Eastern religious and political debate. I will
stress three of these features. First, the Arab volunteers were strongly
anti-Shiite; they contributed to accentuating the common prejudice
among Afghan Sunnis against the Hazara Shia, which led to various
massacres of civilian Hazaras living in Kabul after the fall of the city
in May 1992. The Shiite-Sunni divide has consequently been widened.
Second, under the influence of 'Salafism' (return to the way of the
ancestors) and various brands of Wahhabism, the volunteers strongly
opposed the pervasive Sufi customs among the Afghan population,
and advocated the destruction of many shrines. Third, they did not see
their jihad as waged against communism, but against any 'kafir'
influence, including Christianity and Western culture, although their
presence in Afghanistan had originally been encouraged by the
Americans.

These phenomena accentuated traditional Sunni fundamentalism
and scripturalism among many Afghans, mainly in the Pushtun-
populated areas, due to the fact that the Arab volunteers were primarily
travelling with Pushtun groups (for example, they had been expelled
by Ismail Khan, the Jamiat leader of Herat, in 1986). They contributed
to accentuating the shift from Islamism to a new brand of
fundamentalism, which was mainly a blend of traditional Sunni
fundamentalism with strong anti-Western cultural and political bias,
inherited from the Islamist movements. The new common ground for
the different groups advocating Islamisation was less and less the
concept of an Islamic State than that of Sharia law. Thus they were
reverting to traditional fundamentalism, albeit blended with the anti-
western fervour that characterised the Islamists. The rise of the Taliban
in Afghanistan is a clear example of what I have called 'neo-
fundamentalism', following the crisis of the Islamist political model.

Afghanistan did not escape the general crisis facing the Islamist
movements, which had been apparent as early as the late 1980s. We
can summarise this crisis as follows. First of all, the growing wave of
Islamist protest, instead of uniting the Muslim masses, had, on the
contrary, aggravated the cleavages of the Muslim world. The Iranian
regime had been the natural candidate to lead the Islamist wave,
because of its victory in 1979. But the Iranian revolution did not
inspire similar developments in other Muslim countries except among
some Shiite minorities in Lebanon and Afghanistan. The first Gulf
War, from 1980-88, saw tacit support from the mainstream Arab
Islamist movement, the Muslim Brotherhood, for Iraq. The Shiite-
Sunni divide increased everywhere, from Lebanon to Pakistan. Islamic
solidarity was brought into question during the second Gulf War
(1990-91), when the various branches of the Muslim Brotherhood
adopted different stands according to their national interests, notably in

Egypt, Kuwait, and Jordan. After 1991, the newly-born Islamist movement, the Algerian FIS, lost its political battle in Algeria to the military and the GIA.

The Soviet withdrawal from Afghanistan and the second Gulf War put an end to the 'holy' joint venture that supported the Afghan Mujahideen. Most of the militants who fought or were trained in Afghanistan turned against the US-Saudi coalition: Hekmatyar praised Saddam Hussain, and after 1991, many Middle Eastern militants who came back from Afghanistan to their own countries joined or created radical groups which pledged to fight US and Saudi interests. Sheikh Omar Abdul Rahman, Ramzi Yousuf, and Mir Aimal Kansi, all of whom have been involved in terrorist actions in the USA, were former members of these Afghan Mujahideen support networks. In Algeria, the GIA was founded by Afghan veterans who had also fought in Bosnia and Kashmir.

The Gulf crisis underlined the ambiguity of the Saudi attitude. The Saudis had supported extremely radical movements during the 1980s with the objectives of undercutting the impact of revolutionary Iran in the Arab world by deploying radical Sunni Islamism against Shiism, and of turning an Islamist wave against the Soviet Union (this last goal being one they shared with the US). 1991 saw the failure of these goals: the collapse of the USSR made redundant an anti-communist radical Islam, and the Gulf War exposed both the insularity of Iran and prompted the turning of the Sunni Islamist movements against their Saudi Godfather. But the Saudis did not suddenly stop supporting radical elements. They ceased to fund the more vocal supporters of Saddam Hussain, but kept open many channels of communication with radical groups–Hekmatyar for example–and continued to subsidise various networks of madrassas, religious schools and institutions for the propagation of Islam which were staffed either by radicals or at least by fundamentalists who opposed Western influence.

The consequence of this set of events has been a growing disconnection of militant networks from their sponsoring states, in the Sunni as well as the Shiite world. Iran has acknowledged its failure to export the revolution after Ayatollah Khomeini's death in 1989 and was simply using radical groups abroad as a tool of its nationalist foreign policy, although its rhetoric has remained radical. This growing autonomy on the part of the militant networks has had many consequences. Their brand of militant Islam is both more radical and less sophisticated than the preceding Islamism. Activism has replaced ideology. But they have also been able to mend the fences with traditional fundamentalism, for example on issues such as the role of women and Sharia law. Although like the Islamists they were not trained in traditional religious schools, they had more in common with traditional mullahs than had the Islamists. The Taliban movement cannot be understood if we ignore this shift from Islamism to neo-fundamentalism.

Middle Eastern militants who went to Bosnia after Afghanistan lacked the social roots and the political maturity of their Muslim Brotherhood elders. They recruited mainly among stateless, uprooted or migrant Islamists. The international networks, who still advocated a global jihad, became more and more uprooted, cut off from the mainstream Islamist movements. They dreamt of reviving an ummah which was now more imaginary than real, because they were cut off from the evolution of Islamism in their countries of origin. In the meantime, most of the mainstream Islamist movements in the Middle East, had turned into 'Islamo-nationalist' movements. Caught between more and more repressive authoritarian regimes and radical splinter groups, they adopted a lower profile or played mainly on 'Islamo-nationalism', with less emphasis on international Muslim solidarity and more on domestic politics, presenting themselves as the most fitted to fulfil the national interest: Refah, FIS, and Hamas are prominent examples.

Both for the mainstream movements and for the uprooted militants, Afghanistan appeared more and more as a hopeless case, where Islam was no longer at stake. After 1992, international Muslim militants preferred to expend their zeal in Bosnia or Kashmir.

The Afghan context

The future of Islamism in Afghanistan is likely to be determined by two factors: the general crisis of Islamist political thought and practice in the Muslim world, and the specificities of Afghan politics–rurality, ethnicity and tribalism. Both show that there is no future for Islamism in Afghanistan and that the Taliban model may not survive for very long as a *political* model, but will reinforce the traditional conservatism and puritanism of Afghanistan's tribal south, the Koran belt. We saw that both in the rise and the decline of Islamism, or more exactly in the shift from Islamism to neo-fundamentalism, Afghanistan is part of the Middle East. But there are nevertheless some Afghan specificities if we compare Afghanistan with the rest of the Muslim world. Afghanistan is one of the few Muslim countries where radical Islamist movements rooted themselves in rural society (except south Egypt, and, to a lesser extend, north Yemen, if we consider that the Islah movement is largely based on the Hashed tribe). The Taliban movement is the only contemporary Islamic movement whose basis is a network of rural madrassas. Afghanistan is also one of the few countries (with Syria and Yemen) where the Islamists fought mainly against communist or at least pro-Soviet forces.

The rooting of the Islamist movement in the countryside is not genuine: it is a consequence of the Soviet invasion, which helped the Islamists succeed in mobilising the peasantry, which they had failed to do so five years earlier, in 1975, in their uprising against the Daoud regime. But this rural rooting was also possible because Afghanistan had a vibrant network of rural madrassas which were not dependent on urban support: the Taliban did not, after all, come from nowhere. There were hundreds of small madrassas located in the countryside, mainly in the southern Pushtun belt (from Ghazni to Kandahar) and in the north-west. Teachers and students at these schools were not accepted in the State Faculty of Theology, founded in 1951, whose students came from the approved religious schools in the provincial towns. These madrassas were usually linked with religious networks based in Pakistan, belonging to different brands of Islam, from the orthodox Deobandi school (that of the Taliban), the most widespread, to the small 'panjpir' school of thought (which others regard as 'Wahhabi', and which was established in the North West Frontier Province of Pakistan). During the war, these madrassas turned into military bases, kept their own hierarchies, and usually joined the Harakat-e Enqelab-e Islami, the conservative party of rural mullahs and traditional ulema. Their dislike of the urban Islamist intellectuals was softened by the experience of fighting a common enemy, but they were usually not receptive to Islamist ideology.[3] In fact, in the Afghan Mujahideen movement as a whole, the rural factor has certainly subsumed the urban, except in the Hezb-e Islami. This rural character has been accentuated by the partial destruction of the capital, Kabul, during the internecine wars from 1992 to 1996; and it has again resurfaced with the emergence of the Taliban movement.

This rural dimension tended to accentuate the role played by ethnicity and tribalism among the Afghan Islamists. But the crystallisation of older patterns of segmentation into an almost 'modern' ethnic divide has also been made possible because of the failure to provide a model of an 'Islamic republic' which could have bypassed the traditional evils of Afghan politics, which have been exacerbated by fifteen years of war. Ethnic crystallisation and awareness is not as pristine as often claimed: it is a consequence of the war, of strategic alignments with foreign countries and of the need for small local solidarity groups to identify themselves with larger units. It is also a symptom of the internecine struggle between the Islamists themselves: it is now totally unlikely that the Islamist political model

---

[3] When I travelled in Summer 1984 to the madrassas that formed the cradle of the Taliban movement (including in Panjway, the home town of Mullah Omar), I never found the usual Islamist propaganda. Books were very traditional, solely pertaining to religion, and never to politics, economics or other such topics.

can bypass the ethnic divide, which has grown apace largely because of the absolute failure of the political model.

Despite their original proximity, both Hezb and Jamiat manifest a constant trend in Afghan politics: beyond an acknowledged ideological agenda, political parties embody polarisation along ethnic and tribal lines. The split between the two parties embodied specifically a growing ethnic polarisation between Tajiks (Jamiat) and Pushtuns (Hezb). Of course, to reduce the question of party loyalty to ethnicity is too far-fetched. First, there is a genuine political difference between both parties. Massoud and Rabbani had always maintained good contacts with Western countries and NGOs, while Hekmatyar has regularly been accused of hostility and aggression towards them. Second, it is too reductive to speak of the Jamiat as being Tajik and the Hezb Pushtun. The concept of the 'Tajik' is not well-established in Afghanistan: while ethnologists often call any Sunni Persian-speaker a Tajik, it rarely accords with self denomination; the so-called 'Tajiks' prefer to call themselves 'farsiwan' or Persian-speaker, and give to the term 'Tajik' a more restricted sense: sub-groups of the Sunni Persian speakers from Badakhshan to Faryab. People from Herat do not call themselves Tajik. Massoud himself does not use the term to describe himself. Sub-ethnic identities are stronger: the core of Massoud's troops are Panjsheri, while the larger circle includes people from the Shomali plain to Taloqan. On the same track, the bulk of the Pushtuns never consider Hekmatyar as the leader of the Pushtuns: the fact that he was born in the North and holds only a loose tribal connection disqualifies him as a 'true' Pushtun. But it is clear that there were very few Pushtuns in the Jamiat and not that many 'Tajiks' in the Hezb. It is more obvious that the languages spoken in both parties' headquarters were respectively Persian and Pushto. It is why we prefer to speak of 'ethnic polarisation', meaning that the Afghan population, whose primary identities were very complex and fluid, tended more and more, during the war, to analyse political alignments in ethnic terms, ethnicity being defined here through the main languages spoken: a Pushtun is somebody speaking Pushto, and a Tajik is (now) a Sunni Persian-speaker. Ethnicity is an achievement, not a given fact; it is one of the *levels* of identity, not *the* identity; but it increasingly came to be the relevant reference pertaining to political alignment, even if none of the Sunni parties had ever developed an ethnic ideology.

The Shia radical Islamist parties, such as Nasr and Sepah, also experienced this ethnicisation. When all Hazara parties merged into the Hezb-e Wahdat in 1989 under Iranian pressure, the new party soon stressed Hazara identity before Islamic solidarity; and its relations with Iran deteriorated after 1996. The term Hazaristan appears in some publications of the party, which was joined by former Hazara nationalists who never supported the idea of an Islamic state.

This ethnic polarisation has been the main predicament of the Islamist parties. If ethnicity is the clue to political alignment, what about the universality of Islam? The fight for Kabul between Hezb and Jamiat, from 1992 to 1995, which left the city destroyed, has also killed the idea of an 'Islamic State'. The State was seen merely as one more faction among others.

By the same token, the Islamist parties have been totally unable to implement any 'Islamist' policy, even when they were briefly in charge. When Massoud's force took Kabul in April 1992, it had to sustain, after some months, a two-year siege by its rival Hezb-e Islami, supported by Pakistan. No measures that could be labelled as 'Islamist' were taken by the government chaired by Burhanuddin Rabbani during its four-year tenure, despite the pressure of the pro-Saudi wing of the government, led by Sayyaf: the former communist administration was retained, the same Hindi movies were shown in the half-destroyed cinemas, stewardesses and female anchors continued to work in the state airline and television. The only 'Islamic' measures were the ban on alcohol and the enforcement of a sometimes-purely-symbolic veil for women. A last-chance coalition between both rival Islamist groups, in spring 1996, failed to provide them with an opportunity to establish the model of an 'Islamic State' as advocated by their programmes: Hekmatyar simply closed the movie-houses and strengthened the ban on alcohol. In fact, the Islamist ideology never provided more than a mere blueprint of a 'new order'. The effective practices, constituencies and strategies of both parties had more to do with ethnic polarisation and sheer political rivalries between their leaders than with ideology. Massoud acted in a pragmatic way, driven more by ethnic than by religious prejudices. Hekmatyar, although more adamant about an Islamic agenda, did little to establish Islamic institutions in the areas he controlled. The idea of an 'Islamic State' is thus largely discredited in Afghanistan. And these ethnic feuds, the lack of a real government, and the transformation of Mujahideen commanders into local warlords or highway robbers discredited both Islamist parties.

The internal evolution of Afghanistan reflected the general evolution of Islamism in two other ways. The first is the 'secularisation' of the low-level commanders, as in Algeria, where economic stakes, tribal or clan feuds or even a sheer struggle for power supersede the goal to establish an Islamic State, even if the jihad rhetoric is pervasive. Second, the failure of the Afghan Islamist Mujahideen to establish a stable regime after their capture of Kabul in April 1992 led to the return of a more traditional but exacerbated Islamic fundamentalism, that of the Taliban. Actors who retained an

Islamic agenda shifted from a revolutionary and political approach to advocate the mere implementation of Sharia. This shift from Islamism to what I call neo-fundamentalism is pervasive among the Muslim World. In this sense the Saudi model is now prevailing over the Iranian one. The surge of the Taliban movement is congruent with this wider development.

But the Taliban suffered from the same predicament as the Islamists: ethnic polarisation. The surge of the Taliban movement does not mean that they are offering a new 'Islamic', if not Islamist, model. Their appearance on the political scene coincided also with a wider sense of frustration among the Pushtun population, who never recognised Hekmatyar as its representative, and resented the fact that Kabul was in the hands of non-Pushtuns, for the first time since the creation of the country (if one excepts the brief interlude of Bacha-i Saqao in 1929). The striking fact is that the 'revenge of the Pushtuns' took the appearance of a fundamentalist movement, the Taliban, who, although they are exclusively Pushtun, discarded any ethnic claim and pretended to represent the Afghan Muslim *mellat* (nation). Interestingly enough, if one has to make a comparison, the Taliban's brand of Islam is closer to that of Bacha-i Saqao than to that of any other contemporary actors. In any case, the Taliban's achievement has been to bypass not the ethnic divide but tribal segmentation, which had prevented the Pushtuns from uniting into a single party, as did the Hazaras, the Uzbeks and to a lesser extent, the Tajiks, in the course of the war. Most Pushtun commanders, whatever their ideological affiliation, joined or approved of the Taliban: for instance the former hardline communist General Tanai; the pro-Western Ruhani Wardak; Jalaluddin Haqqani, the 'governor' of Paktia; the pro-Iranian Moazzen; and for a while, the Western-trained diplomat Hamid Karzai. Local Pushtun commanders, whatever their political affiliation, supported the Taliban, like Engineer Bashir Baghlani from Pul-e Khumri, a leading commander of Hezb-e Islami. The only exception among the Pushtun notables has been the Gailani family. By the same token, no well-known non-Pushtun Islamist figures joined the Taliban. This Pushtun constituency marks the strength and the weakness of the Taliban: it antagonises the other ethnic groups (Tajiks, Uzbeks and Hazaras) and it creates an artificial unity among Pushtuns, although rival tribal affiliations remain as strong as before. As usual in rural Muslim societies, charismatic movements waging jihad in the name of the Islamic ummah left untouched the traditional segmentation of the society, but allowed its members to refer to a larger identity.

It is not by chance that the unity of the Pushtuns had been re-forged by a religious fundamentalist movement. The Taliban movement embodied the resurgence of a traditional phenomenon in Afghanistan: the coming together of Pushtun tribesmen, in a time of crisis, under a religious and charismatic leadership. Although the Taliban are all members of local tribes, tribal affiliation did not play a role in the madrassa's recruitment. The Taliban were enlisted when very young in these religious schools, which turned during the war into military bases. Thus a religious and pedagogical hierarchy has replaced their familial and tribal connections. We can compare them with the Murabitun of southern Morocco in the Middle Ages: the equivalent of religious fighting orders. Coming from what is already a very puritan society, they tend to see Kabul as Babylon. The particularly strong fundamentalism of the Taliban, and in particular their rejection of the access of women to public space, is as much linked with their monastic and rural puritanism as with the brand of Islam they advocate. But paradoxically, the way the Taliban have been able to supersede tribal segmentation points towards not a new universal Islamic identity, but an unstated but prevalent Pushtun ethnic identity. Beyond Islam, it is ethnicity as reconstructed by the polarisation induced by the civil war which is the key factor of political alignment.

The Taliban and the future of political Islam in Afghanistan.

As we have seen, the evolution of Afghanistan has always been linked with that of the Muslim world. How do the Taliban fit into this tradition: are they 'conservative' and pro-Western in strategic terms, as is Saudi Arabia, or will they raise the flag of anti-Western Muslim identity?

The emergence of the Taliban is closely related to the balance of power and evolution among the fundamentalist movements. While the Hezb had been supported by the Pakistani Jamaat-e Islami, the Taliban have been helped by a more conservative fundamentalist movement from Pakistan, namely the Jamiat-e Ulema-i Islam. They received discreet support from Saudi Arabia, who became estranged from more radical Islamists like Hekmatyar. The Americans, now strongly opposed to radical Islam, might have been in search of another Muslim card, in line with the Saudis, with the aim of not leaving Islamic fundamentalism with no other choice than to move closer to Iran. Pakistan is still playing the Islamic card in Central Asia and also needs Islamic leverage in its policy to establish a corridor from its territory to Central Asia through Afghanistan. This allows Pakistan also to play on the Pushtun connection (since many high-ranking military officers and civil servants in Pakistan are Pushtun), without playing openly on ethnicity, which might be detrimental to its domestic ethnic balance, where a de facto supremacy of the Punjabis and the Pushtuns is hidden behind a Muslim rhetoric. In this sense, there is still room for Islamic fundamentalism as a strategic tool in the

whole area, but this does not alter the real driving factors which are
state strategies and ethnic assertion (itself a by-product of the present
struggles) more than the expression of given and pristine identities.

The ambivalence of Taliban fundamentalism in strategic terms can
be illustrated in a number of different ways. First, its godfather, the
Pakistani Jamiat-e Ulema-i Islam, could not be labelled as extremist or
anti-Western: it was rather critical of General Zia's policy of
Islamisation and regularly sided with Benazir Bhutto against the
conservative Muslim League or the radical Jamaat-e Islami. Second,
the Taliban struck a deal with the US oil company, UNOCAL, in
order to build a pipeline from Turkmenistan to Pakistan, in an
agreement which is reminiscent of the Aramco alliance in the twenties
with the Saudi monarchy, itself supported by a very fundamentalist
movement, the Wahhabis. Third, the strict and puritan Taliban
conception of Islam does not provide any specific political framework,
nor entail any specific strategy. They are far from the radical
revolutionary movements of Iran or Sudan, which stress the
reinforcement of a strong central state. They 'elected' Mullah Omar as
Amir al-Momineen ('Commander of the Faithful'), the only
institution they recognise; but their actual ruling apparatus is light and
flexible, well-adapted to a tribal and segmented society, which explains
why their rule has been accepted in tribal areas. Their main problem is
with the urban population, who see them (rightly) as poorly-educated
peasants, unable to deal with the complexity of urban life and
administration.

The Taliban have no foreign policy. Their only strategic alliance is
with Pakistan. Theirs is a purely Afghan movement which has been
instrumentalised by Pakistan, whose constant goal since the Soviet
invasion has been to turn Afghanistan into a vassal country by
playing on the Pushtun ethnic group and on fundamentalism.

On the other hand, the Taliban embody a more conservative but as
deeply anti-Western brand of Islam as that of the Islamists. They
acknowledge the Islamist heritage by refusing to hand over or even to
expel the Islamist militants still in Afghanistan, like Osama Bin
Laden. But they are strongly anti-Shia, when all the Islamists tended
to down play the Sunni-Shia rift. In this sense the Taliban are in line
with a wider development in the Muslim world: namely sectarian
relations are deteriorating (as in Syria, Turkey, Pakistan, and Iraq, with
the notable exception of Azerbaijan). This is in line also with the
assertiveness of neo-fundamentalism, insisting on a strict
interpretation of the Sunnah, while the Islamists put more stress on
ideology and politics, thus underplaying theological and even juridical
question. The Taliban also express a deep rejection of the Western
cultural model, but no strategic opposition to the West. Islam is
expressed by them not as an ideology, but as the mere and absolute

application of the Sharia. In this sense, they also embody the failure of Islamism.

Of course, the problem with the Taliban is that they mean what they say. They do not want a King, because there is no King in Islam. They have their *Amir al-Momineen*. They are more likely to expel UN and foreign agencies than to make drastic concessions on women's status. They cannot be manipulated easily by anybody. They might give asylum to Arab radicals in the name of Islamic solidarity. They may forbid the use of drugs but not their cultivation. Their anti-Shiism will not prevent them from establishing links with Iran if needed. In all these regards, the Taliban are not a factor for stabilisation in Afghanistan. But there is no danger of a Taliban spillover elsewhere: the movement is strictly Afghan, Pushtun and tribal. They are the expression of a maverick fundamentalism, strangely unfitted for the contemporary world ummah they think they embody. As elsewhere in the Muslim world, the prevalence of the local specificities–here the ethnic polarisation of a rural and segmented society under the banner of Islam–on a universal version of political Islam, shows the limits of the Islamist model.

THE FUTURE OF THE STATE AND THE STRUCTURE OF COMMUNITY GOVERNANCE IN AFGHANISTAN[1]

M. Nazif Shahrani

'The tribal model of seizure of power by a family is clearly rejected ... The nation is no longer camouflage for the tribe but a political space in which democracy can be constructed ... But what is a nation? Products of a European mold, we are used to considering the nation as a political form that is self-evident, a kind of natural culmination of all societies. It is time to realize that the idea of the nation that Europe gave to the world is perhaps only an ephemeral political form, a European exception, a precarious transition between the age of kings and the "neo-imperial" age'–*Jean-Marie Guehenno*

'The ... autonomous forms of imagination of the community were, and continue to be, overwhelmed and swamped by the history of the postcolonial state. Here lies the root of our postcolonial misery: not in our inability to think out new forms of the modern community, but in our surrender to the old forms of the modern state'–*Partha Chatterjee*

When in February 1989 the last soldiers of the former Soviet colonial occupation forces crossed the Hairatan bridge over the Amu Darya, and when in April 1992 the triumphant forces of the Afghan resistance took power from the puppet·communist regime in Kabul, freedom-loving people in general, and the Muslim peoples of Afghanistan in particular, were euphoric that their cherished hopes for establishing an

---

[1]   An earlier draft of this paper was presented at an international conference on Afghanistan and Regional Security, organised by the Institute for Political and International Studies (IPIS), Tehran, Islamic Republic of Iran, 31 June-2 July 1996. It was also presented as a lecture at the Hagop Kevorkian Center for Near Eastern Studies, New York University on 5 December 1996. I gratefully acknowledge the invitations from both institutions for the opportunity to discuss some of these ideas with lively audiences in both places. Two of my very bright and capable graduate students–Dr Cynthia Werner who read the manuscript and offered incisive comments, and Catherine Petrie who helped in researching sources–also deserve my thanks for their valuable assistance. However, all responsibility for the presentation of facts and interpretations rest with me alone.

independent, Islamic government in Afghanistan would soon be realised. Much to the dismay of most Afghans, the bloody events of the last five years in Afghanistan (1992-97), crowned by the recent carnage–in the Shomali area to the north of Kabul and in the city of Mazar-e Sharif in northern Afghanistan–by the so-called Taliban, have seriously dampened any such hopes and expectations, both inside and outside Afghanistan. Indeed, the insistence by the primarily rural, tribal Pushtun Taliban–a well armed militia created and financed by the now-defunct government of Pakistan under Benazir Bhutto–on trying to reimpose Pushtun hegemony by military means, and (paraphrasing Guehenno) *to camouflage the [Afghan] nation with the [Pushtun] tribes*, especially in the self-governing non-Pushtun regions of western, central and northern Afghanistan, presents new challenges to the viability and territorial integrity of Afghanistan as a multinational state.

The questions that I would like to raise, and briefly discuss in this chapter, are: What has brought this heroic nation of 'freedom fighters' (Mujahideen) to the brink of its political existence as a viable state and society? Why and how did the militarily-successful jihad against the former Soviet occupation forces and their puppet communist regimes in Afghanistan fail so miserably to form a workable national structure of governance? Why did the long-established, ideologically-organised Islamist parties and organisations begin to lose their political relevance or significance, giving way to intense intercommunal proxy wars fought by coalitions of tribal, regional and/or ethnolinguistic-sectarian forces, and financed and managed by foreign powers? More significantly, what specific historical legacies and experiences, together with considerations of current socioeconomic and political contingencies (both internal and external), might prove critical for charting the future course of possibilities and alternatives for workable national (central) and community-based (village, district, province and regional) governance structures in a reunited Afghanistan? The answers to these complex and interrelated questions are by no means simple or readily explicable. But we Afghans, and our concerned friends around the world, Muslim and non-Muslim, must begin to face our national predicaments with honesty, and search for credible solutions with compassion and sincerity. It is with this hope that I wish to share these brief comments as an attempt to address some of these issues.

It is also important to state that this essay is written from my perspective as a professionally-trained 'native' anthropologist, a student, researcher and teacher of Afghanistan studies for some thirty years, and as an Afghan who belongs to a non-Pushtun ethnolinguistic community.[2] The voices and concerns of the non-Pushtun population of Afghanistan were muffled or utterly silenced, both in public media and academic discussions, especially inside Afghanistan, during much of this century. Any criticism of the unjust policies and practices of the Afghan governments directed against the non-Pushtun, especially if expressed by a member of the non-Pushtun community, was condemned (and continues to be in diaspora publications) by the Pushtun-dominated state authorities and/or their spokesmen, as an act of treason and a sign of separatist tendencies. My purpose in this essay is to assess the negative consequences of policies and practices by governments (past and present) and officials under a variety of regimes, during the last hundred years of our national history. My intention is *not* to indict the Pushtun people categorically; rather it is to criticise the oppressive policies of a state run by some of their tribesmen in their name, and for their alleged collective benefit. Further, my aim here is not simply to lay blame, but to suggest solutions to help heal the historical wounds and ensure the future national territorial and political integrity of Afghanistan as a democratic multinational Muslim state in 'the Heart of Asia'.

A political ecological approach

Let me begin first with this question: Why did military success lead to political disaster? Or, as Olivier Roy has recently put it, why 'From Holy War to Civil War'? And, indeed, why the failure to establish a workable national Islamic government in Afghanistan?

Many attempts at answering these questions have been made by media pundits and Afghan experts already. Very briefly, they include the following. Some blame the multiethnic composition of Afghanistan's population, living in hostile mountainous terrain and enamoured of fighting and settling scores with guns–that is, a kind of absurd biological-cum-environmental deterministic solution that says 'Afghans can't help it, violence is in their genes'.[3] Alternatively,

---

2   See M. Nazif Shahrani, 'Honored Guest and Marginal Man: Long-Term Field Research and Predicaments of a Native Anthropologist', in Don D. Fowler and Donald Hardesty (eds.), *Others Knowing Other: Perspectives on Ethnographic Careers* (Washington DC: Smithsonian Institution Press, 1994), pp. 15-67.

3   One of the frequently-cited facts introduced to prove the violent nature of Afghan society is that during the twentieth century, seven out of eleven political leaders of the country met violent deaths (Habibullah I, Habibullah II, Nadir Shah, Daoud, Taraki, Amin, and Najibullah), while Amanullah, Zahir Shah, and Rabbani, three of the survivors, were violently deposed and Karmal was sent into exile. This fact,

some Western experts, many of the better-educated and Westernised Afghan intellectuals, and some prominent Mujahideen leaders (for example Burhanuddin Rabbani and Gulbuddin Hekmatyar), blame the failure of Afghan governments in the past century to build and impose a strong, centralised nation-state as a means to integrate their constantly-feuding rural subjects–that is, nomadic tribesmen and peasants who have jealously tried to guard their freedom and liberty against state interference in their local affairs.[4] A more novel thesis is offered in a recent book by David Edwards, *Heroes of the Age: Moral Fault Lines on the Afghan Frontier*, in which he suggests that 'Afghanistan's political chaos derives less from divisions between ethnic and religious-sectarian groups or from the ambitions of particular individuals than they do from *the moral incoherence of Afghanistan itself* '.[5] According to Edwards, the 'moral incoherence' is the product of the conjunction of three contradictory and incompatible moral systems or codes (the Deep Structure) that undergird Afghan political culture: the ultra-individualistic codes of honour (*nang*), the universalist moral system of Islam, and the codes of kingship-rulership of the state. He richly illustrates his analysis using narratives from the lives of a tribal khan, a Sufi saint and a king, Amir Abdul Rahman. Neither last nor least, and the favourite of many Afghan leaders (I hasten to say with considerable justification), is an approach which blames foreign conspiracies against Afghanistan. This explanation suggests that foreign powers (governments both near and far, and more recently multinational corporations such as UNOCAL of California, Delta Oil of Saudi Arabia, and Bridas of Argentina) have tried to undermine the gains of a militarily successful jihad and Islamic revolution, and have interfered directly in the country's

---

however, tells more about the nature of political succession in the country and the violent nature of Afghan *state* than it does about the peoples of Afghanistan.

4   The argument thus follows that what the country needs at the moment is the establishment of a strong centralised state structure and leadership. Needless to say, the advocates of such a view–including the Taliban, Gulbuddin Hekmatyar and Burhanuddin Rabbani–contend that, given the chance, they could accomplish the task alone! For texts of interviews with former Mujahideen leaders and current Taliban pretenders, news reports, and very often heated discussions of the need for the establishment of an all-powerful central government (*hukumat-e mutamarkiz-e qawi*) in Afghanistan that would disarm the population and impose its will in order to ensure the country's territorial integrity, see Afghan diaspora publications such as *Omaid Weekly*, *Caravan* (bi-weekly), *Afghan News* and *Afghanistan Mirror*, printed in the US and widely distributed around the world.

5   David B. Edwards, *Heroes of the Age: Moral Fault Lines on the Afghan Frontier* (Berkeley & Los Angeles: University of California Press, 1996), p. 3. Emphasis added.

internal affairs in order to further their own policy goals in the region by financing and managing proxy wars in Afghanistan.

Unfortunately none of these explanations is entirely satisfactory in itself. The political and military chaos in Afghanistan is not an isolated or unique phenomenon. Indeed, the tragic experiences of the long-suffering peoples of Afghanistan are part of a much wider affliction common to some post-colonial states and multinational societies, especially smaller and poorer ones, which are unfortunate enough to find themselves in a geostrategic location within the post-Soviet, unipolar New World Order–for example Cambodia, Rwanda, Burundi, Sri Lanka, Azerbaijan, Armenia, Tajikistan, and perhaps more nations to join the list in the not-too-distant future. Therefore, we may need to look for a broader explanation of communal conflicts and occurrences of proxy wars in smaller and poorer post-colonial multiethnic nations. Here, I have found some of Partha Chatterjee's ideas most helpful in examining and understanding better our political miseries in Afghanistan, as well as the post-colonial miseries of other nations in comparable situations.

In his book, *The Nation and its Fragments*, Chatterjee theorises the sources of the intercommunal violence within the frameworks of post-colonial nation-states in the following manner:

The [...] autonomous forms of imagination of the community were, and continue to be, overwhelmed and swamped by the history of the post-colonial state. *Here lies the root of our postcolonial misery: not in our inability to think out new forms of the modern community [or identity] but in our surrender to the old forms of the modern state.* If the nation is an imagined community and if nations must also take the form of states, then our theoretical language must allow us to talk about community and state at the same time. I do not think our present theoretical language [or the political ecology of the New World Order] allows us to do this.[6]

I agree with Chatterjee, and Guehenno, that instead of accepting the nation-state 'as a political form that is self evident, a kind of natural culmination of all societies',[7] we must problematise and question the appropriateness and adequacy of the forms of post-colonial states,[8] and

---

6   Partha Chatterjee, *The Nation and Its Fragments: Colonial and Postcolonial Histories* (Princeton: Princeton University Press, 1993), p. 11. Emphasis added.

7   Jean-Marie Guehenno, *The End of the Nation-State* (Minneapolis: University of Minnesota Press, 1995), p. 2.

8   A critical assessment of the old forms of modern nation-state and their continued relevance as effective political institutions, especially in Asia, Africa and Latin America, is necessary. This is particularly so in view of the fact that in Europe–the original birthplace of this 'ephemeral political form'–the nation-state is losing

critically examine them to determine whether such state structures are part of the problem in breeding communal violence and conflicts in multiethnic societies. And, if the old forms of nation-state are part of the problem, why do we continue to consider such institutional forms also to be a part of the solution for alleviating the crises?

In this essay, I would like to suggest a more holistic or 'political ecological' approach for understanding the predicaments facing not only Afghanistan, but also many other similar nations in different parts of the world. By 'political ecological approach', I mean an examination of factors affecting social identity formation and maintenance (individually and collectively), and the articulation of power relations and social discourses (discursive and non-discursive) between and among individuals and groups within specific political environments. The difficulty of defining 'political environment', unfortunately is far more complicated than that of the 'eco-pond or lake', and the problems of mapping the flow charts of exchanges of power, values, goods and services are ever more complex than before. Fortunately, the so-called post-colonial world system of nation-states has helped create the outlines of our 'political ponds' for us. At the moment, what is at issue is the political ecological viability of some of these arbitrarily-defined political ponds and lakes (nations and countries) within a rapidly changing global environment. In our case, the political pond whose viability is threatened by external political pressures and internal political cannibalism is the state of Afghanistan.

To address these issues we need to examine two major aspects of Afghanistan's contemporary society, state and political ecology–that is, the relationships of its political economy and political culture within the broader national and regional history. First, we need to identify the major sociocultural principles which provide the cultural ideas and norms for conceptualising and ordering identities and informing politics of difference between social groupings, and which articulate the relations of domination, as well as resistance, between social groups and communities.[9] Second, we need to discuss and assess, albeit briefly, the history of the modern state in Afghanistan

---

much of its historic purpose in the face of increasing consolidation of such states within the European Union. See Guehenno, *The End of the Nation-State*, for details. Also see Neera Chandhoke, *The State and Civil Society: Explorations in Political Theory* (New Delhi: Sage Publications, 1995) and George E. Marcus (ed.), *Perilous States: Conversations on Cultures, Politics, and Nation* (Chicago: The University of Chicago Press, 1993).

[9] See Chatterjee, *The Nation and Its Fragments: Colonial and Postcolonial Histories*, p. 166.

and its relationship with its heterogeneous communities of citizens during the last one hundred years–that is, the period of Mohammadzai dynastic rule preceding Soviet intervention, the decade of the jihad struggle against communism and Soviet occupation, and the ongoing post-communist and post-jihad struggle for control of state power.

Constitutive cultural principles, identities and political culture

The most significant principles governing interpersonal relations and collective identities and difference among the peoples of Afghanistan– whether rural or urban, nomad or sedentary, tribally-organised or not– are those ensuing from the mutual bonds of family (*khanadan, khanawada*) and kinship (*kheysh wa qawm*). These social structural principles based on the idioms of kinship (patrilineal descent and affinal ties) are paradigmatic not only in defining personal identities and social relations within particular social groups (beginning with family-household units), but also in defining the boundaries of community-group solidarity–the lines separating the 'we' from 'they'– in all forms of intra- and inter-communal relations.[10] Members of groups and communities so organised share some common interests, in contradistinction to other similarly-conceived and competing entities, not as a result of contractual agreements, but by virtue of their prior categorically-determined inclusion in the specific contextually-defined solidarity groups within the broader social arena. The most durable and pervasive solidarity units resulting from these constitutive principles, and the entities responsible for the social production and perpetuity of these cultural principles in Afghanistan are the extended family formations (*khanawada* or *khanadan*). All other forms of recognised categorical solidarity groups, generally referred to as *qawm* in all major languages of the peoples of Afghanistan–which can mean lineages, clans, tribes, races, linguistic groups, religious-sectarian groups, nationalities and even nation–are similarly conceived, organised and mobilised.[11] The most striking illustration

---

10 For an insightful discussion of similar principles operating among Indian peasant villagers with a caste system, see Chatterjee, *The Nation and Its Fragments: Colonial and Postcolonial Histories,* pp. 164-167.

11 See Jon W. Anderson, 'Tribe and Community among Ghilzai Pushtun', *Anthropos,* vol. 70, no. 4, 1975, pp. 575-601; Jon W. Anderson, 'Khan and Khel: Dialectics of Pakhtun Tribalism', in Richard Tapper (ed.), *The Conflict of Tribe and State in Iran and Afghanistan* (London: Croom Helm, 1983) pp. 119-149; M. Nazif Shahrani and Robert L. Canfield (eds.), *Revolutions and Rebellions in Afghanistan: Anthropological Perspectives* (Berkeley: Institute of International

of the paradigmatic nature of these principles may be evident in the discourse of any number of Afghans when they meet each other for the first time and attempt to establish their mutual critical social coordinates by enquiring *shuma ke astin? ba qawm che astin? az kuja astin?* (Who are you? What is your *qawm* or community? Where are you from?) With answers to these critical queries, the social and spatial coordinates of individuals are easily assessed, fixed and utilised in determining the trajectories of subsequent conversations and interactions.

Within *khanadan* groups and localised *qawm wa kheysh* communities (for example, urban *guzar* or *mahalla*, and rural villages, valleys, regions) members are generally hierarchically arranged, and mutually bound together through the inculcation of a set of shared values.[12] Thus, the unity of a contextually-constituted community is established through assured membership of all segments of the constituent population, albeit with differential rights entailing differential duties and privileges. Indeed, conceptions of politics of difference–whether familial, local, regional, tribal, ethnic or national–in Afghanistan are based mainly on the principles of complementary (segmentary) opposition, and ties of patronage (that is, dependency and hierarchy) between leaders and followers. Ties of loyalty and responsibility–economic, political and moral–between leaders and

Studies, 1984); Robert L. Canfield, 'Ethnic, Regional, and Sectarian Alignments in Afghanistan', in Ali Banuazizi and Myron Weiner (eds.), *The State, Religion, and Ethnic Politics: Afghanistan, Iran, and Pakistan* (Syracuse: Syracuse University Press, 1986), pp. 75-103; M. Nazif Shahrani, 'State Building and Social Fragmentation in Afghanistan: A Historical Perspective', in Ali Banuazizi and Myron Weiner (eds.), *The State, Religion, and Ethnic Politics: Afghanistan, Iran, and Pakistan* (Syracuse: Syracuse University Press, 1986), pp. 23-74; Olivier Roy, *Islam and Resistance in Afghanistan* (Cambridge: Cambridge University Press, 1990); Myron Weiner and Ali Banuazizi (eds.), *The Politics of Social Transformation in Afghanistan, Iran, and Pakistan* (Syracuse: Syracuse University Press, 1994); Olivier Roy, *Afghanistan: From Holy War to Civil War* (Princeton: The Darwin Press, 1995); and Edwards, *Heroes of the Age: Moral Fault Lines on the Afghan Frontier*.

12   However, it is important to note–as Chatterjee, *The Nation and Its Fragments: Colonial and Postcolonial Histories*, p. 166 does in the case of the Indian caste system–that the possibility does exist for the systematic rejection of the supposedly 'shared' values by individuals and groups who are assigned inferior ranking in the system. For Pushtuns of Pakistan see Fredrik Barth, *Political Leadership Among Swat Pathans* (London: The Athlone Press, 1959); Akbar S. Ahmed, *Millennium and Charisma among Pathans: A Critical Essay in Social Anthropology* (London: Routledge & Kegan Paul, 1976); Akbar S. Ahmed, *Pukhtun Economy and Society: Traditional Structure and Economic Development in a Tribal Society* (London: Routledge & Kegan Paul, 1980).

followers are conceived in interpersonal dyadic terms, and are negotiable only within certain limits. The full range of alliances and appositions are often contingent upon the shifting boundaries of the community within the changing context of various factional struggles within or between contending groups–that is, the political ecology of particular times, places and spaces.

While the politics of local kin-based groups (including family-household units), especially in the predominantly rural areas of Afghanistan, are often idealised by natives and rendered in the available literature as egalitarian and harmonious village communities, free from internal dissension and struggle, this image is far from the historical and ethnographic reality.[13] These family and kin-based constitutive cultural principles (sometime expressed in terms of moral codes of honour and shame), are often overlaid, combined or modified by the local (mis)-understanding of, and adherence to, Islamic moral order and rules of Sharia.

Therefore, kinship norms, codes of honour (*nang*), and rules of Sharia as locally understood (even misunderstood), together with language and religious-sectarian distinctions and loyalties represent the essence of traditional political culture and popular consciousness in contemporary Afghanistan. I will also argue that the constitutive principles of *khanawada, khanadan* and *qawm* have had, and continue to have, a powerful and pervasive effect on contemporary political discourse and the behaviour of Afghans at all levels of society–that is, in rural villages and nomadic communities, in the anti-communist and anti-Soviet Islamist resistance groups, in the Taliban militia movement, and in the institutions of national state, including the Mujahideen and the Taliban administrations. Furthermore, the potential effects of these powerful principles of political culture cannot, and should not, be underestimated as we search for appropriate structures of community governance to resolve the current military and political crisis in the country. Indeed, we must now turn our attention to a brief examination of how the persistence and permeation of these constitutive principles of traditional Afghan political culture have influenced the modern forms of the Afghan national state over the last century.

---

[13] See, for example, Shahrani and Canfield (eds.), *Revolutions and Rebellions in Afghanistan: Anthropological Perspectives*; Banuazizi and Weiner (eds.), *The State, Religion, and Ethnic Politics: Afghanistan, Iran, and Pakistan*; David B. Edwards, 'The Evolution of Shi'i Political Dissent in Afghanistan', in Juan R.I Cole and Nikki R. Keddie (eds.), *Shiism and Political Protest* (New Haven: Yale University Press, 1986), pp. 201-229; and Edwards, *Heroes of the Age: Moral Fault Lines on the Afghan Frontier*.

However, at the outset I would like to state clearly that the persistence of family and kin-based loyalties and their pervasive and prominent effects in the political life of Afghans should not be taken as a sign of political backwardness or 'traditionalism' due to the failures of modern institutions of state which should have wiped them clean from its 'modernising' citizens' consciousness. Sociologically or anthropologically, there is nothing inherently wrong with or 'backward' about adherence to 'traditional' familial and kin-based values of mutual support and solidarity in modern society. What we must examine critically is the *negative impact* of our voluntary 'surrender to the old [ephemeral European political] forms of the modern state' upon the cherished cultural values and traditional community governance forms and structures of Afghan society. Indeed, the challenge facing us at this critical juncture in the history of Afghanistan is not how soon we can get rid of the constitutive principles of our own traditional political culture and replace them by 'modern' ones. Rather, the most important challenge we are facing, in my judgement, is whether we have the courage to search for alternative ways of organising a modern national state that can justly accommodate and enhance the continuation of our kin-based political values, along with the persistence of well-organised, armed, and self-governing local communities throughout the nation.

Traditional (imperial) states and community self-governance

Before the arrival and imposition (intrusion) of the modern European forms of the state during the last two decades of the nineteenth century in Afghanistan and its subsequent growth in military strength and institutional infrastructure, local kin-based community governance structures enjoyed considerable autonomy and flexibility, both organisationally and spatially. The geographical distribution of distinctive communities based on languages[14] and sectarian affiliation

---

[14] Tajiki and Turki speakers (Uzbek, Turkmen, Kirghiz and Kazakh) predominantly occupied the area of Afghan Turkestan to the north of the Hindu Kush mountains; speakers of Hazaragi (a dialect of Persian) occupied the central mountain regions; and speakers of Pushto, 'Nuristani' languages, and Baluchi inhabited the regions to the south of the Hindu Kush. There were however considerable numbers of Tajiki speaking peoples in Shomali, Nijraw, Tagaw, Kabul, Logar, Mashreqi and Ghazni regions to the south of the Hindu Kush, as well as in the western (Herat) parts of the country. Before the 1880s and 1890s, there were no significant communities of Pushtuns present in the northern parts of Afghanistan. Since the 1880s, because of the internal colonial policies of the central government in Afghanistan, an unknown, but substantial group of Pushtun *naqilin*

or *madhab*[15] reflected the spatial distribution of power, based on relative demographic and political strength, of each of the communities over time. Intercommunal strife and alliances were common, but given relatively equal access to the available lethal technologies and military capabilities by all the contending groups, a semblance of balance of power prevailed among them. Within the language and/or sectarian communities, dissension against oppressive leaders was expressed through spatial mobility (voting by their feet) or through new alliances. However, on the whole, local communities were, for the most part, economically self-sustaining and politically self-governing. Ties with central or imperial authorities (if and when they existed) were often minimal and indirect. That is, local communities of various sizes and compositions acted as semi-autonomous political entities. The 'familial' or paternalistic model they embodied aimed to preserve their community integrity, and hence

---

(people relocated or implanted by central government) live in colonies in various parts of Afghan Turkestan: see Klaus Ferdinand, 'Nomad Expansion and Commerce in central Afghanistan' *Folk*, vol. 4, no. 1, 1962, pp. 123-159; Nancy Tapper, 'The Advent of Pashtun *maldars* in Northwestern Afghanistan', *Bulletin of the School of Oriental and African Studies*, vol. 36, no. 1, 1973, pp. 55-79; Thomas J. Barfield, 'The Impact of Pushtun Immigration on Nomadic Pastoralism in Northeastern Afghanistan', in Jon W. Anderson and Richard F. Strand (eds.), *Ethnic Processes and Intergroup Relations in Contemporary Afghanistan* (New York: Asia Society, Afghanistan Council, Occasional Paper no. 15, 1978), pp. 26-34; Hasan Kawun Kakar, *Government and Society in Afghanistan: The Reign of Amir 'Abd al-Rahman Khan*. (Austin: University of Texas Press, 1979); Thomas J. Barfield, *The Central Asian Arabs of Afghanistan: Pastoral Nomadism in Transition* (Austin: University of Texas Press, 1981); and Nancy Tapper, ''Abd al-Rahman's North-West Frontier: The Pashtun Colonisation of Afghan Turkistan', in Richard Tapper (ed.), *The Conflict of Tribe and State in Iran and Afghanistan* (London: Croom Helm, 1983), pp. 233-261.

15 Shiite Imamis and Ismailis occupy the marginal high mountain valleys in the central regions and in eastern Badakhshan, and Sunnis predominate in the more fertile parts of the rest of the country: see Robert L. Canfield, *Faction and Conversion in a Plural Society: Religious Alignment in the Hindu Kush* (Ann Arbor: Anthropological Papers no. 50, The University of Michigan Museum of Anthropology, 1973); Robert L. Canfield, 'The Ecology of Rural Ethnic Groups and the Spatial Distribution of Power', *American Anthropologist*, vol. 75, no. 4, 1973, pp. 1511-1528; M. Nazif Shahrani, *The Kirghiz and Wakhi of Afghanistan: Adaptation to Closed Frontiers* (Seattle: University of Washington Press, 1979); and M. Nazif Shahrani, 'The Kirghiz Khans: Style and Substance of Traditional Local Leadership in Central Asia', *Central Asian Survey*, vol. 5, nos. 3-4, 1986, pp. 255-271.

the collective interests of their group through their own local leadership.[16]

The introduction and appropriation of a centralised state apparatus, based on the British Indian colonial model, by a Durrani Pushtun tribal dynasty in Afghanistan, initiated a new model of state-society relations. Until today, the nature and structure of this evolving form of post-colonial state, and its relationship to civil society,[17] have had

[16] See, for example, Lieutenant John Wood, *A Personal Narrative of a Journey to the Source of River Oxus, by the Route of Indus, Kabul and Badakhshan* (London: John Murray, 1841); Lieutenant John Wood, *A Journey to the Source of the River Oxus* (London: John Murray, 1872); Lieutenant-Colonel C.J. Windham, *Precis on Afghan Affairs* (Calcutta: Superintendent Government Printing, India, 1914); Burhanuddin Kushkaki, *Rahnuma-i Qataghan wa Badakhshan* (Kabul: Metbaeh-i Wezarat-e Harbiya, 1923); Tapper (ed.), *The Conflict of Tribe and State in Iran and Afghanistan*; M. Siddiq Farhang, *Afghanistan dar Panj Qarn-e Akher* (Herandon, VA: American Speedy, 1988).

[17] During the past two decades considerations of 'civil society' and its relationship with the state have occupied a prominent place in political theory. However, as to what civil society is, what is the nature of relationship between civil society and the state, and whether there is a civil society outside of Western democracies, there are lively debates in progress: see, for example Jean-Francois Bayart, 'Civil Society in Africa', in Patrick Chabal (ed.), *Political Domination in Africa: Reflections on the Limits of Power* (Cambridge: Cambridge University Press, 1986), pp.109-25; Michael Bratton, 'Beyond the State: Civil Society and Associational Life in Africa', *World Politics*, vol. 41, no. 3, April 1989, pp. 407-430; and Jillian Schwedler (ed.), *Toward Civil Society in the Middle East?* (Boulder: Lynne Rienner, 1995). For the purposes of this essay, I am relying on the definitions of, and relationship between, the concepts of state and civil society as articulated by Chandhoke, *The State and Civil Society: Explorations in Political Theory*, p. 9: '... we need to understand that states are much more than governance. For states invariably seek to control and limit the political practices of society by constructing boundaries of the political. The state attempts in other words to constitute the political discourse. However, politics are articulatory practices which mediate between the experiential and the expressive [and] are not only about controls and laying down of boundaries. They are about transgressions of these boundaries and about the reconstitution of the political; the site at which these mediations and contestations take place; the site at which society enters into a relationship with the state can be defined as civil society. The values of civil society are those of political participation, state accountability, and publicity of politics ... The inhabitant of this sphere is the rights bearing and juridically defined individual, i.e., the citizen. And the protection of the members of civil society is encapsulated in the vocabulary and institutions of rights'. See also Andrew Arato, 'Civil Society vs. the State', *Telos*, vol. 47, no. 1, 1981, pp. 23-47; Andrew Arato and Jean Cohen, 'Social Movements, Civil Society and the Problem of Sovereignty', *Praxis International*, vol. 4, no. 3, 1984, pp. 266-283; Ernest Gellner, 'Civil Society in Historical Context', *International Social Science*

a powerful and lasting effect on the political consciousness and imagination (or lack thereof) of the peoples of Afghanistan. Also important, at least sociologically, has been the tenacious application and utilisation of the constitutive principles of family and kinship (*khanadan* and *qawm wa kheysh*) mores and the ties of loyalties by the rulers of Afghanistan in their state-building efforts. This, however, has not been without paradoxical results for the national political processes. Therefore, I believe a brief discussion of these issues could shed some light on the current political predicament facing the peoples of this beleaguered Muslim nation.

The development of a strong dynastic state and the destruction of self-governing communities

The foundations of a modern centralised state in Afghanistan were laid under the auspices and political tutelage of the British Indian colonial empire, with direct financial and military assistance. This began with the reign of Amir Dost Mohammad Khan (1832-63), and culminated with the reign of his grandson, the 'Iron Amir', Abdul Rahman Khan (1880-1901). The phrase 'Iron Amir'–an infamous description of the violent and oppressive character of the so-called 'founder of modern Afghanistan'–was popularised by late nineteenth and early twentieth-century British authors and is widely adopted by others, including Afghan writers. Towards the end of the Second Anglo-Afghan War (1879-80), General Roberts, the Commanding Officer of the British occupation forces in Kabul, upon being informed of Abdul Rahman Khan's reappearance in Afghan Turkestan (after a decade-long self-imposed exile in the Tsarist Russian-occupied city of Tashkent), telegraphed British authorities in India on 10 January 1880 and suggested that they should cautiously open communication with Sardar (Prince) Abdul Rahman, in whom, the British General thought, 'it was just possible might be found *"our most suitable instrument"* [for governing Afghanistan]'.[18] Indeed, General Roberts was correct in his assumption, and Sardar Abdul Rahman Khan proved to be the 'most suitable [political] instrument' for British policies in Afghanistan.[19]

Journal, no. 129, 1991, pp. 495-510; and Jean Cohen and Andrew Arato, *Civil Society and Political Theory* (Cambridge MA: MIT Press, 1992).

18 Windham, *Precis on Afghan Affairs*, p. 41. Emphasis added.

19 For a revealing description of the events leading to the Viceroy and Governor-General of British India offering 'the Amirship' to Abdul Rahman Khan and formally installing him to the post of Amir of Kabul on 22 July 1880, see Windham, *Precis on Afghan Affairs*, a published summary of all the secret

Thus, the Mohammadzai dynastic centralised state was established during the last two decades of the nineteenth century by Amir Abdul Rahman,[20] who *mortgaged* the control of Afghanistan's foreign affairs to Britain in return for considerable cash and artillery 'to establish himself' as the founder of 'modern Afghanistan'.[21] The Amir initiated and successfully implemented a state policy that aimed to disarm systematically and overwhelm militarily all existing forms of autonomous communities, allegedly in order to create and maintain national unity. He strongly favoured the formation of a powerful centralised state to control and effectively rule over a much-weakened and brutalised civil society. The Amir's policies for accomplishing his state building objectives were blatantly discriminatory, violent and brutal, especially against those non-Pushtun ethnolinguistic communities and against Pushtun tribal communities whom he thought might oppose his direct rule in their territories.[22] His wars of pacification against the Shia communities in the Hazarajat and against the peoples of Kafiristan (renamed Nuristan following their conquest and forced conversion to Islam) in eastern Afghanistan are legendary in their brutality and oppression.[23] In Afghan Turkestan, Kohistan (Shomali), Herat and the eastern Ghilzai Pushtun tribal territories, Amir Abdul Rahman destroyed countless local communities by decimating their leadership through executions, confiscation of

---

communications between British officials in Kabul and their headquarters in India and England.

[20] The 'Iron Amir' was given considerable military and financial assistance by the British Indian government to create a strong buffer state in Afghanistan against any potential threats from the encroaching Tsarist Russian colonial empire to the north–that is, western Turkestan. The modern British weapons, however, were only used by the Amir to brutalise his own subjects, the so-called 'internal enemies of the state', and never in defence of the nation against threats from the outside. The legacies of this well-established strong centralised government have unfortunately persisted throughout this century in Afghanistan. For further details, see Mir Ghulam Mohammad Ghubar, *Afghanistan dar Masir-e Tarikh* (Kabul: Dawlati metbaeh, 1967); Kakar, *Government and Society in Afghanistan: The Reign of Amir 'Abd al-Rahman Khan*; Shahrani, 'State Building and Social Fragmentation in Afghanistan: A Historical Perspective'; Farhang, *Afghanistan dar Panj Qarn-e Akher.*

[21] Windham, *Precis on Afghan Affairs*, p. 77.

[22] See Kakar, *Government and Society in Afghanistan: The Reign of Amir 'Abd al-Rahman Khan*, p. 10.

[23] All of these atrocities were committed in the name of 'fostering Afghan national unity' and promoting the 'dignity of Islam' (Kakar, *Government and Society in Afghanistan: The Reign of Amir 'Abd al-Rahman Khan*, p. 10), and are reminiscent of what is being done by the Taliban Pushtun militia against non-Pushtuns in the country today.

properties, exile or imprisonment in the capital, Kabul.[24] He also
carried out an active policy of internal colonialism by relocating
Pushtun peasants and nomads (both forcibly and by means of offering
free confiscated lands and other financial incentives) in Afghan
Turkestan. Amir Abdul Rahman also opened up Hazarajat and
Badakhshan pasture lands in central and northeastern Afghanistan to
Kandahari *maldar* (pastoral nomads) for use during the summer
months.[25] In this remarkable project of 'state building', the 'Iron
Amir' relied almost exclusively upon the support of his own
immediate family, lineage, clan, tribe and segments of the larger loyal
Pushtun communities. Needless to say, his loyal kinsmen and
supporters were amply rewarded, often at the expense of 'other' tribal
or ethnolinguistic-sectarian communities, especially in the Hazarajat
and in Afghan Turkestan, who lost pastures and agricultural lands and
property.

The ever-growing organs of the state, especially those charged with
economic extraction, and control and punishment, were staffed by
either the Amir's relatives or his loyal 'royal' clients from various
non-Pushtun ethnic groups and Pushtun tribes alike. As such, the
state was run as a dynastic patrimony. Indeed, the dominant
constitutive principles of paternalism, nepotism, tribalism, and
ethnic-regional favouritism suffused all aspects of state and society
relations. By the turn of the century and the end of Amir Abdul
Rahman's rule, the absolute dominance of his family and its larger
Mohammadzai clan of the Durrani tribes of the Pushtun had been
indisputably established in the multiethnic Afghan state. Indeed, Amir
Abdul Rahman had successfully adopted 'the tribal model of seizure of
power' and camouflaged the newly cobbled-together multiethnic nation

---

[24] Kakar, *Government and Society in Afghanistan: The Reign of Amir 'Abd al-
Rahman Khan*, p. 48 reports an account from one of Amir Abdul Rahman Khan's
alleged friends from his days of exile in Russian Turkestan, Kata Khan Uzbek.
On being told of his appointment as governor, 'Kata Khan Uzbek ordered his
servants to fetch all his household property. In reply to a question from the amir,
'Kata Khan said that "the destiny of a Governor in Afghanistan was the
confiscation of his property and the loss of his life; in order to save his own [life]
he preferred to sacrifice his property beforehand".'

[25] This policy of internal colonialism was continued by Amir Abdul Rahman's
descendants without interruption. As a result many Pushtun peasant and *maldar*
communities are established in northern Afghanistan, especially in Badghis,
Faryab, Maimana, Jawzjan and Shiberghan in the northwest, and Baghlan and
Kunduz in the center. The recent declarations of loyalty to Taliban Pushtun militia
in the north by commanders Bashir Baghlani and Arif Khan (Kunduzi) are the
fruits of Pushtun colonialism being reaped in Afghan Turkestan.

with his own tribe.[26] Also, in reference to the new paramount national chieftains, the Mohammadzai Pushtun dynasty of the 'Iron Amir', a new hierarchy was formed which realigned communities (based on kinship, tribal, language, sectarian and regional affiliations) with differential access to strategic state resources. In effect, the autonomous power of local communities, and the relative balance of power among communities themselves, as well as the prevailing balance of forces between them and the central government, were changed drastically in favour of the more powerful, emergent 'modern' dynastic state.

The continued domination of the centralised state by the members of a particular family and tribal-ethnic community was not possible with the internal revenues and national resources of the country. Instead, throughout this century the government leaders increasingly relied on foreign military and economic assistance from willing and able outside patrons (earlier exclusively British, but later Soviet, European, American and some Arab sources) regardless of the many changes of regimes. That is, the pattern of maintaining a strong centralised domestic control over the population through the assistance of foreign powers (often potential enemies of the nation, such as the former Soviet Union, and currently, Pakistan) has been emulated by all regimes in Afghanistan during the past century: beginning with the dynastic shift from Amir Abdul Rahman's family to the Musahiban family (1929-73) of Mohammad Nadir Shah–following the fall of the reformist king, Amir Amanullah (1929), in the hands of a Tajik rebel, Habibullah II (*Bacha-i Saqao*) during a brief interregnum (1929)–to Daoud's republic (1973-78), the Khalq-Parcham Communists (1978-92), the Mujahideen governments headed by Sebghatullah Mojadiddi and Burhanuddin Rabbani (1992-96), to the current militant contenders for the state power, the Taliban militia (from 1996). All of these regimes–monarchic, republican, Communist, and self-styled Islamic– have been moulded and modelled after the familiar old forms of centralised nation-state camouflaged with the 'tribe' of those in power. That is, throughout the twentieth century and the many violent changes of government in the country, the overcentralised administrative structure, and the overwhelmingly punitive, corrupt and extractive functions of state have remained constant. As an Afghan proverb aptly expresses it, *khar amu khar, faqat palaanesh tabdel meshud* (the donkey remained the same, only its tackle changed)–that is, the structure and functions of state and its hostile relations with the society did not change, only the rulers changed places. Therefore, I contend that it is the negative consequences of these old forms of the

---

26 Guehenno, *The End of the Nation-State*, p. 2.

modern state in Afghanistan that lie 'at the root of our [that is, Afghanistan's] postcolonial misery'.[27]

Legacies of Hukumat-e mutamarkiz-e qawi

This brings me to the other significant questions raised earlier in this essay: during the past century in Afghanistan, what have been the legacies of a strong, centralised, punitive and primarily extractive modern state (*Hukumat-e mutamarkiz-e qawi*) which has always 'mortgaged' some of its authority to potential foreign enemies of the nation in order to secure financial and military assistance? How could a critical examination and appreciation of these legacies help us shed some light on a better understanding of the political and military chaos reigning in the country today?

In my view, more than a century of state centralisation policies and practices in Afghanistan have brought about several significant legacies which have had a considerable impact on the current tragic situation in the country.

First, from the perspective of both rulers and their subjects (*rayat*), an official government appointment at any level was seen as a means of extracting and accumulating wealth from the people and not one of dispensing the needed services for their 'citizens' (*ruaya*).[28] Indeed, state officials in all government institutions, including even village school teachers, who were always appointed from the various ministries in the capital, Kabul, and almost always in posts away from their own native territory, were viewed, with few exceptions, by most citizens as outside agents of abuse, corruption and oppression. Therefore, the creation and perpetuation of feelings of mistrust towards government, and distrust of politics in general, amongst the great majority of non-Mohammadzai, especially non-Pushtun *aqwam*, has been a crucial legacy of this century-long experience.[29] By pursuing an ill-defined Afghan (Pushtun) nationalist policy, the state officials often, in practice if not in public rhetoric, denied the existence of

---

[27] Chatterjee, *The Nation and Its Fragments: Colonial and Postcolonial Histories*, p. 11.

[28] Interestingly, the term *rayat* (plural *ruaya*), a Persian-Arabic word widely used in the various vernaculars of Afghanistan, and often translated as 'citizen', in fact means 'subject' or 'an inferior'–that is, one who must submit to the ruler as a subject with considerable responsibilities, but few if any rights.

[29] See also M. Nazif Shahrani, 'Afghanistan's Muhajirin (Muslim "Refugee-Warriors"): Politics of Mistrust and Distrust of Politics', in E. Valentine Daniel and John Chr. Knudsen (eds.), *Mistrusting Refugees* (Berkeley & Los Angeles: University of California Press, 1995), pp. 187-206.

'other', non-Pushtun ethnolinguistic communities.[30] Also, in the
name of creating national unity, the state under its various long- and
short-lived regimes, systematically undermined the identity and local
autonomy of distinct ethnic and sectarian communities.[31] In response,

[30] The invisibility of non-Pushtun groups (even the larger Tajik, Hazara, Uzbek,
Turkmen, Baluch and Nuristani) was particularly evident in official histories
taught in the school systems. These official histories, written from the perspective
of the 'real' Afghans (Pushtuns) as the representatives of the true Aryan race,
depicted Afghanistan essentially as a Pushtun creation that was to serve
exclusively their interests as the 'master martial race'. Members of the non-
Pushtun groups (including the Tajiks who are also 'Aryans') were either denied
any positive role in the national historical narratives or their role was rendered in
a negative light–for example Amir Habibullah II (the only Tajik ruler in the first
nine decades of this century) is described as a thief and dubbed as *Bacha-i Saqao*
('the Water Carrier's Son'). For the only sympathetic account of the life of the
Tajik ruler from Shomali, see Khalillulah Khalili, *'Ayyar-i az Khurasan: Amir
Habibullah, Khadem-i Din-i Rasul Allah* (Peshawar: Jamiat-e Islami Afghanistan,
1980).

[31] Some of the most obvious attempts at undermining larger regional identities
consisted of redrawing and renaming administrative units (sub-districts, districts
and provinces) in the name of 'administrative reforms'–similar to Soviet colonial
policies across the Amu Darya in western Turkestan (the former Soviet Central
Asia) which effectively wiped out the appellation 'Turkestan' from popular
memory in the area. In Afghanistan's administrative reforms, not only did the
name Turkestan or Afghan Turkestan fall into disuse in reference to northern
Afghanistan, but the term Qataghan, a name for a major Uzbek tribal community
occupying the central parts of Afghan Turkestan, as well as the name of the
territory the Qataghan tribe inhabited (the region Qataghan wa Badakhshan) was
also completely altered by dividing and renaming the region into several smaller
provinces. Similarly, the Hazarajat, the land of the Hazara Shiite community was
divided and renamed to undermine their ethnic memory and social existence. The
entire scheme of creating and using administrative units as a basis for 'electing'
representatives for the rubber-stamp parliaments (*majlis-e shura wa sana*) and for
the equally meaningless so-called *Loya Jirga* (Grand National Assembly), was
another clever ploy used by the centralising state to assure Pushtun dominance of
the political process in the nation. That is, a much larger number of provinces and
districts (*wuluswali* and *hukumati*) were created in Pushtun areas with fewer
inhabitants, compared to a smaller number of such administrative units for
significantly larger territories and population in non-Pushtun regions. An important
legacy of this deed is being played out now daily in the media claims that the
Taliban militia are in control of twenty-two (predominantly Pushtun) provinces,
and hence they are ruling two-thirds of Afghanistan. This is an absurdity if one
closely examines the existing demographic and territorial statistics for the
provinces of Afghanistan, even those provided by the former regimes in Kabul.
For comparative examination of facts and figures on provinces of Afghanistan
see Mohammad Siddiq Sarwari, 'Marifi Velayat-e Keshwar', in *De Afghanistan*

the local communities saw the state as the main source of their oppression and they devised complex social mechanisms to insulate themselves from direct contact with government agents and agencies. Indeed, ethnographic evidence clearly shows that local communities isolated themselves from corrupt government officials by creating community-based parallel power structures (that is, a strong Sharia-governed civil society) to resolve internal problems locally through their own trusted leaders, both religious and secular. It was, indeed, these trusted local figures who emerged during the anti-Soviet jihad as the leaders and commanders of the many local resistance units all across the country.[32]

Second, another significant consequence of the discriminatory state policies towards the so called 'minorities' was the politicisation of ethnicity and tribalism. State officials systematically used ethnic and tribal affiliations as a basis for distribution of scarce state resources—economic, educational, and political. Indeed, I would suggest that in Afghanistan, the idea and institutions of the modern state were thoroughly 'tribalised' under the formative influences of the dominant constitutive principles of Afghan political culture–the *khanawada* and *qawm wa kheysh*. This development is ironic in view of the fact that Afghan state authorities in all regimes (monarchic, republican, communist, Islamist, and Taliban) have repeatedly declared their intentions, at least publicly, to pacify, disarm and 'de-tribalise' Afghan society. What is paradoxical, of course, is that the various regimes, at least until the beginnings of jihad struggles against the Soviet invaders and their Afghan communist protégés, had remarkable achievements in pacifying and de-tribalising a large segment of the civil society by means of the 'tribalisation' of the institutions of the centralised state itself. Furthermore, the staffing and operation of this 'tribalised' Afghan state relied heavily on another dominant form of

---

Kalanay (Kabul: Dawlati metbaeh, 1974), pp. 710-762. Some believe that the main reason why the governments in Afghanistan never attempted a full census of the country's population may have been due to their well-founded fear of discovering that their claims of a Pushtun majority in the country would be proved wrong. Therefore, in order to ameliorate the abuses of past and present, there is a strong need for a complete demographic census of the country. There is also a need to reassess the fundamental criteria to be used in redrawing the boundaries of provincial, district and sub-district administrative units and thus to determine population representations in national assemblies in the future state structure of Afghanistan.

[32] See Shahrani, 'The Kirghiz Khans: Style and Substance of Traditional Local Leadership in Central Asia'.

political culture in Afghanistan–the ties of patronage and clientelism based on the distribution and redistribution of state resources.[33]

Third, throughout this century, the processes of centralising the state in Afghanistan, and the creation of a strong national government in Kabul,[34] have been justified–and are currently being justified again by the Mujahideen government and the rival Taliban militia–in terms of a national defence strategy against potential foreign threats, especially from neighbouring countries. Paradoxically, however, the realisation of this dream by the previous central governments, at least for some brief periods, has been always the by-product of the state's increasing and voluntary dependency (economic, technological and military) upon the potential foreign enemy. For example, the monarchic regimes from Amir Abdul Rahman to Zahir Shah (1880-1973), Daoud's short-lived republic (1973-78), and the Communist regimes (1978-92) were dependent upon British India and the USSR. And the Mujahideen resistance parties and Afghan refugee communities (1978-92) were utterly dependent for their sheer survival upon external sources of support such as United Nations agencies, numerous NGOs, and over-friendly nations with their own Afghan clients and agendas to promote in the region–for example Pakistan, Saudi Arabia, the United States, and Iran. Since the collapse of the former USSR and its puppet regime in Kabul, the Mujahideen governments and their many opponents have all followed the same patterns of dependency and foreign patronage to continue their patrons' proxy wars. The post-Soviet list of patrons include new players from the newly independent states of Central Asia, such as Turkmenistan, Uzbekistan, and Tajikistan, as well as Russia, and more recently an increasing number of multinational corporations.[35] Not surprisingly,

---

[33] A rising concern about Taliban practices in this regard, even among Pushtun groups, is the make-up of their so-called Central Shura or Council, and the higher echelons of their administration, which are staffed almost exclusively by Kandahari village mullahs. For a list and brief biographical information on their leadership cadre, see Rameen Moshref, *The Taliban* (New York: Occasional Paper no. 35, The Afghanistan Forum, 1997).

[34] The exceptions are the brief interruption in 1929, and more recently since the beginning of jihad against the Soviets and their client communist regimes (1979-92).

[35] The increasing dependence of the Afghan state, especially since the mid-1950s, upon international assistance, and its consequent impact upon the country's domestic economic and political policies, and the political economy of state and society, have been discussed elsewhere at some length: see Shahrani, 'State Building and Social Fragmentation in Afghanistan: A Historical Perspective'; M. Nazif Shahrani, 'Afghanistan: State and Society in Retrospect', in Ewan Anderson and Nancy Hatch Dupree (eds.), *The Cultural Basis of Afghan*

the central governments of Afghanistan (and unfortunately, various Mujahideen factions as well, especially the Pakistani-created Taliban militia) have used their *borrowed* strength more consistently to crush their domestic enemies (both real and perceived) and disenfranchise them from political participation, than to direct it against any foreign interventionists. In fact, historically no central government in Afghanistan, no matter how strong, has ever been able to withstand foreign invasions. On the contrary, the central governments have often 'invited' foreign enemies into the country to protect their regime against the wrath of their own people. Indeed, the recent experiences of the successful jihad against the Soviets and the communist Afghan government, make the fact amply clear that a dependent centralised government, no matter how powerful, cannot defend Afghanistan's national territorial integrity or independence. Instead, the task of liberating the country has consistently fallen on the shoulders of local communities. Unfortunately, the legacy of the oppressive domestic policies before the communist coup of 1978, aimed at disarming and weakening local autonomous communities, had seriously hampered the possibilities for a far more successful community-based, anti-colonial jihad struggle. That is, more vibrant, better-armed, well-disciplined, self-reliant, and vigorous local communities (or a stronger 'civil society') would have been better able to withstand the Soviet communist threat. Fortunately for the Muslim peoples of Afghanistan, the century-long state policies aimed at the destruction of local autonomous communities were not entirely effective. Emasculated, disarmed and weakened considerably, most of these communities, especially in the rural areas, were nonetheless able to reconstitute themselves quickly in the face of a deteriorating central government power. Indeed, they were able to mobilise rapidly and to fight effectively in the anti-Soviet jihad struggle. And they not only successfully defended their own local communities, but the local resistance groups also collectively regained Afghanistan's national independence. As a result of the decade and a half of successful local community-based resistance struggles, *civil society*, especially in non-Pushtun territories of northern, central and western Afghanistan has been re-established, and is today much stronger then ever before. Their recent fierce resistance against the encroaching Taliban militia in the

---

Nationalism (London and New York: Pinter Publishers, 1990), pp. 41-49. The dependence of Mujahideen organisations upon outside sources of assistance (governmental, NGO, private, Muslim and non-Muslim, neighbours and afar) has similar crippling policy implications for the future of the country, which must be addressed with honesty.

areas north of Kabul, and in northern and central Afghanistan, indicates that they are not willing to return to the *status quo*.

Fourth, and politically a particularly crippling consequence of the corrupt and autocratic dynastic rule by the Mohammadzai clan, has been the creation of a persistent attitude that the members of the defunct royal family and their Mohammadzai clan in particular, and the Pushtun tribes in general, are the only legitimate rulers of Afghanistan. Indeed, they have convinced not only themselves but many Western experts and even the agents of foreign governments, that there cannot be an Afghanistan without Pushtun leadership. Sadly enough, there are some among the non-Pushtun technocrats, and even in the ranks of the former Mujahideen leadership, who have also internalised this moronic 'fact'.

Finally, perhaps the most remarkable legacy of the policies of the old form of 'tribalised' state system in the contemporary political culture of Afghanistan may be their effect upon the rise and formation of many forms of political communities opposing the corrupt and oppressive state system itself. These opposition movements and formations have included ideologically-based secular 'nationalist', Islamist, and various shades of leftist and communist political parties, associations, and organisations. The numbers and variety of such ideologically diverse, organised groups in Afghanistan, at least since the mid-1960s, needs no elaboration. But, again as Chatterjee has pointed out, the roots of 'our postcolonial misery ... [are] not in our ability to think out new forms of the modern community but in our *surrender to the old forms of the modern state*'.[36] Indeed, without exception, all opposition groups and groups with alternative ideologies (communities) have, consciously or not, tended blindly to imitate (or surrender to) the organisational structure (and methods of staffing and operations), commonly used by the 'old forms of the modern [tribalised Afghan] state'.[37]

[36] Chatterjee, *The Nation and Its Fragments: Colonial and Postcolonial Histories*, p. 11.

[37] It is important to note that all Pushtun-dominated Mujahideen political organisations, without exception, and the Taliban militia in particular, are fighting to conquer the whole country and re-establish Pushtun hegemony through a strong centralised state structure based on Amir Abdul Rahman's model. The backers of Mohammad Zahir Shah, the self-proclaimed technocratic elite living in the West, also share the same dreams. The only major Tajik political organisation in the country, the Rabbani-Massoud group, also calls for the establishment of a strong centralised government. So far, the call for a 'federal' state structure that would allow for local and regional autonomy has been hinted only by the Hazara Shia and the Uzbek groups in the country. Unfortunately, any suggestion of local self-governance is immediately viewed (falsely) by the proponents of *hukumat-e*

From military victory to political misery: contingencies

Why and how did the long-established, ideologically-organised, Islamist parties and organisations begin to lose their political relevance or significance, and give way to intense intercommunal proxy wars financed and managed by foreign powers? What explains the legacies of the centralised state and the gains and achievements of the jihad years (1979-92) for imagining the future of the state in post-jihad Afghanistan?

To begin with, I would like to suggest that local community-based Islamist political and military organisations worked admirably well in the context of ideological opposition to colonial occupation forces and a domestic communist regime. The key to the Mujahideen parties' military successes was primarily a new modernist Islamist ideology that could mobilise diverse local communities, and minimally reorganise and operate within the political framework of the existing traditional local community structures of solidarity and loyalties. Communities (local, provincial, regional, ethnic or sectarian) were willing and eager participants in the jihad for two not-entirely-related, reasons: (1) ideological opposition to communism, and the defence of Islam and the Muslim motherland against what they regarded as Afghan communist traitors and their invading Soviet patrons; and (2) for the long-subjugated and abused non-Pushtun communities, opposition to oppressive, colonial and exploitative practices of the modern institution of a Pushtun-dominated[38] centralised state,

---

mutamarkiz-e qawi as evidence of a desire to divide the country or of a scheme which would threaten the alleged territorial integrity of Afghanistan.

[38] During a BBC Persian Service 'Dialogue' programme broadcast on 1 June 1997, when I discussed the issue of Pushtun domination of the state in Afghanistan, the historian Hasan Kakar vehemently objected to my views. In his protest, he recounted the presence of several Badakhshanis who served as ministers of court and finance during Zahir Shah's reign (1933-73). I do not claim that there were no members of non-Pushtun groups serving in ministerial posts in the previous regimes. Quite the contrary: the past regimes made sure, as the Taliban and Mujahideen governments of Burhanuddin Rabbani are doing, that they included token 'representatives' of the various ethnic communities or regions. What Dr Kakar and numerous others forget to ask or explore is what *kind* of Badakhshanis (Uzbeks, Hazaras, Heratis) were those who served in the Pushtun-dominated governments of the past or in the present Taliban regime. The truth is that, at least in the case of Badakhshanis about whom I know, they were the descendants of the children of the Mirs (local leaders of the late nineteenth century) who were brought to Kabul by Amir Abdul Rahman as part of his regional pacification programs to Kabul and kept as hostages and later turned into 'page' or 'slave' boys (*ghulam bachagan*) to be trained as loyal servants of the court. These loyal servants of the court were void of any Badakhshani identity or sentiments. Indeed,

presented another motivating force. During the years of jihad, the Mujahideen consistently expressed and articulated local communities' ideological opposition to communism and Soviet colonialism. However, at the same time the Mujahideen leadership, much to their own detriment as well as the national interest, neglected to address their local community partners' well-founded historic fears of the abusive powers of the centralised state.

On the contrary, upon taking power from the communist regime in 1992, the Mujahideen governments embraced the old forms of the modern state and began to fight others for exclusive control of state power. In this effort, every contending group has tried to secure domestic and foreign allies, even from the ranks of their former communist enemies. Most of them have done so quite successfully. The Taliban, the latest contenders for state power, are following suit not only in recruiting numerous former communist Pashtun military officers and civilian officials, but also in embracing the familiar old forms of the modern state with more determination than ever before. It is this unconditional surrender by the Afghan Mujahideen and their militant opponents, the Taliban militia, to the 'old forms of modern state' and governance structures, combined with their blatant disregard of local, provincial, regional, ethnic and sectarian community governance interests and structures, that I believe to be, among other things, an important factor in the perpetuation of the current intercommunal strife. This tragic situation is further complicated by the fact that all combatants are utterly dependent upon external patrons for the survival of their own party – *qawm*. It is also clear that, in this environment of multiple power centres inside the country, each group is connected to multiple, often competing, sources of international assistance–the many *tribes* of international donors. These friendly donor countries, international agencies, and non-governmental organisations do not necessarily all share the same interests; certainly they do not share the national interests of the peoples of Afghanistan. Indeed, many of them would consider the return of peace to war-torn Afghanistan to be detrimental to their own national and regional geostrategic interests, and indeed it might be so. Furthermore, as long as the feuding Afghan parties continue to adhere to, and surrender to, the old forms of the modern state, the flames of war will be fuelled by outside forces that benefit from instability in the region. Therefore,

---

they had become *mankurt* ('slave, who could not remember his past life'), to borrow an apt term from the famed Kirghiz author Chengiz Aitmatov. This does not by any means indicate that the Pashtun communities were not also subjugated or abused by the otherwise Pashtun-dominated state. Indeed, I have no doubt that some of them were and still are.

one of the major contingencies for even beginning to address the current military and political impasse in Afghanistan seems to be a radical change in the political economy of the warring factions and the sources of their effective support. However, much to my own personal dismay, based on the behaviour of Afghanistan's neighbours and some distant 'friends', especially the increasingly belligerent attitude of the governments of Pakistan towards the non-Pushtun communities in Afghanistan, any appreciable change in the political ecology of the current proxy wars seems remote, to say the least.

The possibility of a new relationship between civil society and the future state

On the bases of our brief examination of Afghanistan's political culture; the legacies of the century-long experiences of the relatively strong centralised, but economically and militarily dependent state structure and political economy; the legacies and achievements of the jihad era; and the current political ecology of post-jihad proxy wars— we have to ask ourselves: what might be a reasonable way out of the current impasse for the long-suffering peoples of Afghanistan? Or what could be the relevance of these legacies (as outlined above) for imagining the shape of the future state in post-jihad Afghanistan?

A military solution, so favoured by the Taliban Pushtun militia and their militant Pakistani government patrons, even if successful in conquering the non-Pushtun territories in northern and central Afghanistan, which appears unlikely in the near future, will not result in the resumption of peace and the reconstruction of Afghanistan.[39]

---

[39] The Taliban's insistence on forcing misguided, punitive and Pushtun-tribal misunderstandings of Islam (imported from the Northwest Frontier Province of Pakistan) upon the great majority of very pious, knowledgeable, orthodox practitioners of Islam (in non-Pushtun communities as well as many Pushtun communities in many parts of the country) is one of the main reasons for the likelihood of continued turmoil. Their policy of virtually 'imprisoning' Afghan women in their own homes, and denying them any and all forms of human rights and basic civil liberties, in clear contradiction to the most fundamental teachings of Islam, is another reason why the freedom-loving Muslim peoples of Afghanistan will not stand for these un-Islamic and inhumane practices of the Taliban. The Taliban fondness for focussing on trivial 'Muslim'-cum-rural-Pushtun-tribal customs, urged on allegedly by their other patron, Saudi Arabia–for example forcing men to grow long beards, outlawing all forms of expressive and plastic arts (music, drama, photography, painting, sculpture) and preventing young children from playing with certain musical toys, flying kites, or keeping pet pigeons–together with their lack of any vision for addressing the monumental

The return of the 83-year-old ex-king Zahir Shah and the reinstatement of his family to the Afghan throne, lobbied for and cheer-led by the US congressman Dana Rohrabacher (Republican of Orange County, California), and many Afghan technocratic supporters of the old King in Europe and America, with alleged financial support from the California-based multinational oil company UNOCAL, is unlikely to get anywhere. The various peace initiatives and proposals put forth by the United Nations special envoys to Afghanistan (including the latest one by Dr Norbert Holl), by Zahir Shah, and by some 'independent' Afghan cultural organisations in Europe and America working towards peace in Afghanistan, seem to lack any innovative ideas and creative thought and do not hold any promise in the foreseeable future. The reason is simple: all of these proposals contain two often-tried and tired components: (1) forming a broad-based transitional central government made up of an apolitical (politically indifferent?) group of technocrats; and (2) charging the transitional government with the eventual task of creating a permanently elected central government.[40] In this well-worn formula, the entire problem is reduced to getting the parties to agree on the right kind of mix of ethnolinguistic and sectarian representation, in the so-called 'broad based coalition government'. Unfortunately, such governments have been formed time and again over the last five years, and more may be proposed and formed during the months and years to come, but without any positive outcome to bring peace in Afghanistan.

Therefore, by way of a conclusion, and suggestion for a possible way out of the current national predicament faced by the peoples of Afghanistan, I would like to reiterate the following crucial points.

First, the old forms of modern state in Afghanistan, created by Amir Abdul Rahman, perpetuated by his Mohammadzai clansmen, and desired so strongly by most of the contenders in the current conflict in Afghanistan, although organised after the modern European models–as in most other post-colonial situations–have had little or no functional or ideological resemblance to European models. Their re-institution, with or without broad-based representation, is unlikely to serve the interests of the great majority of local communities fighting to

---

social and economic problems confronting the nation, militate against optimism about peace under a Taliban militia-controlled state.

40   The suggested mechanism for legitimising the future state is also a well-worn and not very democratic 'traditional Afghan' institution: the *Loya Jirga* (Grand National Council).

preserve their hard-earned rights to local self-governance, particularly among the non-Pushtun citizens of the country.[41]

Second, the old forms of the modern state in Afghanistan, to all intents and purposes, not only denied the existence of traditional community structures, solidarities and loyalties, but often oppressed and attempted to destroy them. Ironically, both history and recent memory show us that it is the presence of these strong, well-armed and organised local community structures in Afghanistan that have assured national independence–not the presence of any kind of strong, but dependent, centralised modern state apparatus with or without Pushtun kings. Indeed, disarming local communities is not only dangerous for the long-term security of such communities vis à vis other belligerent and hegemonic forces,[42] and/or oppressive and autocratic central governments, but also for national defence against foreign threats.

Third, much attention has been given to alternative Islamist ideological formulations, both in Afghanistan and elsewhere in the Muslim world. However, with the minor exception of the Islamic Republic of Iran, there is little or no systematic attempt to think of alternative structures of community governance or appropriate forms of state apparatus for the realisation of Islamist ideologies. The plain

---

[41] In my judgment, the most crucial issue in the post-jihad intercommunal fighting in Afghanistan is not merely adequate representation of the non-Pushtun in the central government apparatus. This reminds me of an important point made by Edward Said while delivering a series of lectures as a Patton Lecturer at Indiana University in Spring 1995. When commenting on Yasser Arafat and Nelson Mandela as leaders of resistance movements in their respective countries, he said the difference between them was that, 'Nelson Mandela went to prison so that his people could be free, while Yasser Arafat left his people imprisoned so that he could be free'. In a similar vein, I contend that what is at issue is both the freedom of local communities to choose representatives to participate in the national political organs and the institutions of the national state, and to act as free leaders of their communities; and, also the freedom of the communities themselves to be able to manage their own local affairs, instead of relinquishing that right to the central government to 'imprison' them again, as it was the case prior to the onset of the recent jihad.

[42] The rapid and sudden fall to the Taliban militia in September 1995 of Herat, the only effectively-disarmed non-Pushtun region during the post-jihad era under the peaceful civilian rule of Governor Ismail Khan, a local resistance hero, is a good example of the sad consequences of returning to the *status quo ante*. Indeed many Afghans consider that the Taliban militia's policy of disarming the local communities, resisted even by the Pushtuns in the eastern Kunar province on the Pakistan border, is dictated by Pakistan as it would benefit Pakistan, if she should be 'invited' by the Taliban to intervene more directly and openly in order to help them establish themselves as the 'legitimate rulers of Afghanistan'.

facts are that the Europeans are moving beyond the old political forms of the modern nation-state, but Muslim movements, despite their anti-Western revolutionary ideologies and rhetoric, are still clinging on to the same old forms with even greater determination.

Fourth, the challenge therefore facing the peoples of Afghanistan, and Islamist movements elsewhere–especially in view of the prospective military success of Taliban militia with their misguided interpretations and implementations of Islamic beliefs and practices–is not only the question of determining what individual(s), or which party or ethnic-tribal group will or should lead Muslim communities into the next century. It is also the challenge of seriously considering whether we ought to abandon the 'old forms of state' for a new and more equitable structure of community governance–a kind of governance structure that is accountable, protects all its citizens' rights, and allows us to talk about the complementarity of strong autonomous local communities (civil society) and new forms of national state at the same time.[43]

It is, then, to the challenge of creating an Islamically-informed and culturally appropriate community-based national governance structure that our people and leaders must rise, in order to fulfil the cherished hopes of the long-suffering Muslim peoples of Afghanistan. As to what would constitute an appropriate and adequate state structure, there are no easy answers to offer. However, I am willing to outline below some of the fundamental parameters that ought to be considered in imagining the shape, structure and functions of the future state in contradistinction from those of the old forms.

I find recent suggestions and semblance of a debate taking place in some of the Afghan expatriate print and electronic media in the USA as to whether Afghanistan should strive for the establishment of a 'strong centralised' national government (for some preferably led by the rampaging Taliban militia, and along the 'old forms of the post colonial state'), or a more loosely-structured 'federal' system, to be both hopeful and excessively limiting, to say the least. Those opposing the federal model (such as the Taliban supporters) seem to argue that it would lead to the disintegration and fragmentation of Afghanistan along ethnolinguistic or sectarian cleavages. The proponents of federalism, on the other hand, claim that the only way to safeguard Afghanistan's territorial integrity is through the establishment of a federal government. What is limiting in such debates, is that the concepts of 'centralism' and 'federalism' are constructed by both sides in a seriously monolithic and predetermined manner. Both as sociological concepts, and as forms of political

---

[43] See Chandhoke, *The State and Civil Society: Explorations in Political Theory.*

practice, the two models of governance offer a wide range of structural and organisational possibilities for state and community governance. As evident from our brief review of 'centralism' in the history of Afghanistan, however, such conceptual models, whatever their original rationale, are not in practice immune from the 'tribalisation' of the institutions of the state and abuse by power holders.

Therefore, instead of debating what ready-made Western or Eastern model of state should be adopted for Afghanistan,[44] we should evaluate the strengths and weaknesses of the emergent and existing local and regional self-governing communities, paying particular attention to their legitimate concerns and fears regarding their ties to the national governance structures. The most crucial issues at this moment in Afghanistan's national history, are: (1) whether we want a militarily strong central government (as advocated and being created by the Taliban militia under the auspices of our potential foreign enemies), that will oppose the existence of any and all peaceful, self-reliant and self-governing local and regional communities, and once again spend its *borrowed* military might to vanquish, expel, and disarm a significant segment of its disenfranchised citizens by labelling them unreliable or undesirable (based on tribal, ethnolinguistic or sectarian differences); or (2) alternatively, favour a kind of central government that would be willing to help strengthen local self-governance and incorporate all such communities into a powerful pyramid of national governance. If we are willing to heed the legacies of the past century, and pay attention to the most basic elements of the constitutive principles of our national political culture, then our choice of national governance structure should be clear–that is, we must choose to build our future national state on the proven strengths of our 'civil society', the powerful self-governing community structures that have re-emerged as part of the blessings of our nations' most recent struggles against communism and Soviet intervention. Further, we must encourage the formation of a central government based on democratic principles of free election and power sharing among all interest groups in the country (tribal, ethnolinguistic, sectarian, and gender) on an equitable basis–that is, by applying the Islamic principles of 'shura' or consultative rule.

Such a national government must be committed, at a minimum, to work towards the following national goals: (1) drafting and ratifying a new national constitution reflecting the post-Communist

---

[44] As was done very recently in Dennis Kux and George Tanham, 'Afghanistan: The Swiss Solution', *The Washington* Post, 18 June 1997. Similar views have been also presented by Ghulam Ali Ayeen, an Afghan elder statesman living in the US, in a series of articles published in the *Omaid Weekly*.

and post-jihad national needs, aspirations and political, ecological, and economic realities in Afghanistan; (2) guaranteeing the constitutional rights of *community self-governance* at the local, district, provincial, and regional levels throughout the country[45]–that is, allowing local communities to run their own local civil, judicial, security and educational administrations by themselves, to register and keep their small arms, and to maintain law and order with the help of a local community police force; in other words, the people's rights both to elect representatives for legislation (nationally and locally), and also for implementation and administration of the laws must be guaranteed; (3) creating a national administrative structure to ensure a uniform implementation of new constitutional laws by local self-governing authorities throughout the country–that is, the new representative and accountable national government, unlike that of the past, should not be directly involved in implementing national laws and local ordinances; instead, the new central government should serve to *monitor* and ensure the universal application and enforcement of all national laws in a judicious manner by locally elected and appointed government officials; (4) instead of disarming local communities, possibly recruiting some members to form a national army, with the rest coordinated into local community-based national guard detachments to defend the country against external threats.

It is only through liberating ourselves from the legacies of the old forms of the modern centralised, and often 'tribalised' state structures, and acknowledging and incorporating the tremendous strengths of our re-emergent civil society into a new community governance-based state structure that we may be able to rise to the challenges facing us at this historic national crossroad. The price for *not* acting responsibly, and supporting the bloody rampage of the Taliban in their campaign to re-establish Pushtun supremacy in the country, is huge: it is nothing less than the very viability and national integrity of Afghanistan, and the preservation of the newly gained freedoms by all the citizens of a reunited Afghanistan. So, let us (Afghans) take heed from the poem of our compatriot, Abdul Rahman Pazhwak, and make sure that Afghanistan does *not* again become a land 'where the people

---

[45] It is significant to note here that, as Chandhoke, *The State and Civil Society: Explorations in Political Theory*, p.9 points out, without the protection of juridically granted and enforceable rights of free expression, freedom to form associations, freedom to dissent, freedom to generate and disseminate public opinion, civil society is crippled. Armed with these weapons–rights, rules of law, freedom and citizenship–civil society becomes the site for the reproduction of a critical rational discourse which possesses the potential to interrogate the state.

are imprisoned and the country is free'! Therefore, we must aspire to establish models of community self-governance and national state structures that guarantee both the freedom and liberty of all the peoples inhabiting Afghanistan, as well as the territorial integrity and full independence of the nation itself. Absolutely nothing short of that should do.

INDEX

243